Teaching mathematics

The Open University Postgraduate Certificate of Education

The readers in the PGCE series are:

Thinking Through Primary Practice
Teaching and Learning in the Primary School
Teaching and Learning in the Secondary School
Teaching English
Teaching Mathematics
Teaching Science
Teaching Technology
Teaching Modern Languages
Teaching History
Teaching Music

All of these readers are part of an integrated teaching system; the selection is therefore related to other material available to students and is designed to evoke critical understanding. Opinions expressed are not necessarily those of the course team or of the University.

If you would like to study this course and receive a PGCE prospectus and other information about programmes of professional development in education, please write to the Central Enquiry Service, PO Box 200, The Open University, Walton Hall, Milton Keynes, MK7 6YZ. A copy of *Studying with the Open University* is available from the same address.

Teaching mathematics

Edited by Michelle Selinger
at The Open University

London and New York
in association with
The Open University

First published 1994
by Routledge
11 New Fetter Lane, London EC4P 4EE

Simultaneously published in the USA and Canada
by Routledge
29 West 35th Street, New York, NY 10001

Reprinted 1995

Typeset in Garamond by Florencetype Ltd, Stoodleigh, Devon
Printed and bound in Great Britain by
Biddles Ltd, Guildford and King's Lynn

British Library Cataloguing in Publication Data
A catalogue record for this book is available from the British Library

Library of Congress Cataloguing in Publication Data
A catalogue record for this book is available from the Library of Congress

ISBN 0-415-10252-9

Contents

Foreword

The form of teacher education is one of the most debated educational issues of the day. How is the curriculum of teacher education, particularly initial, pre-service education to be defined? What is the appropriate balance between practical school experience and the academic study to support such practice? What skills and competence can be expected of a newly qualified teacher? How are these skills formulated and assessed and in what ways are they integrated into an ongoing programme of professional development?

These issues have been at the heart of the development and planning of the Open University's programme of initial teacher training and education – the Postgraduate Certificate of Education (PGCE). Each course within the programme uses a combination of technologies, some of which are well tried and tested while others, on information technology for example, may represent new and innovatory approaches to teaching. All, however, contribute in an integrated way towards fulfilling the aims and purposes of the course and programme.

All of the PGCE courses have readers which bring together a range of articles, extracts from books, and reports that discuss key ideas and issues, including specially commissioned chapters. The readers also provide a resource that can be used to support a range of teaching and learning in other types and structures of course.

This series from Routledge, in supporting the PGCE Open University programme, provides a contemporary view of developments in primary and secondary education and across a range of specialist subject areas. Its primary aim is to provide insights and analysis for those participating in initial education and training. Much of its content, however, will also be relevant to ongoing programmes of personal and institutional professional development. Each book is designed to provide an integral part of that basis of knowledge that we would expect of both new and experienced teachers.

Bob Moon
Professor of Education, The Open University

Introduction

Michelle Selinger

The last fifteen years have seen great changes in mathematics teaching in the United Kingdom. The publication of *Mathematics Counts* (the Cockcroft Report) in 1982 brought to the fore a shift of emphasis in the way in which pupils were taught and learnt mathematics. In the report a wide range of teaching styles were encouraged, some of which had only been happening in a few classrooms up and down the country. Pupils in secondary-school classrooms were introduced to 'investigating' and the use of practical equipment was increased in addition to the usual textbook exercises that had previously been the only diet for many pupils. Pupils were encouraged to discuss their work, teachers began to rearrange their classrooms so that pupils could work in groups and exchange ideas. A whole range of new schemes were developed by publishers, often involving groups of teachers on their writing teams, in order to incorporate the new teaching styles. Individualised schemes were developed for mixed-ability groups particularly in years 7 and 8 and the emphasis was placed on setting mathematics in 'real' contexts and with an increased stress on the practical use of mathematics. The subsequent introduction of the National Curriculum and the introduction of national testing at 7, 11 and 14 have also had an influence on the mathematics curriculum and the way in which mathematics is taught.

This book sets out just some of the debates, issues and controversies surrounding mathematics teaching and learning in secondary schools today. It forms part of the Open University's PGCE course in secondary mathematics and is therefore aimed at all those who are about to embark on or are currently training to be mathematics teachers or those who are considering teaching as a career. However, those who are already teaching in schools may well find that some of the chapters start to raise new issues for them that might lead them to question their practice or to confirm their beliefs.

The majority of the chapters have been specially commissioned for this text, the remainder being reprinted from books and journals. The authors are mainly practising teachers and lecturers in teacher education. The chapters cannot take up all the issues involved in teaching mathematics; instead, the collection is focused on just some of the debates surrounding the main issues that are currently central to mathematics teaching. It provides a forum for a range of perspectives on topics such as published schemes, computers and calculators, mathematical investigation, cultural and social issues and curriculum content, as well as considering the historical development of mathematics education and how research can develop classroom practice.

Parts II–VI form the core of the book; each part addresses a particular question and sets up a debate with which the reader is invited to engage. Some points of view can be very persuasive – until another point of view that might conflict is put to the reader or listener. Debates serve an important function in helping to establish an independent point of view. In teaching, decisions have to be made about which starting points to offer pupils. These decisions are based on intuitions, some of which are informed by experience, others by discussion with colleagues about pupils' past performance and others by the teacher's own 'gut' reactions. Sometimes gut reactions can go hopelessly wrong, while at other times they can succeed. It is hoped that by reading and considering others' opinions on a particular topic, the reader will form opinions about teaching mathematics that can be tested against the arguments presented here. It is possible to resonate with two differing points of view, seeing merits as well as disadvantages and flaws in both. However, opinions can be strengthened or changed as a result of reflecting on these arguments and they can also inform views about mathematics teaching in general and lesson planning in particular.

Each question is introduced with a brief discussion on the particular issues presented and a rationale for presenting these particular views. There are of course many other perspectives to each of these issues, but the purpose of the selected chapters is to enter the reader into the debate and to allow them to formulate their own ideas and opinions and to follow up those that appeal to or interest them as they embark on their teaching career.

Part I

A historical perspective

Chapter 1

Secondary mathematics education in England

Recent changes and their historical context

Barry Cooper

INTRODUCTION

Secondary-school mathematics is not fixed and unchanging. During the past hundred years there have been several periods of intense debate about its nature. Definitions of 'good practice' have changed as a result, in respect of both content and teaching styles. These periods of change have been characterised by conflict between those of opposing views, and frequently, as a result of the uses of mathematics in society and the economy, have involved voices from outside mathematics education. As a result, the mathematics curriculum at any time is a compromise between the demands of various groups with different degrees of power and influence. Since the concerns of these groups change, as do their power and influence, this compromise is inherently unstable, and new periods of change are always likely (Cooper 1983). Such periods have been described by a variety of authors from a variety of perspectives (see, for example, Howson 1982; Price 1983, 1986; Cooper 1985a; Noss 1990; Ernest 1992). My purpose here is to describe some of the changes of the past decade and to provide some historical background for these.

I shall concentrate on two particular aspects of secondary mathematics: (i) curriculum differentiation and (ii) practical work, investigations and problem solving; giving a broadly chronological account of their development. I shall not be able to discuss directly many other important issues in mathematics education such as the uses of computers (ICMI 1986), initiatives concerned with gender (Burton 1986) or ethnicity (Shan and Bailey 1991) or debates amongst mathematics educators about ethnomathematics (D'Ambrosio 1991), all of which interact in various ways with these two areas.

DIFFERENTIATION

'Differentiation' means different things to different people. For sociologists the term tends to be used to refer to some process whereby pupils are ranked on academic and behavioural criteria in schools and/or the stratification of curricula by criteria such as social class, 'ability', sex or previous attainment (Young 1971; Cooper 1985b; Hammersley 1985; Dowling 1991a). Its effects are generally seen as negative. In recent debates on mathematics education, and in particular in government documents, the term has come to mean the provision of work appropriate for individual pupils (Murphy and Torrance 1988).

In terms of differentiation in the first sense, it is possible to sketch a move through a variety of usages. In Victorian England it was generally assumed – and explicitly argued – by those in power that children should receive an education appropriate to their socio-economic *origins*, and, of course, to their sex. Gradually, there was a move away from this as a publicly stated position. It came to be argued that children should receive an education appropriate to their expected occupational *destination* and/or their 'ability'. More recently, the official position shifted again, with the word 'attainment' often replacing 'ability' in documents on the curriculum. I shall illustrate some of these shifts.

The Victorian period

In 1868, at a time when only a minority – mainly male – attended secondary schools, the Taunton Commission, drawing on descriptions of parents' wishes, had effectively argued for mathematics in these schools to be related to pupils' origins. 'Mathematics' should be included for the upper-middle and professional classes, 'arithmetic' and 'the rudiments of mathematics beyond arithmetic' for pupils from the mercantile classes, and 'very good arithmetic' for the sons of 'smaller tenant farmers, the small tradesmen, [and] the superior artisans' (see Maclure 1973: 92–5). For the working classes the Revised Code of 1862 had specified elementary arithmetic (see Maclure 1973: 80).

Between the wars

Between the wars, children aged over 11 attended either one of a variety of selective schools or the elementary school. The selective schools tended to be the preserve of the middle classes (Lacey 1970: ch. 2; Halsey *et al.* 1980). In these schools mathematics consisted of arithmetic, geometry, algebra and, in some, trigonometry – these usually examined separately (Howson 1982: 162–3). Girls, and the 'less able', were more likely than their colleagues to study arithmetic alone. Most working-class children were educated in the elementary schools, with senior departments taking children to 14. The recommended 'mathematics' course for these children was 'practical' and 'non-academic' in orientation, emphasising applied arithmetic:

The course will fix and extend the knowledge and skill in arithmetical operations gained in the Junior School, and teach the children to apply their new powers to the affairs of daily life and school; it will also have to prepare them to deal with situations requiring numerical knowledge that lie ahead of them. Their experience of accounts, gained in school affairs such as meals, concerts, savings banks and societies, school journeys, excursions, gardening or poultry-keeping will introduce ideas that are current in the larger world of finance, and will be used to lead up to such questions as buying by instalments, investments, pensions and insurance. The use of graphical methods will provide them with a new means of representing and interpreting arithmetical data. Their work in practical subjects, mechanical drawing, surveying and design will serve as a basis for the study of Geometry.

(Board of Education 1937: 144–5)

Post-war

After the 1944 Education Act, the elementary school gradually disappeared. There remained grammar schools, technical schools and secondary modern schools and the private sector. The 11+ exam determined which school pupils attended, alongside the parents' ability and willingness to use the private sector. Again, broadly speaking, middle-class children were more likely to attend the grammar school and working-class children to attend the secondary moderns (Halsey *et al.* 1980). The mathematics in the grammar school remained broadly similar to what it had been pre-war: academic and abstract. Gradually, though, the traditional Euclidean approach to geometry was losing ground to a more informal approach. Trigonometry was now more likely to be studied, and the slow progress towards a 'unified' mathematics examination at 16 continued (Howson 1982: 163).

Mathematics in the secondary moderns at first owed much to the elementary tradition. One early book on these schools, by the Chief Education Officer for Southampton, had no section on mathematics, just one on arithmetic (Dempster 1949). Neither did mathematics appear in either the list of contents or the index. However, by the end of the 1950s, for a variety of reasons, pupils in the A streams of these schools were being entered for GCE examinations and were receiving a curriculum similar to that of the grammar school. Differentiation *within* the school remained. Mathematics was differentiated by 'ability', with 'less able' children being entered for a variety of vocational certificates (Murphy and Torrance 1988). In one boys' school, for example,

the content of school mathematics appears under three headings: the mathematics *necessary* for everyday life, as, for example, money, simple length, time, etc.; mathematics *useful* in everyday life, as, for example, in interest rates, proportion, averages and statistics; and mathematics as *a mode of thought*, as in problems in arithmetic, algebra and riders in geometry. This school provides all except the near-ineducable with the first of these mathematical aims, and as many boys as possible with the second. Only, however, with a few of the boys is it possible to attempt the third aim. The claim of any topic for inclusion . . . depends . . . on whether it is within the powers of comprehension of a boy and whether he is likely to experience a sense of achievement through the work associated with it.

(Chapman 1959: 113–14)

There was also differentiation by sex within this sector. The Newsom Report (Central Advisory Council for Education 1963: 234–40) showed that not only did girls spend less time on 'mathematics' than boys, but that girls in single-sex schools were also much more likely to be restricted to arithmetic.

The 1960s reforms and comprehensive schools

The 'modern maths' reform movement of the 1960s, coupled with the move towards comprehensive schools and the tendency within English education for curricula for lower status groups to drift towards emulating those of higher status groups, led to considerable change in this stratification (see Cooper 1985a, b). By the mid-1970s there, first, had been a revision of grammar school mathematics to please some key audiences within universities and some sections of industry, and, second, the School Mathematics Project (SMP) had become the new orthodoxy in secondary schools via its rewrite of its numbered books as a lettered series for 'average' children. This dominance of SMP had occurred in spite of there having been a variety of other projects which had aimed their work at 'average' and 'below average' pupils rather than at the 'top 20%', as SMP initially had (Cooper 1985a). Notwithstanding the differentiation of its materials, the SMP's work led to 'average' pupils receiving a more varied mathematical diet than before. Not only were fewer children being restricted to arithmetic but also more were coming into contact with 'modern' topics, such as sets, matrices, transformation geometry and statistics, in the context of an approach to mathematics via relations and functions.

A debate also occurred about mixed-ability teaching in mathematics (Schools Council 1977; Evans 1985) and the use of workcards to individualise pupils' assignments (Watson 1976: 22–8). Some projects worked towards making it possible for every pupil to have access to an individualised curriculum suited to 'ability'. SMILE, for example, advertised itself in terms of the appropriateness of its materials for particular ability levels: 'the children seem to be happy with their own "tailor-made" matrix and prefer it to work set from a formal textbook when a few bright ones are bored and the less able are completely lost' (Frost 1975). The Kent Mathematics Project, also developing individualised curricula, talked of 'mathematical ability' being 'developed', a significant shift in usage (Banks 1975).

HMI's survey of mathematics (DES 1980: 23) revealed some of the consequences in schools of this curriculum development. 'Average' pupils were now often studying more than just arithmetic. However, there remained a tendency for more 'able' pupils to be more likely to study 'modern' topics, reflecting the belief in schools that these topics were of no relevance to and/or too difficult for 'average' pupils (see Cooper 1983: 218–19).

Some commentators believed that 'average' pupils were now studying quite 'inappropriate' versions of mathematics. A vigorous reaction occurred, steadily growing from the mid-1970s. The industrialists involved in supporting the SMP project had been mainly concerned about the supply of graduates, and had accepted the arguments of Thwaites, the founder of SMP, that reducing the discontinuity between school and university mathematics should be a key goal, believing this would help ease their problems in obtaining mathematically trained employees (Cooper 1985a). Now, however, the employers of apprentice-level labour were entering the debate, unhappy with the skills of their recruits and often blaming this on the introduction of 'modern mathematics'. Within mathematics education, various voices began to attack what they saw as the overly academic nature of work for 'average' pupils. Hayman, in her Presidential Address to the Mathematical Association in 1975, argued that much of the 'disorder' in comprehensive schools resulted from pupils being asked to study inappropriate mathematics. Her remedy was simple: 'we must stop trying to teach abstract mathematics . . . to all pupils, and concentrate on mathematics for some pupils and competence in arithmetic as a first priority for the majority' (Hayman 1975: 153).

There was a widespread belief, fuelled by the media's selective treatment of research reports, by the Black Papers, and by comments by industrialists and politicians, that standards in basic arithmetic and elementary mathematics were falling (*The Times Educational Supplement* (*TES*) 22 October 1976). Many commentators saw this as a result of the introduction of the calculator coupled with the move to 'modern mathematics' in primary schools as well as secondary schools.

The press pursued the theme of falling standards in mathematics with relish. For example, the *Daily Mail*'s Education Correspondent, explaining why he had removed his son into the private sector, argued that 'progressive theories, first trumpeted as a way of raising standards . . . had quickly [become] perverted into an excuse for lowering them' (*Daily Mail* 2 October 1976). He continued, discussing his son's work, 'suddenly the kitchen table is being covered with pages of sums for homework'. He added that one local primary-school teacher had not been able to tell him what mathematics syllabus she was supposed to be teaching. Reassuring, familiar terms appear here: sums, homework, syllabus. These appealed to parents' own experience, whereas 'sets', 'matrices', 'discovery' did not, and therefore could easily come to be associated with 'out-of-touch' 'trendy' teachers.

A key event was Callaghan's Ruskin College speech in 1976, opening the so-called 'Great Debate' on education. Amongst other themes, he raised the issue of a possible 'core curriculum' noting the 'strong case' for this. He pointed to concern about the aims and methods of informal instruction. He expressed concerns about standards of numeracy, raising the possibility that a 'professional review' of the mathematics needed by industry at various levels was required (*TES* 22 October 1976).

Cockcroft

In the mid-1970s the demands for an enquiry into school mathematics grew, fuelled by a continuing attack on 'standards' in schools (see, for example, *Daily Mail* 1–4 November 1976; *The Sun* 9 March 1978). They were met in 1978 (*TES* 17 March 1978). The committee, chaired by the mathematician W.H. Cockcroft, included representatives of industry and commerce as well as mathematics education professionals. Its remit was to 'consider the teaching of mathematics in primary and secondary schools in England and Wales, with particular regard to the mathematics required in further and higher education, employment and adult life generally, and to make recommendations' (Cockcroft 1982: ix). It reported in 1982. Concerning differentiation, it made much of the large differences between children in mathematical attainment at particular ages. It argued 'modern' topics had spread too far down, reaching, via CSE, pupils who found them difficult to understand and for whom their purpose was not clear. This had resulted from wanting pupils to have their options kept open for as long as possible, but led to a sense of failure for these pupils. There had been too great a difference between syllabuses, now there was too little. In place of top-down syllabus construction by deletion, syllabuses should be created bottom-up, working from a foundation list of topics that would form 'by far the greater part' of the syllabus for the 'lowest forty per cent of the range of attainment in mathematics' (Cockcroft 1982: 134). The positive justification for this was that pupils would remain confident in mathematics if they were set work which was within their capabilities. Except that logarithms are replaced by the use of electronic calculators, the list is very similar to that set out for the senior elementary school in the 1930s. There was criticism of this aspect of Cockcroft (e.g. Ruthven 1986).

The subsequent HMI (1985) document, *Mathematics from 5 to 16*, argued that 'mathematical content needs to be differentiated to match the abilities of pupils', again via extensions rather than deletions. This would allow pupils to progress as 'far and as rapidly as their abilities will allow', via allowing them to experience success rather than failure (para. 3.3).

The move to the GCSE

The introduction of the CSE in the mid-1960s as an exam for children in the middle of the 'ability' range had led to a situation where pupils were effectively being selected at 13+ for either GCE O level, CSE or non-exam courses (Woods 1976; Ball 1981). There was growing concern about the effects of this form of differentiation (Murphy and Torrance 1988) and gradual moves towards the idea of a common exam at 16 (Whitty 1985: ch. 6). Eventually, the decision was made in 1984, after several years of debate, to go ahead with a common, yet differentiated, exam at 16 from 1988. This would be run by Regional Consortia of the GCE and CSE Boards, with their examinations being based on agreed National Criteria.

In 1983 the Joint Council of the GCE/CSE Boards produced its proposed National Criteria for the expected 16+ exam (*TES* 18 February 1983). Those for mathematics involved two lists of syllabus items, one containing the minimum required for a 'mathematics' exam, the other being the content to be added if Grade 3 (equivalent to the minimal O level 'pass' grade) were to be available to candidates. Yet more would have to be added for Grades 1 and 2 to be available. Sir Keith Joseph, then Secretary of State for Education, questioned whether the Lists 1 and 2 were small enough for 'average' and 'below average' pupils (*TES* 26 August 1983).

When the criteria for GCSE mathematics appeared in 1985, there were again two lists (1, 2) of syllabus items (DES/WO 1985). Courses had to be 'appropriate' and 'worthwhile'. Papers would be differentiated so that – according to the rhetoric – pupils would be able to be entered for papers which enabled them to demonstrate what they knew and could do, rather than what they didn't and couldn't. List 1 would be for pupils expected to receive grades E, F and G; List 2 for those expected to receive grades C, D and E. For those expected to receive grades A or B a syllabus 'well in excess' of these lists would have to be studied. Here 'abstraction, generalisation and proof' are emphasised, along with the need for a firm foundation for A level and beyond.

Much of this was seen positively by mathematics educators. Isaacson, for example, argued that:

> Most importantly, syllabus content will be substantially smaller, especially at the lower assessment levels. This should mean there will be time to teach for understanding, to consider a wide range of applications in realistic situations, to develop problem-solving skills, to do mathematics for fun and build on children's natural interest in puzzles and games, to enjoy the aesthetic aspects of mathematics, and to present work in

attractive and appropriate ways.

(Isaacson 1987: 5–6)

A dilemma exists, however, for those concerned with equal opportunity and/or 'mathematics for all' (Damerow and Westbury 1985). While it may be likely that 'average' and 'below average' pupils will have more experience of success if they are asked to study less in a given time, i.e. if pacing is slower and if teaching is made less formal and more 'relevant' to their concerns, it is also the case that 'success' on such a restricted curriculum will still count as 'failure' from another perspective (Young 1971; Murphy and Torrance 1988).

The National Curriculum

As part of the move towards the National Curriculum, the Secretary of State set up the Task Group on Assessment and Testing (TGAT) in 1987 to advise on 'the practical considerations governing assessment within the National Curriculum' (DES/WO 1988a). Its broad recommendations were accepted by the Government, in spite of attacks from the Right and elsewhere (Centre for Policy Studies 1988; Howson 1989). Working Parties on the National Curriculum were to work to its guidelines. There would be Profile Components and Attainment Targets (ATs), with ten levels of attainment in each of the latter. Differentiation, in the context of testing, was to occur via the tests being designed in such a way that a pupil, at a given age of testing, would be able to demonstrate achievement at a variety of levels of attainment. In theory, as Howson (1989: 24) points out, a low-attaining 15-year-old and a high-attaining 9-year-old could be following the same curriculum.

After much argument about draft proposals (Ball 1990), the first version of the mathematics National Curriculum appeared in 1989, with fourteen ATs, each with ten levels. It was now possible to see what particular pupils were expected to learn as mathematics. 'Average' pupils were expected to have reached around level 6 at age 16. Taking the example of the Statements of Attainment (SA) for AT1, concerning 'using and applying mathematics' in relation to number, algebra and measures, a pupil who left school having reached level 5 would have been variously selecting materials, recording findings, interpreting information and explaining work done; but a pupil reaching above level 5 would also be involved in the higher level activities of 'designing' and 'planning'. In fact, some examples given for the SAs do include 'devising' and 'designing' below level 5, but, nevertheless, the difference of emphasis is clear. Higher attaining pupils would be involved more in the conception side of the conception-execution dimension (Braverman 1974). They were to devise and design tasks, and carry them through, while lower attaining pupils were to carry through tasks given to them by others. It has been suggested, following the general arguments of Bowles and Gintis

(1976), that pupils are being prepared via such differentiation for different positions in the capitalist labour market (Noss 1990). Such a position is lent support by the evidence presented in Ranson (1984) that Department of Education and Science (DES) officials and politicians were becoming concerned in the late 1970s and early 1980s that practices in schools and colleges were generating 'unrealistic' career aspirations. For example, a DES official, referring to the inner city 'riots' of this period, argued:

> We are in a period of considerable social change. There may be social unrest, but we can cope with the Toxteths. But if we have a highly educated and idle population we may possibly anticipate more serious social conflict. People must be educated once more to know their place.
>
> (Ranson 1984: 241)

Clearly, given the existence of such agendas – concerned with 'cooling out' many pupils' 'unrealistic' aspirations – teachers concerned about equal opportunity must constantly ask themselves questions about the intended and/or unintended effects of curriculum differentiation. A recent – and fascinating – example of a critical examination of differentiation in a text-based scheme can be found in Dowling's work on SMP 11–16 (Dowling 1991a).

INVESTIGATIONS, PROBLEM SOLVING AND PRACTICAL WORK

I shall treat investigations, problem solving and practical work together, partly because of lack of space, but also because they are linked via the idea of relative pupil activity as opposed to passivity. Problem solving here signifies not tasks of the type $2 \times 2 = ?$, but rather the type of problem that arises when decorating a room or planning a journey, as well as 'pure' mathematical investigations such as the exploration of number patterns. 'Practical' work might involve drawing and cutting out shapes, using dice to investigate probability, designing and carrying out a survey or using mathematics in the context of another subject such as craft, design and technology. It can be favoured for purely pedagogic reasons as an aid to the understanding of concepts, or because it is believed that the school curriculum should have greater links with the world of work. The word 'practical' therefore signifies different things to different people, and the reader should bear this in mind. Although I shall say little about differentiation in this section, it is important to note that different pedagogical approaches are likely to be received differently by pupils from different social and cultural backgrounds. Because of this, debates about pedagogy are also, implicitly at least, debates about differentiation (Bourdieu and Passeron 1977).

Pre-Cockcroft

Until the 1970s, mathematics traditionally had been taught via the textbook, consisting for each topic of some introductory text, some worked examples and some exercises for the pupil. The pupil was positioned as ignorant, the writer as an expert on known mathematics and the role of the teacher plus text was to introduce the pupil to known knowledge and techniques. Often the pupil learned how to perform algorithms with little understanding of underlying principles, though many projects such as the SMP worked very hard to avoid this from the 1960s onwards. The traditional text had worked on the assumption that some concepts and techniques must be learned before others. Furthermore, pre-1960, most tasks were closed, having a right answer and not requiring much beyond the mechanical application of techniques and tricks learned from the text itself. The result was that lower-attaining pupils seldom progressed much beyond basic arithmetic, while higher-attaining pupils were more likely to experience more powerful mathematical techniques. Furthermore, in this form of pedagogy, it is only late in the *successful* learner's educational career that it is disclosed that knowledge is contested and subject to criticism and change (Bernstein 1971).

For most of the twentieth century, practical work, if it occurred at all, was seen in schools as suitable for the 'less able' only, and as unnecessary for the 'able'. It was of low status in schools, and generally in English culture (Weiner 1981). This can be traced back to the nineteenth century (Damerow and Westbury 1985). Practical work was, however, often recommended in official and professional publications, where 'progressive' educational ideas were represented.

Concern over the effects of 'traditional' pedagogic approaches in mathematics is not of recent origin. Perry campaigned for a more 'practical' – in the sense of useful to scientists and engineers – mathematics curriculum at the turn of the century (Price 1986). The Mathematical Association, then concerned with 'able' pupils, argued against 'premature' rigour and formalism after the First World War. Rather, pupils should approach any branch of the subject through a series of stages, of which three were especially relevant in schools (Mathematical Association 1938). In Stage A, the emphasis should be on experiment, e.g. geometrical drawing. In Stage B there should be more emphasis on deduction. The idea of proof should be introduced. Stage C would take this further, introducing more rigour. Practical work here serves an introductory *pedagogical* purpose and then is to be moved away from.

Similarly, there were recommendations for a practical approach for 'average' and 'less able' pupils. The Board of Education's handbook (1937) suggested some geometry for the Senior Elementary School pupils, building on 'work in practical subjects'. The basically arithmetical curriculum was to be related, for these pupils, to 'the affairs of daily life' (p. 144). After the

Second World War, many secondary moderns in Chapman's (1959) survey reported a 'practical' approach. Some rural schools, for example, based their mathematics around farm and garden concerns. Some reported linking mathematics with other subjects as recommended in the section on 'ordinary' pupils in the HMI (1958) report. Pupils taking O level would have been exempt from this approach.

The actual practice in most schools at this time was not likely to have been very 'practical'. For example, HMI (1958: 111) note that some modern schools had emphasised a 'rigorous and exclusive insistence on the practice of mechanical skills, in long sequences of similar sums'. It is likely that only in a minority of schools were other approaches to mathematics teaching practised.

The belief in an approach to learning via 'activity' grew from the 1950s, and had a considerable influence in primary schools. The work of Piaget was often used to support this perspective (see, for example, Schools Council 1965: 5–9). The Association for Teaching Aids in Mathematics (ATAM) – later to become the Association of Teachers of Mathematics (ATM) – campaigned for this approach in mathematics education. Much of their work was aimed at the earlier years of schooling, and concerned structural apparatus for arithmetic (Griffiths and Howson 1974). But they also concerned themselves with the secondary years, arguing strongly for the use of models and practical work as aids to conceptual understanding and against pupils being taught to apply rules without understanding. A flavour of their perspective can be gained from two articles by Hope, a lecturer at Worcester Training College (later a co-founder of the Midlands Mathematical Experiment).

> We are not concerned with mere instruction designed to convince the child sufficiently for him to accept the teacher's dogmas, but with the child's creative activity by which he discovers and convinces himself [sic] and others of the truth and importance of his discoveries.
>
> (Hope 1958a: 11)

> One would like to see more reference to things to make, experiments to carry out, fields of mathematics to investigate . . .
>
> (Hope 1958b: 21–2)

Key words of later debates – activity, making, experimenting, discovering, investigating – are here, though it should not be assumed that their meaning has remained constant. The Mathematical Association was also at this time arguing that pupils needed 'actual experience and experiment again and again' in its report on secondary modern mathematics (Mathematical Association 1959: 19).

As noted earlier, at the same time as the ATM was struggling to reform pedagogy from inside the education system, others were turning outside to seek support for major change. Thwaites, the founder of the SMP, brought together a temporary coalition representing both pure and applied mathematicians from the universities, teachers from the public schools and personnel from industry and commerce. A concern with applications was reintroduced into the debate on selective school mathematics. 'Realism' became one key issue in the series of influential conferences on selective school mathematics in the late 1950s and early 1960s (Cooper 1985a). Hammersley, an applied mathematician later to attack 'modern mathematics', speaking at the Oxford conference of 1957, illustrates this.

> Mathematical examination problems are usually considered unfair if insoluble or improperly described; whereas the mathematical problems of real life are almost invariably insoluble and badly stated, at least in the first instance. In real life, the mathematician's main task is to formulate problems by building an abstract mathematical model consisting of equations, which shall be simple enough to solve without being so crude that they fail to mirror reality . . .
>
> (quoted in Cooper 1985a: 99)

Some SMP writers wanted more 'realistic' problems to be set in school mathematics. Their concern with applications was to be represented in their texts, alongside the introduction of 'modern' algebraic topics such as sets, groups and relations. SMP Book 5 (1969), for example, includes linear programming (as an example of mathematical modelling) and, in a chapter on practical arithmetic, sections on heating a house, investment, growth of money, hire purchase, buying a house, income tax and rates – as well as work on statistics. A concern with practical applications of mathematics was also to strongly characterise the approach of several other projects (Watson 1976; Cooper 1985a).

Notwithstanding this concern with applications, during the reaction against the 'modern mathematics' reforms, a central element was to be the issue of the preparation of pupils for work. It was to be suggested again and again that mathematics teaching was not achieving this. Cockcroft commissioned surveys of mathematics at work to use in its deliberations (see Dowling (1991b) for a critical examination of these). However, more than one version of school mathematics can be derived from a concern with preparation for work. Depending on the image of work accepted, either a stress on arithmetic and rule-following or a stress on more 'progressive' pedagogies can be argued (see Ernest 1992). It is because of this that, while some have been arguing that the needs of the economy are for more work on basic skills, others have been able to argue that their preference for an investigative and problem-solving approach is economically useful – in so far as it creates flexible, creative workers.

Investigations and an investigational approach to teaching mathematics are also not particularly new ideas. Polya's (1945) *How To Solve It*, concerning problem solving, and his subsequent work had a considerable influence on many teachers. We have already seen that the ATM was trying to move people in this direction in the 1950s, and a well-known popularising book discussed investigations in the teaching of algebra in 1964 (Sawyer 1964). SMP's early texts also were moving in this direction. Alongside the introduction of structural algebra we find a concern to change teaching and learning styles. Their O level Book 5 (SMP 1969) argues 'these texts pay . . . attention to an understanding of fundamental concepts . . . we hope that our texts are more attuned than is usual to the child's natural learning processes and that they encourage teachers to try out fresh teaching methods'. They continued, 'the approach from experiment, the initial emphasis upon experience and upon single concepts and the avoidance of manipulation and drill during the first years were dictated by an awareness of natural learning processes . . .' (p. v). Book 3T (1970) began with practical/experimental work on tessellations, and included 'investigations'. It included 'topological projects' to be carried out 'with three or four other pupils (or, if you prefer, on your own)' (p. 241), thus reflecting the increasing interest in group work and pupil discussion at this time (see, for example, Barnes *et al.* 1969). Other projects and individuals also favoured this general approach (Watson 1976). Furthermore, by 1970 arguments were also appearing from the computer science community for the use of the programming language Logo to allow pupils to actively construct their understanding of geometrical concepts (Papert 1972).

Later, in the 1970s, there was a development of coursework, project work and teacher assessment as part of changing practice in public examinations, especially under the CSE Mode III arrangements (Murphy and Torrance 1988). In spite of all this, mathematical pedagogy changed very slowly in secondary schools, though content changed faster. The HMI survey reported on 'practical' work:

> The use of realistic source material such as timetables, catalogues, newspapers, magazines, maps or instructional manuals was very limited. Material of this kind, and an experimental or practical approach to some of the topics in the course, were found in some ten per cent of GCE courses, in twenty to twenty-four per cent of CSE courses and in some thirty to forty per cent of non-examination courses.
>
> (DES 1979: 132)

A clear relationship between 'ability' and the use of 'practical' work can be seen. On pedagogy generally:

> The work was predominantly teacher controlled: teachers explained, illustrated, demonstrated, and perhaps gave notes on procedures and examples. The pupils were led deductively through small steps and closed questions to the principle being considered. A common pattern,

particularly with lower ability pupils, was to show a few examples on the board at the start of the lesson and then set similar exercises for the pupils to work on their own. There were few questions encouraging wider speculation or independent initiative.

(DES 1979: 136)

Cockcroft

Bringing together what had been said 'many times and over many years', the Cockcroft report (1982), in the now famous paragraph 243, argued that mathematics teaching 'at all levels should include opportunities for':

- exposition by the teacher
- discussion between teachers and pupils and between pupils themselves
- appropriate practical work
- consolidation and practice of fundamental skills and routines
- problem solving, including the application of mathematics to everyday situations
- investigational work

Problem solving was to 'relate both to the application of mathematics to everyday situations within the pupils' experience, and also to situations which are unfamiliar' (para. 249). 'Investigations' were not presented as equivalent to 'projects', i.e. as being necessarily an extended piece of work, but rather as concerning a willingness to ask 'what if?' questions generally in lessons (para. 250).

The subsequent HMI (1985) document, *Mathematics from 5 to 16*, recommended that 'appropriate practical work', 'problem-solving' and 'investigative work' should all form part of classroom approaches. Problem solving and investigative work were seen as not clearly distinguishable, but it was suggested that the former involved relatively convergent tasks and the latter more divergent ones. It was argued:

It is worth stressing to pupils that, in real life, mathematical solutions to problems have often to be judged by criteria of a non-mathematical nature, some of which may be political, moral or social. For example, the most direct route for a proposed new stretch of motorway might be unacceptable as it would cut across a heavily built-up area.

(HMI 1985: 41)

Several Government initiatives resulted from Cockcroft's argument for a use of a wider range of pedagogic approaches having a considerable influence in schools. In 1985, Keith Joseph announced the appointment of 350 Advisory Teachers for Mathematics, who were to play a significant role in acting as catalysts for pedagogic change (Straker 1988). The DES also funded the influential LAMP project (1983–6), whose brief was to develop and encourage 'good practice' in the teaching of mathematics to 'low attaining pupils' and to investigate ways of disseminating its work. The project, based at the West Sussex Institute of Higher Education, and involving a dozen teacher–researchers given partial release from their schools, had a considerable direct influence in the surrounding counties and, via its report *Better Mathematics* (Low Attainers in Mathematics Project 1987), a more indirect influence throughout the educational system.

The GCE/CSE and GCSE National Criteria

One of fifteen aims set out by the Joint Council of the GCE/CSE Boards in their National Criteria for the 16+ was for pupils to 'apply combinations of mathematical skills and techniques in problem-solving' (*TES* 18 February 1983). On assessment, it was proposed that coursework would be optional, but if chosen must account for at least 20 per cent of marks. Written exam papers were to account for at least 50 per cent. Sir Keith Joseph, then Secretary of State for Education, argued for a greater emphasis on 'extended pieces of work, mathematical investigations and problem-solving, alongside teaching the use of mathematics as the language of science' (*TES* 26 August 1983), probably reflecting his concern that 'non-academic' pupils receive a more 'practical' curriculum (Whitty 1985: 184). He wanted more thought given to whether timed, written papers should be the only compulsory element in exams at 16, and whether they need be at least 50 per cent of the total assessment.

Not surprisingly, therefore, when the National Criteria for GCSE mathematics were published (DES/WO 1985), one emphasis was on applying mathematics, problem solving and investigative work. Generally, assessment schemes were to 'assess not only the performance of skills and techniques but also pupils' understanding of mathematical processes, their ability to make use of these processes in the solution of problems and their ability to reason mathematically' (p. 1). Aim 2.7, reflecting the concern over 'real' problems that had characterised earlier debates, was that pupils should be able to 'recognise when and how a situation may be represented mathematically, identify and interpret relevant factors and, where necessary, select an appropriate mathematical method to solve the problem'. Aim 2.13 was to 'develop [pupils'] mathematical abilities by considering problems and conducting individual and co-operative enquiry and experiment including extended pieces of work of a practical and investigative kind'.

These aims were reflected in the detailed assessment objectives. From 1991 all GCSEs in mathematics would have to include assessment other than 'time-limited written examinations', in order that oral, practical and investigational work could be properly assessed (assessment objectives 3.16 and 3.17). Meanwhile, from 1988, all Examining Groups had to offer at least one scheme that would allow this. Coursework was now official. However, many in mathematics education circles believed the GCSE criteria had not gone far enough. Margaret Brown, an advocate of graded assessment (Pennycuick and Murphy 1988), attacked the proposals in the *TES* (10 May 1985), arguing that not enough emphasis had been given to practical and investigational skills, that coursework should not be optional and – returning us to the issue of differentiation – that there was a danger of pupils being sorted into rigid bands by the fourth year because of the stress on there being three separate levels of assessment, each with its own syllabus.

By the mid to late 1980s, in some schools investigations and/or an investigational approach became a very significant part of the approach to mathematics, though in others 'investigations' were dealt with in separate periods – to prepare to meet the GCSE coursework requirements – and otherwise mathematics continued as before (Cooper 1990). A few schools became well known for focusing on an investigational approach. Some mathematics departments willingly practised assessment by coursework, while in other schools there was considerable dispute within departments over the stress that should be put on this, partly motivated by some teachers' anxieties about how to use this approach.

The 'New Right' and others organised a number of attacks on investigational approaches. In a well-publicised book attacking the GCSE, for example, Coldman and Shepherd attacked the 'gradual intrusion and acceptance of empirical methodology' in the mathematics curriculum (North 1987: 63). The GCSE, they argued, was 'the latest stage in a disastrous process that has seen school mathematics drift towards becoming a low-level empirical science' (p. 63). Prais (1985) continued to argue his case that British standards were too low in arithmetic and basic mathematical skills. These arguments were to reappear in the subsequent debates over the details of the mathematics National Curriculum.

The debate over the National Curriculum in mathematics

For a more detailed account of the National Curriculum debate than given here see Ernest (1992), Ball (1990) and Noss (1990). The Mathematics Working Party was set up in July 1987, and comprised '9 mathematics educationists, 3 head teachers, 4 educational administrators, 2 academics, 1 industrialist and 1 member of the New Right' (Ernest 1992: 45). Broadly speaking, what occurred during its period of work was a shift away from an initial statement which tended in the 'progressive' direction towards a more 'traditional' view of pedagogy. The final report of the Working Party (DES/WO 1988b) argued that profile component three (PC3), 'Practical applications of mathematics', which gave central importance to processes in terms of 'personal qualities', 'communication skills' and 'using mathematics', should form 40 per cent of the assessment weightings. In spite of this receiving the support of a 'large majority' of respondents in the subsequent 'consultation' exercise (NCC 1988: 12), PC3 disappeared under attack from elements of the 'New Right', reappearing in reduced form as the two of the fourteen ATs concerned with 'Using and applying mathematics' (DES/WO 1989). Similarly, the argument that long multiplication and division algorithms were unnecessary, given the calculator, received much criticism from the same source. Eventually, Baker, then Secretary of State for Education, instructed the National Curriculum Council to include these as 'paper and pencil methods for long division and long multiplication' (NCC 1988). As Ball (1990) shows, professional and industrial members of the working party failed to achieve the degree of emphasis that they had wanted on 'real-life' problem solving and investigations. It is important to note, though, that the emphasis of the *Mathematics: Non-Statutory Guidance*, published after the *Standing Orders for Mathematics*, is very much in these 'process' areas. Since then, the fourteen ATs have been reduced to five (NCC 1991), of which one concerns 'Using and applying mathematics', and the focus of debate has shifted to the testing of pupils at the four key stages, i.e. at the ages of 7, 11, 14 and 16.

At the age of 7, we have seen a move away from relatively time-consuming practical tests to more traditional paper and pencil tests (*The Guardian* 4 July 1991; *The Independent* 3 December 1991; *TES* 6 December 1991). For GCSE the government has moved to reduce the amount of coursework assessed by teachers within the schools. In July 1991 the Prime Minister suggested in a speech to the Centre for Policy Studies that no more than 20 per cent of marks should be awarded on the basis of coursework, linking this to concern over 'standards' (*The Independent* 4 July 1991). Later that month Lord Griffiths, a right wing economist who had headed Margaret Thatcher's Policy Unit, was appointed chairperson of the Schools Examinations and Assessment Council (SEAC). Several months later, after considerable argument, it was decided that the coursework limit would not be reduced to 20 per cent in most subjects but that it would be in mathematics (*The Independent* 31 October 1991; *TES* 29 November 1991). This occurred in spite of the Mathematics Committee of SEAC apparently having wanted a 70 per cent limit – though their Chair, the right wing educationist John Marks, did not, according to *The Times Educational Supplement*, endorse this view (*TES* 6 December 1991). Again, during the planning of the standard assessment tasks (SATs) for 14 year olds at key stage 3, there was a move away from oral and practical testing to the use of pencil and paper tests, in spite of concern about the likely negative effects of this on girls' results in particular (*TES* 1 February 1991, 29 November 1991). Clearly, what all these changes have in common is a move away from the assessment by teachers of a wide range of educational outcomes towards the assessment – externally in the case of GCSE – of a more limited range of skills.

Nevertheless, looking back over the post-Cockcroft period of change, there can be no doubt that, in spite of these more recent events, there were major changes in mathematics in some secondary schools, away from a 'transmission' pedagogy (Barnes 1976). As a result of the Cockcroft report, the advisory teachers, the LAMP project, the requirement for a coursework element in the GCSE, the INSET activities surrounding the GCSE and the marketing of many books on investigations and 'activities', there certainly was a shift in the ways in which many mathematics teachers conceptualised their work and also some shift in actual practice. But how general was it? We can gain some idea from the HMI's report on the first year of the National Curriculum in mathematics, though we must bear in mind that some teachers may have moved away by then from more open-ended practical and investigational work as a result of the demands of the National Curriculum (Scott-Hodgetts 1992). HMI note, reporting on the implementation of key stages 1 and 3, that 'increased attention was paid to practical work which was more in evidence in Year 1 than in Year 7, where it was often not an integral part of the mathematics curriculum' (HMI 1991: 22). Furthermore,

> activities which encouraged pupils to investigate and solve problems were increasingly adopted during the year in both Years 1 and 7. However, they were still usually 'bolt-on extras' and not fully integrated into the whole mathematics programme. There were few schools which had developed problem solving as the major thrust of the mathematics curriculum.
>
> (HMI 1991: 22)

Evidence of more 'traditional' approaches can be found; 'in a significant number of mathematics lessons, especially in Year 7, there was undue emphasis on the practice of manipulative skills in a narrow way' (p. 22). Oral work tended to involve 'closed questions', and 'mathematics in many secondary classrooms was too often a solitary and silent activity' (p. 24).

In their subsequent report (HMI 1992) on the second year of the National Curriculum, oral discussion was found to be a feature of only one in twenty lessons in Years 7 and 8. Some improvement had occurred in 'using and applying mathematics' but these ATs 1 and 9 were 'only evident in 14% of the work seen in Year 7 and Year 8' (p. 26). Furthermore, 'low attaining pupils spent about half of their time in mathematics manipulating numbers and practising skills isolated from contexts' (p. 26).

As noted earlier, it is possible that in some schools there has been a recent move away from practical work and investigations as a result of the introduction of the National Curriculum, the increased emphasis on national testing of basic skills and competition between schools for pupils. Because of this, it might be rash to assume that the findings of the HMI reports can be taken as a measure of the effect of Cockcroft and its supporters on teachers' *desire* to change their practice. On the other hand, there is possibly enough in the National Curriculum documents, especially the original *Mathematics: Non-Statutory Guidance* (NCC 1989), to allow teachers to legitimate an approach based on Cockcroft's recommendations. HMI's findings therefore suggest that many teachers had not yet taken Cockcroft's paragraph 243 on board.

But we must also ask whether there had begun to be a routinisation of 'problem solving' and 'investigations', possibly motivated by the need teachers – many of them not well-qualified mathematically (Straker 1987; Merson 1989) – felt for a way of coping with the increasing demands on them. Hewitt (1992; see also Chapter 5) has recently argued that investigations have been developed in a way that draws the pupils' attention away from the mathematical content of problems (see also Lerman 1989). The recent national pilot tests for key stage 3 seem, similarly, to attempt to routinise problem solving in 'real-life' contexts in a manner which removes the 'real' from the problem (Cooper 1992). To move secondary mathematics away from a decontextualised 'transmission' pedagogy may yet prove a more difficult cultural change than many had hoped, especially given the current government's preferences for highly visible and easily tested outcomes in education. On the other hand, many teachers discovered in the 1980s that pedagogic approaches involving more pupil activity and greater reference to 'real' contexts could motivate their pupils in ways that 'traditional' approaches could not (see *Better Mathematics*), and these teachers are unlikely to give them up readily. The next few years, in which the battle over preferred pedagogies will be fought out, are likely to be critical for the future of English mathematics education – and, of course, for pupils' mathematical development.

REFERENCES

Ball, S.J. (1981) *Beachside Comprehensive*, Cambridge: Cambridge University Press.
—— (1990) *Politics and Policy Making in Education*, London: Routledge.
Banks, B. (1975) '. . . and how the KMP progresses', *The Times Educational Supplement*, 3 October: 51.
Barnes, D. (1976) *From Communication to Curriculum*, Harmondsworth: Penguin.
Barnes, D. *et al*. (1969) *Language, the Learner and the School*, Harmondsworth: Penguin.
Bernstein, B. (1971) 'On the classification and framing of educational knowledge', in M.F.D. Young (ed.) *Knowledge and Control*, London: Collier-Macmillan.
Board of Education (1937) *Handbook of Suggestions for Teachers*, London: HMSO.
Bourdieu, P. and Passeron, J-C. (1977) *Reproduction in Education, Society and Culture*, London: Sage.
Bowles, S. and Gintis, H. (1976) *Schooling in Capitalist America*, London: RKP.
Braverman, H. (1974) *Labour and Monopoly Capital*, New York: Monthly Review Press.
Burton, L. (ed.) (1986) *Girls Into Maths Can Go*, London: Holt.
Central Advisory Council for Education (1963) *Half Our Future*, London: HMSO.
Centre for Policy Studies (1988) *The Correct Core*, London: Centre for Policy Studies.
Chapman, J.V. (1959) *Your Secondary Modern Schools*, London: College of

Preceptors.

Cockcroft, W.H. (1982) *Mathematics Counts*, London: HMSO.

Cooper, B. (1983) 'On explaining change in school subjects', *British Journal of Sociology of Education* 4(3): 207–22.

—— (1985a) *Renegotiating Secondary School Mathematics*, Barcombe: Falmer.

—— (1985b) 'Secondary school mathematics since 1950: reconstructing differentiation', in I.F. Goodson (ed.) *Social Histories of the Secondary Curriculum*, Barcombe: Falmer.

—— (1990) 'PGCE students and investigational approaches in secondary mathematics', *Research Papers in Education* 5(2): 127–51.

—— (1992) 'Testing National Curriculum mathematics: some critical comments on the treatment of "real" contexts for mathematics', *The Curriculum Journal* 3(3): 231–43.

D'Ambrosio, U. (1991) 'Ethnomathematics and its place in the history and pedagogy of mathematics', in M. Harris (ed.) *Schools, Mathematics and Work*, Basingstoke: Falmer.

Damerow, P. and Westbury, I. (1985) 'Mathematics for all – problems and implications', *Journal of Curriculum Studies* 17(2): 175–84.

Dempster, J.J.B. (1949) *Education in the Secondary Modern School*, London: Methuen.

DES (1979) *Aspects of Secondary Education in England*, London: HMSO.

—— (1980) *Aspects of Secondary Education in England: Supplementary Information on Mathematics*, London: HMSO.

DES/WO (1985) *GCSE: The National Criteria: Mathematics*, London: HMSO.

—— (1988a) *National Curriculum: Task Group on Assessment and Testing: A Report*, London: HMSO.

—— (1988b) *Mathematics for Ages 5 to 16*, London: HMSO.

—— (1989) *Mathematics in the National Curriculum*, London: HMSO.

Dowling, P. (1991a) 'A touch of class: ability, social class and intertext in SMP 11–16', in D. Pimm and E. Love. (eds) *Teaching and Learning School Mathematics*, London: Hodder & Stoughton.

—— (1991b) 'The contextualising of mathematics: towards a theoretical map', in M. Harris (ed.) *Schools, Mathematics and Work*, Basingstoke: Falmer.

Ernest, P. (1992) 'The National Curriculum in mathematics: its aims and philosophy', in M. Nickson and S. Lerman (eds) *The Social Context of Mathematics Education*, London: South Bank University Press.

Evans, J. (1985) *Teaching in Transition*, Milton Keynes: Open University Press.

Frost, D. (1975) 'What is SMILE?', *The Times Educational Supplement* 3 October: 49.

Griffiths, H.B. and Howson, A.G. (1974) *Mathematics, Society and Curricula*, Cambridge: Cambridge University Press.

Halsey, A.H. *et al.* (1980) *Origins and Destinations*, Oxford: Oxford University Press.

Hammersley, M. (1985) 'From ethnography to theory: a programme and paradigm in the sociology of education', *Sociology* 19(2): 244–59.

Hayman, M. (1975) 'To each according to his needs', *Mathematical Gazette* 59: 137–53.

Hewitt, D. (1992) 'Train Spotter's Paradise', *Mathematics Teaching* 140.

HMI (1958) *Teaching Mathematics in Secondary Schools*, London: HMSO.

—— (1985) *Mathematics From 5 to 16*, London: HMSO.

—— (1991) *Mathematics: Key Stages 1 and 3: A Report by HM Inspectorate on the First Year, 1989–90*, London: HMSO.

—— (1992) *Mathematics: Key Stages 1, 2 and 3: A Report by HM Inspectorate on the Second Year, 1990–91*, London: HMSO.

Hope, C. (1958a) 'Filmstrip in mathematics', *Mathematics Teaching* 6 (April).

—— (1958b) 'The printed word', *Mathematics Teaching* 6 (April): 20–2.

Howson, A.G. (1982) *A History of Mathematics Education in England*, Cambridge: Cambridge University Press.

—— (1989) *Maths Problem: Can More Pupils Reach Higher Standards?*, London: Centre for Policy Studies.

ICMI (1986) *The Influence of Computers and Informatics on Mathematics and its Teaching*, Cambridge: Cambridge University Press.

Isaacson, Z. (1987) *Teaching GCSE Mathematics*, London: Hodder & Stoughton.

Lacey, C. (1970) *Hightown Grammar*, Manchester: Manchester University Press.

Lerman, S. (1989) 'Investigations: where to now?', in P. Ernest (ed.) *Mathematics Teaching: the State of the Art*, Basingstoke: Falmer.

Low Attainers in Mathematics Project (1987) *Better Mathematics*, London: HMSO.

Maclure, S. (1973) *Educational Documents*, London: Methuen.

Mathematical Association (1938) *A Second Report on the Teaching of Geometry in Schools*, London: Bell.

—— (1959) *Mathematics in Secondary Modern Schools*, London: Bell.

Merson, M. (1989) 'Teacher match and education policy', *Journal of Education Policy* 4(2) 171–84.

Murphy, R. and Torrance, H. (1988) *The Changing Face of Educational Assessment*, Milton Keynes: Open University Press.

NCC (1988) *Consultation Report: Mathematics*, York: NCC.

—— (1989) *Mathematics: Non-Statutory Guidance*, York: NCC.

—— (1991) *Consultation Report: Mathematics*, York: NCC.

North, J. (1987) *The GCSE: an Examination*, London: Claridge Press.

Noss, R. (1990) 'The National Curriculum and mathematics: a case of divide and rule?', in P. Dowling and R. Noss (eds) *Mathematics Versus the National Curriculum*, Basingstoke: Falmer.

Papert, S. (1972) 'Teaching children thinking', *Mathematics Teaching* 58: 2–7.

Pennycuick, D. and Murphy, R. (1988) *The Impact of Graded Tests*, Basingstoke: Falmer.

Polya, G. (1945) *How To Solve It*, Princeton: Princeton University Press.

Prais, S. (1985) 'Schooling standards in England and Germany: some summary comparisons bearing on economic performance', *National Institute Economic Review*, May: 53–76.

Price, M. (1983) 'Mathematics in English secondary education 1860–1914', *History of Education* 12(4): 271–84.

—— (1986) 'The Perry movement in school mathematics', in M. Price (ed.) *The Development of the Secondary Curriculum*, London: Croom-Helm.

Ranson, S. (1984) 'Towards a tertiary tripartism', in P. Broadfoot (ed.) *Selection, Certification and Control*, Barcombe: Falmer.

Ruthven, K. (1986) 'Differentiation in mathematics: a critique of *Mathematics Counts* and *Better Schools*', *Cambridge Journal of Education* 16(1): 41–5.

Sawyer, W.W. (1964) *Vision in Elementary Mathematics*, Harmondsworth: Penguin.

Schools Council (1965) *Mathematics in Primary Schools*, London: HMSO.

—— (1977) *Mixed-ability Teaching in Mathematics*, London: Evans/Methuen.

Scott-Hodgetts, R. (1992) 'The National Curriculum: implications for the sociology of mathematics classrooms', in M. Nickson and S. Lerman (eds) *The Social Context of Mathematics Education*, London: South Bank University Press.

Shan, S-J. and Bailey, P. (1991) *Multiple Factors: Classroom Mathematics for*

Equality and Justice, Stoke-on-Trent: Trentham.

SMP (1969) *The School Mathematics Project, Book 5*, Cambridge: Cambridge University Press.

Straker, N. (1987) 'Mathematics teacher shortages in secondary schools: implications for mathematics departments', *Research Papers in Education* 2(2): 126–52.

—— (1988) 'Advisory teachers of mathematics: the ESG initiative', *Journal of Education Policy* 3(4): 371–84.

Watson, F.R. (1976) *Developments in Mathematics Teaching*, London: Open Books.

Weiner, M.J. (1981) *English Culture and the Decline of the Industrial Spirit, 1850–1980*, Harmondsworth: Penguin.

Whitty, G. (1985) *Sociology and School Knowledge*, London: Methuen.

Woods, P. (1976) 'The myth of subject choice', *British Journal of Sociology* 27(2): 130–49.

Young, M.F.D. (1971) 'Curricula as socially organised knowledge', in M.F.D. Young (ed.) *Knowledge and Control*, London: Collier-Macmillan.

Part II

How might student activity be initiated and sustained?

To enter a classroom and to engage pupils in working on mathematics with interest and enthusiasm is every teacher's dream. How might this come about?

Even though usage may vary, most school mathematics departments have a published scheme available. In Chapters 2, 3 and 4, the debate about the value of such schemes is considered. The following issues are addressed.

1 How should published schemes be used?
2 Should published schemes be the only source of mathematical activity in the classroom?
3 Are pupils learning effectively through a scheme?
4 What are the benefits of group work in such an environment and how should it be organised?
5 Are there improved benefits from devising a home-made scheme?

In Chapters 5, 6 and 7, the focus is on the role of investigation in mathematics. In Chapter 5 Dave Hewitt argues that many mathematics investigations become focused on numerical results, finding patterns and generalising. In Chapters 6 and 7 which follow, two practising teachers explain how they use mathematical investigation in very different ways from that described by Dave Hewitt. Anne Watson encourages her pupils to engage with mathematics and to think mathematically, and the investigations she sets up are vehicles for the pupils to become independent thinkers. Mike Ollerton uses one starting point as a vehicle for inviting pupils to explore mathematics at their own level and how the starting point can become a springboard to a whole range of mathematical activity. Their discussions offer the reader a snapshot of their classrooms and their way of working with pupils.

Chapter 2

Schemes

LAMP (Low Attainers in Mathematics Project)

PUBLISHED SCHEMES

We have found cause for concern in the adverse effects that a close adherence to a published scheme can have on both children's learning of mathematics and teachers' professional development. Seven of these concerns are outlined below.

1 Investigatory or enquiry elements of schemes are often left out by teachers, frequently because of 'syllabus pressures'. This is an age old problem which can be easily exemplified from most post-war publications. In trying to resolve this some schemes have attempted to include enquiry as a compulsory component of their course. However, there are two problems with this.

(i)   Because the more stretching investigatory elements of some schemes are not reached until initial material has been completed by pupils, it is often only the quicker children who get a taste of this kind of work. *All* children need and benefit from mathematical exploration.

(ii)   When given greater status, and often in order to 'help' the teacher, investigatory elements can become prescriptive and limiting, precluding the teachers' and children's own questions and losing all sense of real enquiry or exploration. The following writing illustrates this concern.

> What is it that some schemes offer pupils when they include their 'Investigations' chapter or booklet? All too often these consist of a long list of questions beautifully annotated and carefully structured so ensuring that pupils will be able to work independently and have enough to get on with, but offer no encouragement to ask questions of their own.
>
> If all the questions come from text, worksheet, blackboard or are asked by me then what is the essence within the mathematical experience undergone by my pupils that warrants my calling it an investigation?

2   New schemes are often chosen because they are seen to cater for a particular organisational classroom priority. However, the 'prices' that are paid for these priorities may well have adverse effects on the children's mathematical experiences. For example, if the priority is to ensure that pupils can 'get on' independently of their teacher, there is a danger that a scheme which provides for this may also lead to the mathematical content being unnaturally fragmented.

3   By their nature most schemes are answer oriented, some to make life easier for teachers, some to encourage pupils to 'work back' from solutions and some to enable pupils to mark their own work so as not to hamper their speed of progression. One teacher writes of the answer-oriented view his scheme has given his pupils:

> As work is self-marked, only questions with a single answer are asked . . . but some of the cards do say 'what do you notice?' Pupils quickly learn that there is AN answer to this too and either look up answers or ask a teacher, who provides the words.
>
> Responses not in the exact form of words in the answer sheets are marked wrong by pupils. Any teacher intervention in this process, with positive encouragement to speculate, is viewed with suspicion. Authority rests with the answer sheets!

4   Many mathematics schemes now include microcomputer software packages. There is, however, a danger that computers are not realising their potential as powerful vehicles for mathematical enquiry and development in the classroom. Although many of the programs within the packages can provide excellent starting points for exploration, some are no more than simulations of what are considered to be successful classroom activities. When these activities are 'translated' for use on a computer they sometimes lack flexibility, precluding and limiting opportunities for pupils to follow up their own ideas or organise their own work. All too often the packages in general are used as 'rewards' and devices to 'keep the pupils occupied'.

5   The teacher's role can be undermined by a close adherence to a polished scheme. A teacher wrote:

> My horror stories are not so much the schemes as the teachers who:
>
> go in knowing that 25th March means p. 47 Book 2;
>
> rely on their scheme to prepare their lessons for them;
>
> feel that published schemes know better than they do;

are so bound by the structure of a scheme that they can't, or don't want to try anything else;

think it's the scheme's and examination's job to motivate their pupils;

feel too comfortable to be open minded about change.

Much of the undermining occurs because a scheme is seen to take over classroom responsibilities that should be those of the teacher. Responding to the immediate needs of individual children, controlling material, deciding what should happen next and what pathways of learning should be encouraged are all essential parts of the teacher's role and cannot be generalised by an external system written for unknown children and teachers.

6 Frequently an adherence to a scheme is seen as a necessary support for so-called 'weak teachers'. However, even as a short-term solution this can be unsatisfactory and often counter-productive. This is also true of the understandable concern frequently expressed about probationary teachers of mathematics as this head of department indicates in the following.

If, as I believe, teaching is improved through reflecting on our classroom experiences, then to consider a scheme as something that will 'make it OK for a probationary teacher' is arrant nonsense, since it denies the ways in which teachers develop their abilities.

Most schemes, by APPEARING to make a probationary an effective teacher – ie able to keep the class 'happy' and 'occupied at their tasks' can undermine that teacher's development, hiding the real need for it. That is a most pernicious effect.

Schemes need to be 'patchy' in order that the teacher has to take responsibility for the development in children of the processes and strategies of mathematical activity.

For all teachers, support and development are essential.

A considerable part of the teaching of mathematics is done by non-specialists. These are sometimes strong teachers of their first subject, and it is commonly assumed that they will benefit from even more guidelines and will need a strictly prescriptive mathematics scheme. We have found, however, that the development of these teachers is also undermined by such a provision. When allowed the time for an element of 'retraining', their development is also facilitated and they can become significant members of a mathematics department, bringing unique insights and making valuable contributions. A tutor on such a retraining course wrote:

It was interesting to see that teachers arrived with a very limited idea of mathematics and mathematics teaching.

Having been given the opportunity on the course to engage in mathematics themselves in an exploratory and creative way, and thus experience the positive aspects of the subject, they began to realise their own capabilities in mathematics.

This experience also enabled them to see how successful teaching approaches from their own subject area could be used in this new area of the curriculum.

One teacher told me about how she taught English, describing how she collected materials, utilised the pupils own ideas and generally fuelled their creativity. The realisation slowly dawned on her that she could teach mathematics in the same way.

Statement 1   Schemes are offered in good faith by advisers, headteachers and other concerned agencies to teachers of mathematics as 'solutions' to classroom problems. In practice, because in the end schemes fundamentally undermine the principles of teacher development, they become major inhibitors to improvement in the quality of mathematics teaching.

7   New schemes are often taken on in order to initiate change in static teaching situations dominated by exposition and textbooks. Sometimes this is in order to respond to a national initiative such as the recommendations of the Cockcroft Committee, or GCSE. We have found that where a department is aware that the new scheme is merely a starting point for discussion and development it has been beneficial. However, in many cases even when schemes have been taken on in this spirit they have failed to facilitate development. Key teachers leave, financial investment inhibits rejection and busy teachers with other responsibilities who would have been in a strong position to contribute to departmental development become reluctant to endanger what is for them a familiar, administratively efficient system. In these all too frequent cases the scheme becomes a substitute for genuine teacher development rather than a vehicle for it, and the quality of the children's mathematics learning may well not be improved. Teachers begin to teach 'the scheme' rather than teach mathematics.

Statement 2   No mathematics scheme alone can meet the needs of pupils and an adherence to any scheme may prove detrimental to their mathematics. The mathematical development of pupils can only be encouraged, sustained, evaluated and assessed by the personal involvement of their teachers. It is not possible to produce a definitive scheme which will apply to all pupils or situations, even within specific ability ranges.

HOME-MADE SCHEMES

Faced with the above problems, or in efforts to increase departmental involvement or in order to deal with a school-specific problem (mixed ability, team teaching etc.) many departments decide to produce their own scheme, often based on a prescribed sequence of home-made workcards, booklets or worksheets. We have found that in time there is a real danger of these schemes becoming as habitual as published schemes, and that in many cases the same problems are to be found. Added to these is the strength of attachment that is derived from the expenditure of personal time and effort. This makes change and flexibility that much harder to achieve. A head of department wrote as follows.

> Teachers cannot afford to be sentimental about the form – of organisation, resources, methods etc. – when they accept responsibilities for the mathematical growth of their pupils. They need much greater confidence in themselves so that they can 'kick around' and experiment with new methods and materials. They need to develop their power to live, change, grow and respond so that they can meet changes and disturbances which are present in life. This they can hardly begin to develop if most of their energies and beliefs are invested in methods, organisations and 'materials'.

A teacher who inherited a highly acclaimed home-produced scheme wrote about it while looking at paragraph 243 of the Cockcroft Report.

The scheme demands that the following happen:

1. Exposition
We have 'lead-lessons' for each year group.

2a. Discussion between teacher and pupil
This happens in all other lessons, but the scheme does dictate the nature of that discussion; it tends to be 'answer giving', 'how to do it', rather than shared talk.

2b. Discussion between pupils themselves
Grouping around tables allows this, but it is used as the worst punishment to make pupils work in silence for a time. Does this mean discussion is a privilege not a necessity?

3. Appropriate practical work
Some tasks demand painting, drawing, using dice, pinboards, cutting up paper, making models, but who are these appropriate for? All pupils tackle these activities simultaneously. Have you ever seen 120 children all using glue at the same time? It is terrifying!

4. Consolidation and practice of fundamental skills and routines
'Basic skills' are on particular sheets in the first and third year, tackled fortnightly. So if 'basic skills' are 'sums' the scheme has these.

5. Problem solving
The nearest the scheme has to this is some sheets which offer a mixture of tricks, jokes and some reasonable 'starters' (with an answer!)

6. Investigational work

'Investigations' occur in fourth and fifth year work. 'Find out about . . .'
occurs frequently but in practice means 'ask a teacher' or 'look it up'.
Several tasks at the end of topic books are headed 'investigations' but (i)
few pupils get this far, and (ii) the answers are on the answer sheets.

Certainly, our scheme could be said to satisfy Cockcroft paragraph
243! Is this 'good practice'?

Home-made schemes, and even departmental schemes of work, are often
designed to be as flexible as possible, but without continual re-evaluation
and modification involving the *whole* department, a scheme can quickly
stagnate and its content take on a higher significance than was meant. A
teacher wrote:

I'm really concerned about the power of the written word. Once something has been formalised it can take on a far greater importance than was
perhaps originally intended.

Last summer two teachers put together a 3rd year scheme of work –
some of it based upon what they had done with their own groups over
the year. It meant very little to me when I first read it. I didn't understand why it was organised the way it was, why the content included
particular topics and not others, or why the activities listed had been
chosen.

The entire document seemed useless to me. I abandoned it, along with
several other teachers in the department, and instead we got together and
tried to sort out what we going to do.

If I'd been involved in the formation of the departmental scheme of
work I'd have realised the flexibility that was implicit in its structure.

Statement 3   A scheme cannot be a substitute for an ongoing dialogue with
colleagues. This generates more ideas and an increased awareness of pupils'
needs. The continuing process of development is more important than the
particular details of the curriculum. There are no short cuts and the process
takes time.

USING RESOURCES

A teacher described an incident with a bottom set, second-year class as
follows.

Two girls came up to me and asked if they could do some 'sums'. They
were fed up with what they were doing. I had some very old textbooks in
a cupboard that were full of exercises containing dozens of 'sums' ranging
from the four rules to quadratic equations. They were meant as practice
for pupils of considerably higher age and ability than these girls, but I

rather dismissively told them they were there and that they could choose something from them to do if they wanted.

When I got back to them they were happily engaged in experimenting with their calculators in order to obtain answers to an exercise entitled 'Changing Vulgar Fractions into Decimals'.

Not only were they not put off by the title but the only piece of sound knowledge they had was that a half equals 0.5. From this piece of information they were successfully completing the exercise.

Pupils in this class were used to asking their own questions about their mathematics and hence when offered material that would seem to be extremely uninviting they accepted it, as they normally would, as a challenge. Their personal motivation was sufficient for them to sustain exploration on their own and achieve good results.

Statement 4 When teachers and pupils are accustomed to exploring mathematical ideas and have established a positive attitude to learning, then almost any material can be used as a stimulus for mathematical enquiry in the classroom.

There is, at present, a wide variety of useful resources available for teachers and pupils in mathematics lessons. These include ideas within existing schemes and textbooks, resources in the form of thematic and topic booklets, books and periodicals containing ideas and 'starters', catalogues and timetables, reference material, magazine and newspaper articles, games and practical materials including calculators and computers, as well as the resources that the children bring with them to school in terms of ideas, interests and miscellaneous items. Spending limited departmental funds on 'packaged' schemes often means that no money remains for these forms of resources. This has implications in terms of teacher awareness about what is potentially useful in their mathematics classroom, and about what physical accommodation is necessary in order to work at the subject in the ways indicated throughout this report. In the first case we have found that when given the opportunities for teacher development, teachers have become more discerning and more demanding consumers of published material and equipment. In the second, it is essential that senior management do not look upon mathematics as a subject that can be taught in any room in the school as long as it has a blackboard and some chalk.

Statement 5 It is part of the professional concern of all teachers to take responsibility for choosing appropriate materials which will encourage pupils to learn mathematics. It is this professional responsibility which needs encouragement, time and resources to develop.

SUMMARY

The situation

1 There is cause for concern about the adverse effects that a close adherence to a published scheme can have on children's learning of mathematics.

2 Investigatory or enquiry elements of schemes are often left out by teachers, frequently because of 'syllabus pressures'.

3 It is often only the quicker children who get a taste of the more stretching investigatory elements of some schemes, because they are not reached until initial material has been completed.

4 In many schemes investigatory elements have become prescriptive and limiting.

5 By their nature most schemes are answer oriented.

6 Schemes are offered in good faith by advisers, headteachers and other concerned agencies to teachers of mathematics as solutions to classroom problems. In practice, schemes can become major inhibitors to improvements in the quality of mathematics teaching, because ultimately they undermine the principles of teacher development.

7 The mathematical development of pupils can only be encouraged, sustained, evaluated and assessed by the personal involvement of their teachers.

8 No mathematics scheme alone can meet the mathematical needs of pupils.

9 It is not possible to produce a definitive mathematics scheme which will apply to all pupils or situations, even within specific ability ranges.

10 Home-made schemes, if not constantly reviewed, will suffer from the same problems as published schemes.

11 When teachers and pupils are accustomed to exploring mathematical ideas and have established a positive attitude to learning, then almost any material can be used as a stimulus for mathematical enquiry in the classroom.

12 There is, at present, a wide variety of useful resources available for pupils in mathematics lessons.

13 When allowed the opportunities for teacher development, teachers have become more discerning and more demanding consumers of published material and equipment.

Recommendations

1 A scheme must not take over classroom responsibilities such as responding to the immediate needs of individual children, controlling material and deciding what should happen next and what pathways of learning should be encouraged. These responsibilities are those of the teacher and cannot be generalised by an external system.

2 Schemes and schemes of work should be continuously evaluated and modified. This process must include the *whole* department, and is more important than the particular details of the curriculum. There are no short cuts and the process takes time.

3 Resources in the form of ideas, thematic and topic booklets, catalogues and timetables, books and periodicals, reference material, magazine and newspaper articles, games and practical materials including calculators and computers are needed. The spending of limited departmental funds on 'packaged' schemes should be seriously questioned by schools as this often means that no money remains for these other forms of resources and this can lead to inflexibility.

4 It is essential that mathematics is recognised as a subject which has special accommodation requirements.

5 It must be seen to be part of the professional concern of all teachers to take responsibility for choosing appropriate materials which will encourage pupils to learn mathematics. It is this professional responsibility which needs encouragement and funds to develop.

Chapter 3

Small groups

Steve Turner and Maggie Furness

In this chapter we describe how we use a 'small group' approach in school.

Do you remember sitting in a class of thirty, bored to tears, wondering when the teacher would shut up so that you could get on with your examples? Or were you the type of pupil who kept your head down, understanding little of the discussion, only to feel embarrassed or belittled when the easy question came your way again?

If you are going to be a maths teacher, you were probably successful at school and more likely to associate with the first type of pupil. On the other hand, you came back on the 'other side' so you may well have been one of the types not mentioned so far, the lucky ones, close enough to the middle of the group to find the lessons interesting and challenging. Even so, don't delude yourself; even in a well-settled group there can be a substantial body of dissatisfied customers of the types mentioned, especially where exposition is used in front of thirty well-disciplined faces.

Of course, we know that with investigatory or problem-solving tasks a whole class can be engaged together actively in the introduction and conclusion discussions. Whoever is asked to speak to the group can, with skillful forethought on our part, produce explanations of ideas that benefit both the rest of the class and perhaps more importantly themselves. They will have tackled some ideas at their own level and pace and with helpful interactions and interventions should have found value in what they were doing. However, much of the work in the facts, skills and concepts area needs exposition. Any amount of discovering can never be as efficient as a discussion thoughtfully led by someone who already has mastery of the content. So how do we avoid the pitfalls mentioned above?

We try to use the SMP 11–16 Booklets to develop discussion between pupils and between pupils and ourselves. The various games give excellent opportunities for pupils to work together. When a pair is blended well, both contributing to the learning of the other, they stay together as a working partnership, which can produce more effective learning for the pair than the sum of the individuals.

At the start of Year 9 it is clearly unrealistic to change over to whole class, teacher-led working. The pupils, however, have mostly reached a stage where reflective discussion of the learning produced in the various real contexts can be the key to effective work. If more practical tasks are to be introduced to supplement the questions in the books and the teacher's time is to be used efficiently, it is clear that a working group needs to contain about six pupils. In trying this it soon became obvious that the groups needed to be smaller to amend the sometimes high noise of several people wanting to speak at the same time. The 'chemistry' of groups of six was almost impossible to manage, but smaller groups meant that teacher interactions had to be cut short and tended to be too directional.

The answer was to move into pairs, then as working rates become established, to move similar pairs into adjacent seats. Self-marking would then be completed in sixes along with the self-assessments used in our developing profile scheme. While the pairs are still together the teacher can then move in as required to instigate a discussion to conclude the chapter and to help pupils to generalise key points from the work completed. A check on progress and errors can also be made and recorded before introduction to the next piece of work. Pupils then collect whatever is required and carry on in their pairs. If homework is to be set from the texts, a certain amount of negotiation has to take place between the pairs in order to keep fairly close together. This process can of course be helped by careful use of extension questions both from the texts and from the teacher's own ideas.

When one person has been absent they can usually catch up in a mutually agreed period of time, sometimes having to work alone until that time or often joining in a new topic and catching up the last one at home on their own. Obviously groups and pairs change sometimes but discussion is facilitated and the space produced to enable real two-way discussion to take place. Even a teacher's limited absence causes only a minor hiccup where they too have to work hard to catch up with work completed by the groups. This general system, together with any other details of working routine preferred by individual teachers and groups, now forms the basis of the first lesson discussion when new classes are formed.

There are so many nice active learning tasks in the textbook section of the course that we must spend time with pupils discussing them. The best time for these discussions is often when pupils can take the lead; just after the tasks are completed and each pupil has written a short paragraph summarising what they feel they have learned from that section of work. The good habits of a well-organised classroom and pupils who can gather their own materials transfer from the first two years. A high level of familiarity with the course content by the teacher is as important as with the booklets, but because the class are working at a relatively limited range of tasks (all from the same book) this can be developed much more conveniently by a newcomer than is the case with the booklets.

With the pupils spending so much time working together it is important to assess individual learning. We are trying to do this by developing tests which have sets of items relating to the various understanding objectives which the course addresses. These are completed after each book is finished and a structured revision section of work is covered. Each objective set requires an 80 per cent success rate to pass and leads to certification which will eventually form the content side of our statement of achievement which each school leaver will receive. We have found that this can help pupils to feel more secure about mastery and motivate them to work more thoughtfully at areas they found difficult initially, in order to pass our retests.

The general feeling among pupils that they are responsible for their own progress continues. They feel they can initiate extra work when required to ensure their own mastery of the subject. We feel we have created an environment which provides the mathematical athletes an opportunity to pursue excellence yet also gives the stability and security required for the plodders to make and be aware of their own real progress. We feel sure that both types of characters introduced at the start of this article are beginning to genuinely enjoy their mathematics.

Chapter 4

Teaching for the test

Alan Bell

The National Curriculum is intended to produce a more uniform and a more sharply focused curriculum. Teachers will perhaps need to become more aware of what particular ideas and skills pupils are learning through the varied investigative and realistic activities they perform in the classroom, and to ensure that gaps get filled. There will undoubtedly be pressure to teach towards the attainment target items.

Teaching for the test is generally deplored – and widely practised. Its evils are greatest when the learning is short term, fading away as soon as the test is over, and when the learning is specific to the items in the test, not generalisable to other similar tasks. Producing tests which reflect the real tasks which we want pupils to be able to deal with in the immediate and longer-term future, and which tap knowledge in such a way that we can be confident that the attainment they record is effectively permanent, is the challenge currently facing the teams developing SATs – and, more importantly, facing those who will have to decide how effective a testing system they are prepared to finance.

The teacher's task will still be to obtain diagnostic information and to respond to it with teaching which has lasting effects. Work on diagnostic teaching at the Shell Centre at Nottingham has been developing teaching methods of this type. Our trials of these methods and materials have demonstrated both their considerable power compared with more usual methods and the very low level of effectiveness of some methods currently in widespread use – in particular, schemes where the pupils work largely on their own from individualised booklets.

Results from the APU surveys and from the research on mathematical understanding at Chelsea, Nottingham, and elsewhere round the world, have given us a few unwelcome surprises because they reveal rather slow progress in the mastery of fundamental ideas and some rather persistent areas of misunderstanding.

The following examples illustrate some of the common and persistent misunderstandings.

'Mushrooms cost 40 pence per pound. If I buy 25 pence worth, what weight will I get?' Ninety per cent of a middling third-year secondary class gave a correct estimate for the answer (i.e. $\frac{1}{2}$ lb, $\frac{3}{4}$ lb or similar); but, asked what calculation was required, only 10 per cent answered correctly, $25 \div 40$, most of the remainder giving $40 \div 25$, on the assumption that division must be of the larger by the smaller number.

There is also the Concepts in Secondary Maths and Science question on meat price (the price of minced beef is shown as 88.2 pence for each kilogram, what is the cost of a packet containing 0.58 kg of minced beef?) and its result: only 29 per cent of the 15 year olds correctly chose multiplication; 42 per cent suggested division, believing that this was the operation which would produce the necessary smaller number from 88.2.

A third example. Asked to put in order of size, smallest first, the decimals 0.236, 0.62 and 0.4, many pupils chose 0.236 as the largest, treating the decimal point as merely a separator between two integers (as in 3 hours 15 minutes), and some chose 0.4 as the largest, because it only involved tenths while the other numbers went into hundredths and thousandths.

This research gave important guidance about what can reasonably be expected at different stages, and much of this has been incorporated in the construction of assessment projects and in the National Curriculum itself. The diagnostic teaching project has followed up the implications for teaching and has developed the methods which are the focus of the trials to be described here.

The method involves teaching with an awareness of what are the actual difficulties and misunderstandings which the pupils need to overcome, and dealing with them intensively. We start by offering problems of the type we want the pupils to become able to deal with, and noting where the difficulties and breakdowns occur. It is useful at this stage to have some prior knowledge of the likely misunderstandings, and this is where the results of previous research come in. However, what one needs to know is not merely what points of common difficulty have been shown by research, but what are the actual problems of one's own pupils.

Good diagnostic test questions, written and oral, show these up clearly; and the sort of questioning which listens, follows up and probes the pupils' ideas is needed. One must get beyond the stage at which the pupils give back what they think the teacher wants, and encourage them to talk freely about how they see the situation. The conflict lesson itself usually starts with the posing of some quite hard problem which the pupils first think about individually, and write down their response, then discuss in small groups, again recording their conclusion, and subsequently discuss as a whole class. The group work helps to ensure that pupils' wrong ideas are actually brought out and expressed, and that they can be subjected to challenge and criticism in an unthreatening situation.

The class discussion exposes a wider range of ideas, and also ensures that if any whole group has agreed to a wrong idea, either other groups or the teacher can challenge it and pose corrective questions. Summing up by the teacher can be helpful, but should not be excessive, since the aim is that the pupils should reach well-founded convictions based on their own perceptions, not take over superficially understood ideas from the teacher. Even without any summing up, a well-focused discussion can lead to subsequent arrival at correct ideas, as the pupils turn over the experience in their minds.

So far, materials have been prepared and tested for several well-known areas of difficulty in the mathematics curriculum, such as decimals, directed numbers, multiplication and division problems involving decimals, rates (such as price, speed and measure conversion) and graphical interpretation. Some work has also been done in algebra, probability, ratio, fractions, shape recognition and other topics.

The first of the four sets of trials to be described involved teaching decimals to two parallel 12–13-year-old classes, covering a wide range of ability, by two contrasting methods, called 'conflict' and 'positive-only'. In the conflict method, each lesson began with some questions designed to expose any misunderstandings which the pupils might have in the topic in question. This was followed by a discussion in which pupils with correct and incorrect answers were encouraged to explain their viewpoints and to argue their cases to each other.

When the correct approach had been clarified there followed a consolidation phase, in which further questions were worked in the light of the understanding now gained. The positive-only method also focused on the known difficulties, and the same questions were used, but the correct approach was explained to the class before work began. More questions were covered to compensate for the time taken up by discussion in the conflict method, thus ensuring that equal times were spent on the two methods.

The same teacher taught both methods; he did not find this easy, and the presence of a colleague in the classroom as an observer offering comments helped him to keep to the appropriate method for each class. The eight lessons for each class covered three areas of decimal knowledge: scale-reading, decimal sequences and comparison of decimals. In scale-reading, the common misunderstandings include counting marks instead of spaces, writing $1.6\frac{1}{2}$ for 1.65 and 2.3 for 2.03 and assuming that every space was 0.1 even when five or twenty of them, rather than ten, made up a unit. The main problems in decimal numbering were those indicated above.

The effects of the two teaching methods were judged from the results of a test given before and after the teaching, and again some weeks later. Between pre-test and delayed test, the 'conflict' group improved from a mean score of 44 per cent to 80 per cent, a gain of 36 per cent, while the 'positive-only' group rose from 52 per cent to 76 per cent, a gain of 24 per cent (significant level of difference; 1.2 per cent). Note that in this case, both teaching methods focused on the misconceptions, the only difference being in the presence or absence of conflict-based discussion. This result certainly calls into question the widespread assumption that teachers should not display or dwell upon errors lest they should lead to confusion. It shows, on the contrary, that errors which arise from some definite misunderstanding or tendency of thought need to be exposed and thoroughly discussed if they are to be eradicated – and that even if this takes considerable time, it is cost-effective in terms of better results.

The second round of trials to be described was on a larger scale, seven classes being taught using a conflict-discussion method, and two with a typical expository method (in which the pupils mainly worked on problems while the teacher came round and helped).

The topic was rates, and the common misconceptions related to the desire to divide larger by smaller, the confusion of the roles of the two quantities constituting the rate (pence per gram versus grams per penny) and the interrelations between speed, distance and time (some pupils assumed that for a given distance, more speed means more time). The teaching material included a number of new tasks aimed at exposing misunderstandings and arousing conflict, such as making up verbal problems to fit given numbers and 'marking homework' – an exercise in which pupils have to correct a supposed homework, identifying the errors and explaining how they might have arisen.

The results were similar to those in the previous case, but the differences were greater: the conflict groups gained, on average, 20 points between pre- and post-test and lost only one point between post and delayed tests, while the exposition-and-exercises groups gained 10 points by the post-test stage, then lost 5.

This general pattern of results, in which the conflict group gained some-what more initially and lost much less over time, was repeated in the remaining two sets of comparative trials to be described here. These were on reflections and on fractions, and in both cases the comparison was with teaching based on the SMP 11–16 booklet scheme. The 'conflict' material was devised by the teachers concerned to cover the same ground as the relevant SMP booklets (*Reflections* 1 and 2 and *Fractions* 1 to 3).

The work on reflections was conducted with two parallel first-year mixed-ability classes in the same school, though in this case the classes did not have the same teacher. The 'conflict' teaching focused, as before, on observed misconceptions (such as that horizontal or vertical objects always have horizontal or vertical images, and that any line which divides a figure into equal parts is a line of symmetry). But it also aimed to establish, explicitly, through the conflict-discussions, the correct principles for relating object and image (straight across the same distance, with appropriate interpretation).

But whereas the booklets contained large numbers of fairly easy questions, the conflict teaching was begun by giving one or two much harder questions of the same general type, to be argued out in small groups; further questions were then made up by the groups; finally there was a discussion among the whole class.

The two classes were matched on the NFER Mathematics II test, but on the reflections pre-test they were not particularly close. The mean scores of the groups are shown below.

	Pre	Post	Delayed
Conflict	48	79	82
Booklets	32	70	54

It is clear that the scores of the conflict group might well have been even higher if there had been more headroom in the test.

For the final set of trials, on fractions, two groups were formed by dividing the class of thirty-two pupils in their last term at junior school into two parts, matched on the NFER test (means 103.2, 103.7) and also by performance on the fractions pre-test. Both groups were taught by the same teacher, one using the SMP *Fractions* booklets 1, 2 and 3, and the other by a conflict and investigation method. Some of the tasks used in the latter method were as follows.

> Divide a square into halves as many ways as possible (use squared paper); discuss, explain and justify.

> Share 3 bars of chocolate among 4 people: draw diagrams, symbolize . . . share $2^3/4$ bars among 4 people . . . make up your own questions.

> Which is bigger, $4/5$ or $3/4$? (devise your own method)

These challenges were given to groups of three or four pupils, each one being the basis of a whole lesson, with additional similar questions being generated by the pupils. After discussions in the groups, a whole class session was held in which each group explained and defended its methods and conclusions. The teaching lasted three weeks, with a post-test at the end (this was in June/July). The delayed test was given in September, after the summer holiday. Figure 4.1 shows the mean scores of the two groups at each of the three stages. We see again the pattern of similar initial gains from the two methods, but full retention in the conflict group contrasting with substantial loss from the SMP booklets.

The teacher's notes include some comments on how pupils' involvement and motivation changed. With the booklets, initial enthusiasm declined, whereas the conflict group became highly involved and were arguing over the points outside the lessons. Except for the second set of trials – on rates, which involved nine classes – these comparisons were on a fairly small scale, with only one class undergoing each method.

Considering the variability in conditions and the random hazards nor-

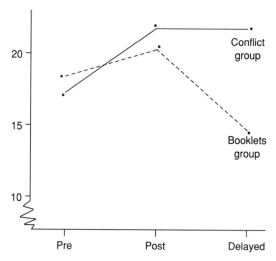

Figure 4.1 Mean scores on fractions test

mally associated with classroom trials, these results pose some important questions for mathematics departments.

The first set of trials shows that deliberately provoking conflict can have a beneficial effect, and the second shows the superiority of the diagnostic-conflict-discussion method over a typical teaching method. The third and fourth examples show again the effectiveness for long-term retention of this method, and conversely the very poor retention resulting from the use of individualised booklets. We know that the SMP booklet system is popular with pupils and with teachers, but also that many are somewhat uneasy about the depth of learning achieved with it.

Success on checks and tests closely related to the learning materials is not a reliable indication of long-term learning. Teachers should, perhaps, conduct some form of more detached or delayed evaluation to check on pupils' real progress. It may be felt that there is no time for a method which involves intensive discussion of particular points. But on the evidence presented here, we have to ask whether we can afford to waste pupils' time on methods which have such little long-term effect when, with diagnosis, conflict and discussion, we could be doing so much better.

Chapter 5

Train spotters' paradise

Dave Hewitt

I have been in many classrooms where children have been encouraged to use their intelligence and creativity to find some mathematical properties. Children have been asked to look at particular situations and are encouraged to find connections, make conjectures and test to see if those conjectures are correct. They are encouraged to make generalisations and to express these in algebraic form. In such lessons, I am impressed by how much children are able to discover for themselves and how well they can articulate their findings. There is an atmosphere of involvement in mathematics, children are being challenged and are expressing a sense of achievement in what they are doing. Quite often they continue working on their problem at home and involve their parents. They may arrive the following day eager to share new things the family have discovered. Such times have so many ingredients of lovely mathematics lessons. Yet I feel saddened rather than joyful.

I will mention five such lessons.

In one lesson, children are asked to draw a number of networks and to see whether they can be traversed without taking the pen off the paper or going over any line twice. After a while the teacher asks them to draw up a table giving the number of nodes, how many are odd and even, the number of arcs, the number of regions and whether the network is traversable or not. The challenge for the children is to look at the table and see whether they can see any patterns.

In another lesson, children are looking at the number of matches required to make a square such as shown below.

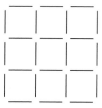

The children draw different sized squares and collect their results in a table. A number of patterns are found and many children articulate rules.

In a third lesson, the class are asked to draw a number of circles with different radii. Using some string, they measure the circumferences of each circle and make a table of the radius, diameter and circumference. The children are asked to try to find a connection between the radius and the circumference.

The fourth lesson involves choosing a number, say 68, reversing the digits to get 86, and adding the two numbers together:

$$68 + 86 = 154.$$

If the answer is a palindrome, stop. Otherwise, repeat the process with the answer:

$$154 + 451 = 605$$
$$605 + 506 = 1111.$$

In the case of 68, it took three iterations to arrive at a palindrome. Thus the number 68 is called a *level 3* number. The class are divided into groups and, between them, are asked to find out what level are all the numbers from 1 to 100. They are asked to collect the results in a table and to look for patterns.

In the fifth lesson, children are listing the different outcomes that are possible if they throw 1, 2, 3, . . . coins. They are asked to collate their results in the table shown as Table 5.1. Then they are told to look for patterns and predict how the table would continue.

Table 5.1 Number of ways of getting:

	0 heads	1 head	2 heads	3 heads	4 heads	. . .
1 coin						
2 coins						
3 coins						
4 coins						
. . .						

Despite the fact that in each of these lessons children were well motivated and involved in mathematics, I am saddened because the children ended up doing a similar activity irrespective of the initial mathematical situation.

Is the diversity and richness of the mathematics curriculum being reduced to a series of spotting number patterns from tables?

Whatever the initial mathematical situation, once the numbers are collected into a table, a separate activity begins to find patterns in the numbers.

Their attention is with the numbers and is thus taken away from the original situation. After a period of time, some children have difficulty reminding themselves where all the numbers came from. I suggest that, for many children, what they find out about the numbers remains exactly that; it does not mean they have learnt anything about the original mathematical situation, only about sets of numbers in a table.

Children can find many patterns in their table, even if they have made some errors in the entries. They may find all sorts of rules, none of which apply to the original situation but then some children have long ago turned their attention away from that. Spotting patterns in the numbers becomes an activity in its own right and not a means through which insights are gained into the original mathematical situation.

Networks may come under a heading of topology; the square of matches is essentially a geometric situation; circumference of circles may come under a heading of measures or geometry; palindromic numbers within number theory; and the coins within combinatorics or probability. These initial situations span a broad cross-section of mathematical areas and yet I argue the case that each of these lessons was really under the same heading of spotting number patterns since that is what the pupils ended up attending to.

In all these lessons, the children were doing several particular examples and collecting results from these. I presume the structure of collecting results in a table offers the possibility of making general statements about these results. The trouble is that the general statements are statements about the results rather than the mathematical situation from which they came. The existence of the table places value on collecting several results rather than looking in any depth at a particular one. More might be learnt about the original mathematics if one particular situation was looked at in depth, rather than rushing through several in order to collect results.

If I consider the network

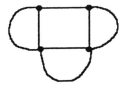

I can learn that it is traversable. However, instead of rushing on to consider another network, I could explore this one further. Are there other ways I can traverse this network? What if I keep the same starting node, where can I finish up? What if I try starting from the other nodes? How often do I visit each node? What would change if I rubbed out one of the arcs? Does it matter which one?. . .

If I take some matches and start putting them down so as to make this square:

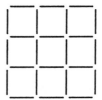

In what order do I place them down? Do I repeat certain patterns of matches? How often? Is there a stage when I am half way through? Can I look at the final square and imagine half the matches a different colour? What about a third? A quarter? How many horizontal lines are there? How many vertical? Why? Can I see the square one size less within this square? What if I paint the extra ones blue? Can I see the square two sizes less within this one?. . .

Imagine taking the diameter line of the circle and picking up a copy of it leaving the circle with the original diameter staying where it is. Imagine I could bend the diameter although I cannot alter its length. I try to bend it so that it curves round the circumference of the circle. If this bent diameter starts at A, how far round the circumference do I think it will go? Will it go as far as B? Suppose I put a mark where it has got to and continue with another copy of the diameter, how far now? How many diameters would I need to go once round the circumference and return to A? What if I did a drawing of this and put it in a photocopier which reduces the size?. . .

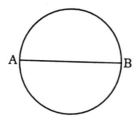

If I consider adding together 68 and its reverse 86,

68 +
86
—

what numbers appear in each of the columns? If they are the same numbers, why do I get the same number in each column of the answer? When will I get the same? What effect does the 'carry' have? How could I change the numbers so that I do not get a carry? If I stick with the original number being two-digit, when do I get two-digit answers? Three-digit answers? Can I get four-digit answers? If the answer is three-digit, what digits could I get in the hundred column?. . .

Let me consider the situation where I have exactly one head with a number of coins. If I know how many ways there are of getting one head with two coins, do I have the same number again when I introduce a third coin which happens to be tails? If the third coin was a head, what would the other two coins have had to be? What if I consider a larger number of coins and introduce one more coin which is a tail? A head?. . .

There is so much mathematical richness that can be gained by looking at a particular situation in some depth rather than looking at it superficially in order to get a result for a table and then rushing on to the next example. By staying with the particular situation, I can learn about the mathematics inherent in it rather than learning about numbers in a table. I practise and develop different abilities rather than practising and developing the one ability of spotting number patterns. I see geometry as geometry, combinatorics as combinatorics rather than everything as spotting number patterns. I am being asked to be creative and adaptable in different situations, to see that different situations require different questions to work on them.

Train spotters go in search of trains and collect numbers. At the end of the day, they are left with numbers . . . not a train in sight.

Chapter 6

What I do in my classroom

Anne Watson

I stand by the whiteboard and ask the pupils to be totally silent. I ask them to work inside their own heads. I ask them to watch what I am doing and try to decide what it is. I write

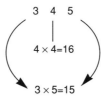

on the board. Then I pause and suggest they think about where I started, what numbers I chose, what I did, and what the result is. Then I write

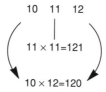

I remind them not to shout out. I suggest that if they think they know what is happening they should construct some similar examples in their heads, or think of a word description of the situation, or think about an algebraic description. Meanwhile I tell them I am going to do another one and they must continue to watch.

The event is rigidly controlled on the surface. There is a social element to the control. It is a quiet, settled start to a lesson. If everyone is peaceful, I am happy and likely to be a friendly and attentive teacher. An observer might say that I am 'controlling the class'.

But there is more to the notion of control than this. I have no control over what goes on inside their heads. They can choose to ignore what is being done on the board and merely pretend to watch. They may be misreading what is there or thinking about the mathematics in what, to me, is an unexpected way. They may have such a blockage about multiplication that they cannot begin to work with it. They may be already bored and day-dreaming. They may be mentally doing comparable calculations with 3, 5, 7 or 3, 4, 6.

I have given them the freedom to engage with the task or not. I have also given them the freedom to work with it how they choose. The first of these freedoms exercises me most at the start of a new piece of work. How can I make it more likely that they choose to get involved? The second of the freedoms is more complicated. Some may say that it is not a freedom which it is in my power to give. This could be because the pupils have to follow a National Curriculum and have to end up being able to do certain things, and the teacher should be making sure they can do these things. Another view is that it is not in my power to give a freedom which is already theirs, namely the way they think.

I want to offer them various ways of working with mathematics, help them appreciate the value of different approaches and enable them to make sensible choices about methods. I also have to maintain a balance between the freedom to think and construct meanings for themselves and the exter-nally imposed agenda of the school, society, government or the subject itself.

Freedom to engage

I try to engage the interest of the whole group. In my secondary classroom this may range from a pupil whose reading age is 7 to another who grasps quite complex ideas rapidly. What I offer should involve all and offer all a learning opportunity. 'What is this woman up to?' is a way into the mathematics of the example above.

I can appeal to trust, either explicitly – 'just listen to me for 5 or 10 minutes and I will offer you something absorbing to do' – or implicitly by their knowledge of me and the things that have happened as a result of my offerings in the past. There are some pupils who will only be quiet if they believe it is worthwhile.

I might show them how interesting I find a particular thing: 'Here's something I find exciting.' They might groan, but interest is aroused.

I can appeal to accepted practice. 'In this school it is expected that pupils should listen when the teacher is talking and do what is expected.' In the example above I would resort to this if one or two were delaying the start. I may not gain their interest but I would have a better chance of involving the others.

I can appeal to their need to be involved in doing something worthwhile, to end up with a good qualification, to exercise that thing between their ears which, I remind them, is more powerful than any computer.

I can appeal to the desire to learn which is, I believe, in all of us although it may take some work to uncover it.

A strong element in the example above is intrigue, which I introduce in an attempt to arouse their curiosity.

> I hold a large triangle in one hand and an imaginary telephone in the other. I pretend I am talking long-distance: 'I have designed your triangle. Yes, it has one side of 60 cm, another of 70 cm . . . yes that's right 70 . . . and an angle of 35 degrees and another of . . . hello! hello! . . . I seem to have been cut off. Are these three pieces of information enough to reproduce the triangle?

Apart from confirming the conviction that their teacher is slightly mad, this is a very positive start to an activity. There is a real detective job to do here and pupils often set themselves up in pairs with a wall of bags in between to give and receive instructions. It is my job to show ways to construct triangles given certain pieces of information and to remind them that they need to produce one and only one possible triangle. If the triangles match I ask if it is a fluke; is there any other way they could have put it together? Often the response is: 'no, because . . .' and this shows me that some analytical thinking is going on.

In both the examples I have given, the pupils can start working on the situations from their present state of knowledge or, more realistically, from the relevant knowledge with which they feel most comfortable. They can also choose their way of working. There is access through trying simple examples, complicated examples, imagery, theorising, appeals to other knowledge, past experiences and so on. It is common to find pupils choosing an access point which is well within their present knowledge and they may need encouragement to work on a higher level. It is rarer to find someone choosing an access point which they cannot cope with. This is most likely to happen if someone is truly stuck and has tried to adopt another's way of working.

I ask 'what are you trying to do?' or 'what is the question you are trying to answer?' in an attempt to help unpick what has been done so far. The pupil's attempt to articulate should either reveal the extent of the muddle or itself enable sense to be made and a way forward to be found.

Sometimes 'starting from where the pupils are' is interpreted to mean that mathematics should be presented in a social context. It is true that access is easier if the pupils are on familiar territory and can see a wider relevance in what they are doing, but one person's familiar context can be a bias against access for someone else. It is also difficult to find contexts which offer a range of mathematical possibilities. A physical activity can be a relatively unbiased way to provide a context.

> A group of about six pupils has to give instructions to another pupil to walk along the edges of an imaginary hexagon on the floor. The pupil doing the walking is told to be a real nuisance and only do exactly as told.

This encourages complete, accurate instructions or sends the pupils to paper to work out what they will have to say. Co-operation is essential, apart from the walker, and it also gives someone a real part to play who may otherwise not have much to contribute to the work at this stage. Physical starters are a very good alternative to models or diagrams because they allow movement in the classroom, varying the atmosphere. Also they appeal to all pupils' need to be a part of something and reflect the three-dimensional world in which, and from which, mathematics happens.

My main aim, however, is to get the pupils to involve themselves in the mathematics and not just the context. A favourite context involves the mathematical aspects of planning an outing or meal or disco. Of course I try to make sure that the event actually happens but in the end, whether it does or does not happen, the mathematical outcomes must be valid and valued on their own.

Young people cannot be expected to know instinctively what is valuable. Teachers may have different ideas about value in mathematics but pupils need to know what they are. I value contributions to discussion from everyone and use my broader overview of the subject to work with their offerings and weave them together in public. There are two reasons for this: one is to show that everyone is worth listening to and the other is to show that apparently disparate ideas can be synthesised to open a new way forward. How can I convince them that this is a worthwhile thing to do if they never see me doing it?

> The class is sitting in a circle and I ask them to imagine a cube inside their heads. Move it around, I say, spin it, tip it up and so on. (Some half-close their eyes.) Now hold it still and look at it carefully. I am going to ask you to say one thing about your cube and everyone else will listen. If someone says something you do not believe, you must not shout out, you must try to see if you can move your cube to look like theirs. Listen to everyone.

I once used this opener with the idea that they were all going to go on and explore cross-sections of cubes, but one pupil told us, amid everyone else's geometrical descriptions, that his cube was pink. I completely changed my lesson plan in order to respond to his contribution and steered everyone towards thinking about a painted cube instead.[1] I was not naive about this. I am sure he was using 'pink' as a way to avoid the topic but by taking him seriously I gave him a social investment in the work which followed and, as I expected, he did very well with it.

Once pupils have some kind of personal investment in a mathematical activity they are more likely to work enthusiastically with it. One example of this might be to use a collection of heights and shoe sizes to create a database for correlation work. Another example might be a lesson I saw in Russia in the winter of 1992. At the time, getting materials for anything was hard work. In fact, even getting food was hard work and there was little else in the shops that anyone could afford. The pupils had been asked to make skeleton models of cubes and tetrahedra for homework. They had used imagination in finding suitable raw materials. Some were made with used matches, others with waxed string and others with struts made from spindled paper. The time and emotion invested in the structures must have been enormous. They were proud of their creations and eager to work with them. They were all totally involved in seeing how various points on the edges of their shapes joined to make certain intersecting lines. At 14 they were doing work I had done for A level. The conclusion I drew was that the pupils had put so much effort into the work already that they were determined to get as much out of it as possible.

Access, though important, is not the only part of the story. It is pointless having easy, multi-level access to a boring task or to one with limited mathematical outcomes.

Ways of working

I like pupils to see mathematics as a network of ideas and learning it as a kind of adventure game in which they are finding out as much about ways of thinking and working as they are about mathematics. Ideally, each fact, method or theory met and learned should lead on to something else. The same method or process can be applied to another area of mathematics and the same bit of knowledge can be used in a different context or viewed from another angle. Frequently it is the pupil who, by choosing a particular way to work, decides to move in the direction of something new.

Although some mathematical ideas are building blocks for other ideas I do not believe that mathematics can or should be learned in a linear fashion. It is often by working with a complex idea that a simpler one suddenly makes sense or a technique begins to feel comfortable. Mathematicians frequently start looking at complex worlds and work backwards, sometimes having to invent new branches of mathematics with their own simplicities and complexities in order to move forward again. I am not, however, suggesting that mathematics should be learned by chance or has to be rediscovered from scratch by everyone. I try to choose activities which offer a space or a new concept to be explored, something to be discovered and something to be worked with for all.

From resources, other teachers, my own imagination and experience and even from other subjects I choose those activities which

- provide as few obstacles as possible between the learner and the mathematics;
- encourage learners to work directly on the mathematical concept involved rather than practise algorithms in the first instance;
- provoke discussion;
- allow assumptions to be discussed;
- appeal to all the senses;
- provoke thought.

Consider something which appears on a relatively high level of the National Curriculum: trigonometry. What opportunities could this topic offer the motley group before me? How can I give them all access to this area of mathematics? I have no time for the argument that there are some pupils who will never be able to 'do' trigonometry. I know this is probably true but I do not consider it part of my job to decide in advance who those people are. There are things to be discovered, calculators to be used, triangles to be drawn, problems to be solved, angles to be measured, numbers to be divided, even lines to be measured. A huge variety of mathematical activity ensues which can end up with some finding the shortest route to the top of a pyramid, others exploring trigonometric functions, others constructing triangles with compasses, and perhaps others measuring angles as accurately as possible with protractors. I do not need to say that trigonometry is only for the brightest. I do not need to accept the implied hierarchy of the National Curriculum. All I need to do is make sure that the introduction provides many ways forward and rich and worthwhile mathematics for everyone to work on. The National Curriculum just reminds me that they should have the opportunity to 'do trig'.

A teacher cannot assume that pupils automatically possess a range of ways of working or ways of thinking. At some stage these have to be offered and valued, whether it is in pre-school discourse with a parent, in early integrated teaching or through specific subjects later on. It is a part of teaching to be explicit about useful learning practices and stratagems, to celebrate when they are used successfully and to remind pupils about them from time to time. Pupils should be given opportunities to develop their learning skills. For instance, I could structure an activity in a way which forces them to communicate about their ideas or discoveries. I could build the idea of remembering into the activity, or I could offer them part of a story so that they have to do some thinking and reasoning in order to tell the whole story. I could offer something which has to be done collaboratively; for instance, finding the prime numbers by eliminating the multiples on a large grid. It is so much quicker if three or four are having a go at it and sharing results.

This is exactly what I often do with trigonometry. I offer triangles to draw and measure and ratios to find. I offer calculators with buttons to be pressed and I ask them to put the two together and find links.

Pupils often say to me 'I think I have found something' and then launch into some explanation of a connection in their work.

I am not saying that everyone ends up with some understanding of trigonometry, or that this is all that is necessary for a complete understanding. I am saying that all pupils can be offered this area of mathematics in which to work and the outcomes vary.

If I have chosen the starting point wisely they will all have something to do. I like to think that I spend most of my lessons going round the room talking to individuals about their mathematics, pushing, provoking, praising, etc. In reality I do not always have that amount of energy and there are other things to do, like talk about work done, or not done, previously. Sometimes I work from one place and ask them to come and tell me about their work. Eventually I walk around the room and there are various things which may happen then. I may quietly stand behind them and watch. If they are usefully involved and discussing with a neighbour I really enjoy listening to the discussion. Young people love to argue and I am glad if I have given them something to argue about. They know that eventually they will have to explain their ideas to me, so the argument is seen as useful for both of them.

Often it is 'What did she mean by . . .?' and I may intervene with 'What do you think I mean?' followed by discussion about instructions or assumptions. If I have a particular outcome in mind, or several possible outcomes, I may guide them to make certain assumptions. Otherwise I may just remind them that whatever they decide they ought to be explicit about it and stick to it for a while. Awareness of what is fixed and what changes is not automatic. Teachers have to help.

Pupils regularly start mathematical tasks by making everything much more complicated than it needs to be. I try to encourage my groups to start with a simple example. Through the years this becomes a saying of mine which they recognise and repeat back to me. 'What do you think I am going to say about this?' 'That we should have started with a simple one.'

It is during these discussions with individuals or small groups that I can do most to encourage and value their work. 'Yes, that's a good start, now what do you think you will do next?' encourages planning. 'What do you think will happen next?' encourages prediction. 'Why don't you go over and talk to so-and-so about that, you're both working on the same sort of thing' encourages discussion and broadens the pupils' perceptions of where to get help and who they can work with. 'This reminds me of something you did a few months ago; can you remember what it was?' encourages a holistic view of mathematics, pointing out that past work was worthwhile and highlighting the importance of memory.

I have dozens more phrases like this but I am not always aware when I use them. Originally they come from a conscious sense of what they need to do to be better learners of mathematics. Gradually, through use, they become automatic for me and even for some pupils and their constant use creates and maintains the atmosphere of my classroom.

Their own questions are more motivating than mine can ever be, but asking the right questions is a skill which has to be developed. Often they get bogged down in number-crunching or the minutiae of an activity and miss something bigger and more exciting that could result from an overview. It is as if they are glued to a television screen and have no idea what is on the wall above and behind it. They want to respond to my questions and suggestions instead of being curious for themselves. Occasionally they ask if they could work from a book instead.

> Why are you so happy to answer questions asked by someone who may live hundreds of miles away and certainly doesn't know you rather than get curious and answer your own questions?

Telling and showing

The questions and workings should be about mathematics and teachers cannot expect pupils to know what is or is not mathematics. In fact, many teachers and other adults would disagree with each other's definitions of what is or is not mathematics. How do my pupils learn that to plan the critical path for a trip to Tanzania is mathematical but to choose the colour of a hat is not? (And am I sure that this distinction is true?) In my classroom *I* am the expert on mathematics, so as well as asking questions about ways of working and mathematics I feel I ought to show my pupils, from time to time, what I know and can do.

Sometimes I do this almost traditionally on a board or from a book. More often I seize the opportunities offered by the pupils' work or questions. There are three main types of situation which can occur.

The first is when pupils ask me how to do something. I can choose to show them directly or to get involved in a question-and-answer session with them in which I take them through the reasoning involved for them-selves. This may not be the way they would get to it if left to themselves but it is a model of mathematical reasoning which they can see at work in me.

The second is when people are stuck or have gone up a blind alley and cannot get out. I may offer an alternative route which may be a new method or may refer to some piece of knowledge they do not yet have.

> Some Year 9 pupils were working on the design of the largest water tank they could make from a 10 m square of metal. One decided that a cylinder would be best but did not know how to work out the volume. I decided that a lesson on area of circles from first principles was not appropriate, she wanted to know then and there so I told her, pausing only to point out generalities about volumes of prisms. This was the first time she had

met *pi*. It did not bother her that she did not know where it came from. She went on to make cylinders and calculate their volumes.

The third is when I see someone working on something which, with my larger overview, I recognise as leading somewhere interesting. If I think there will be a positive response I might take the opportunity to direct the work slightly so that it opens up a new area of mathematics to be explored.

The best moments in the classroom happen when this third situation has been initiated by the learner and the questions are a result of that process.

> A Year 10 class had been using a graph plotter to explore families of functions. I had emphasised the questions 'what is the same?' and 'what is different?' in order to get them to think about intercepts and gradients. Later some of them went on to look at quadratic curves and other powers of *x*. Three times in one lesson I was asked 'how can I find the gradient of a curve?', so three times I sat down to give a simplified introduction to calculus.

Discussions

From time to time a change of pace is required. Perhaps several pupils are stuck or there is so much exciting mathematics going on that I would like them to share it.

Teachers sometimes over-estimate the ability of pupils to take part in discussions. A good discussion in which everyone can take part needs preparation.

I can prime participants beforehand: 'that is an interesting point and I would like you to decide how best to explain it because in a few minutes I will ask you to explain it to the whole class.'

I can ask them to work with a friend and practise their explanations first in order to increase their confidence.

These strategies work with all ages and with all levels of attainment. I have used them with adults as well as youngsters and I have always found that if I trust them to make good use of this opportunity, they will. I also see it as part of my role as a teacher to encourage listening, describing, conjecturing, sharing ideas, etc.

Behaviour in a discussion will be conditioned by the influences around pupils throughout their lives. This shows up as a difference in response by those of different genders, different races or different social backgrounds. It is possible to structure what happens so that the lesson is not dominated by those who are most skilful or confident. As a pupil you may have been in a lecture or class in which everything else stopped while the teacher spent time talking about an obscure point raised by someone in the front row. You could neither hear nor understand so began to daydream. In those situations I remember thinking 'get on with it!' or 'why can't this be sorted out later?'

and suspecting the other pupil of showing off. As a teacher I look for ways to avoid it happening.

One of my phrases is 'every time you put your hand up you turn someone else's brain off!' You probably know the feeling that if someone else is going to answer the question you might as well not bother, or if you cannot work it out that quickly you probably cannot work it out at all. So I have to make sure that no one is bored, having known the answer for ages, while I wait for someone else to grapple with it. 'If you think you know the answer,' I say, 'think about what would happen if . . .' or 'how would you express it as a general rule?' or 'try to think of a convincing explanation'. My aim is to convince them that knowing an answer is only a step to somewhere else. Their thinking does not have its pace set by me or by anyone else. They are free to think further into the mathematics and this is much more desirable than joining in a race to answer. By introducing this alternative type of response to teachers' questions or other pupils' comments I am reducing the competitive effect that mathematics sometimes produces and increasing the amount of thinking time that I give everyone. There is no emergency about my questions.

> Take your time, think it through, plan what you are I going to say if I ask you for an idea towards an answer. Plan how you might explain this to your art teacher. What would you have to say if you wanted to explain it to a younger person?

Sometimes everyone can contribute to the discussion.

> Thirteen A level students considered the laying down of salt on a seabed starting with 100 tonnes and then laying down 1 per cent less per year. All had started on the problem, some numerically and some theoretically. I asked them all in turn to say how they had tackled it.

> 'I started working the first few years out and then thought there must be a better way', 'I tried to see if there was a formula' and 'I realised I had to keep multiplying by 0.99' contrasted with 'I worked out the first ten years because I wanted to see how quickly it moved to a limit' and 'I worked out 1 per cent of one hundred and kept on subtracting it'.

This last contribution allowed me to highlight a common confusion between compound and simple rates of change and also the delicate use of language required in mathematics questions. In this case English was the second language for the learner so the delicate understanding of language was also an issue. All approaches held something of value but I did feel a bit like a conductor trying to keep an orchestra together during the feedback.

Equal opportunity

I am not the perfect teacher. I have shared with you in this chapter some things which work in my classroom. I have attempted to describe why I organise things in this way based on what I know of children and what I know of mathematics.

People do not have equal opportunities to make something their lives. Much of what they do is based on their environment and this affects their self-esteem and expectations. I want my classroom to be a place of fairness, value and opportunity. I want my pupils to develop adaptable techniques to help them solve problems and learning skills to help them understand new concepts. I would like them to be more confident as a result of their experiences. I continue to search for ways to do this through mathematics.

NOTE

1 A cube is made up of uniform smaller cubes. If it is dipped in paint how many cubelets will have one, two, three or more faces painted?

Chapter 7

Contexts and strategies for learning mathematics

Mike Ollerton

As a teacher of mathematics I am interested in finding ideas and tasks that I can use with groups of children who inevitably have wide ranging interests, have different motivations, will show a variety of responses to problems I suggest and whose potential achievement or depth of understanding arising from the development of a piece of mathematics will be substantially diverse.

I do not wish to try to 'keep a class together'; indeed I want to adapt my teaching method in order to embrace the differences that exist and to use the variety of responses in positive ways to inform me about the types of conversations and interactions that I can have with my students so that I can share in the process of helping individual students to move on. 'Without all the colours there would be no rainbow' (Bishop Desmond Tutu).

The following quotation is one that I subscribe to and one which encourages me to think carefully about the implications for my curriculum planning.

> At various points in this document comments are made about the undesirability of overemphasising the practising and testing of skills out of context; the ability to carry out operations is important but there is a danger that skills come to be seen as ends in themselves. If mathematics is only about 'computational skills out of context' it cannot be justified as a subject in the curriculum.
>
> (HMI 1985)

I find this a very powerful statement with strong messages about the value of learning skills within contextualised and holistic frameworks and for planning modules of work that can be sustained for two, three or four weeks, rather than in deconstructed and fragmented ways. By fragmented I mean that for one or two lessons children are responding to a set of short questions in an exercise, such as 'solve the following equations', and then the following day or week they are working on another skill such as adding fractions or working out areas of triangles. Their experience is reminiscent of the soldier in Henry Reed's poem 'Naming of the Parts'. It begins:

To-day we have naming of parts. Yesterday,
We had daily cleaning. And to-morrow morning,
We shall have what to do after firing. But to-day,
To-day we have naming of parts. Japonica
Glistens like coal in all of the neighbouring gardens
And today we have naming of the parts.

If mathematics is to have any meaning then inter-weaved with the learning of skills there must be recognition about how such skills are connected. As Peter Lacey, Professional Officer at the National Curriculum Council, rightly points out, 'The purpose of mathematics is to solve problems. Being able to do things with numbers is only useful when pupils can apply these skills to the solution of problems' (*Times Educational Supplement* 9 October 1992). Peter's excellent article raises important issues about the need for mathematics to be learnt in ways that cause skills to be used and applied.

Therefore finding ways of causing the learner to make connections and provide opportunities for the transfer of skills is essential if teachers are going to promote the effective learning of mathematics. I want to find wholesome ways of developing my students abilities to think mathematically. In order to achieve this I set out to create learning environments which encourage students to use and apply mathematics in ways that make learning a meaningful process containing appropriate challenges.

Planning for development

An important part of my planning is concerned with finding tasks that:

- are a suitable starter for everyone in the class to work on;
- provide rich opportunities for many developments;
- cause a variety of content skills to be worked on;
- create opportunities for students to explore ideas and ask questions;
- support different types of teacher interventions ranging from asking questions to explaining and telling;
- learners can take ever more responsibility for developing;
- will have a variety of outcomes, some of which may be unexpected;
- enable content to be processed;
- draw upon 'real' cross-curricular type contexts, such as using information from a newspaper, or problem-solving contexts;
- wherever possible have a practical beginning in order to provide concrete experiences from which abstractions can be made.

Context and starter task

To illustrate the thought processes that I use when planning a module of work, I have examined ideas which can be generated from the Fibonacci sequence.

The sequence itself can be constructed from the exploration of a variety of tasks. The particular starter that I choose to use will vary according to who I am working with, and what my relationship with the 'class' is like. Whatever I choose to do, I want to be responsible for making these decisions and not to have them made for me. It is important that I am in control of my teaching and the starter tasks are central to achieving this control. I choose to work with certain ideas because I have used my professional judgement about the value of a task and not because they happen to be the next chapter in the book.

I have two favourite starting points for generating the Fibonacci sequence of numbers. The first is 'going up steps', where the rule for going up a set of steps is that you can either go up a single step or a double step. Thus for a step size of four the solutions are as given in Figure 7.1, making five possible ways.

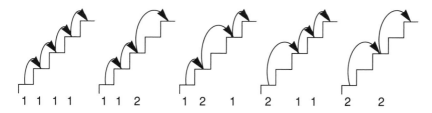

1 1 1 1   1 1 2   1 2 1   2 1 1   2 2

Figure 7.1 The solutions for a 'going up steps' problem with a step size of four

The other starter that I use is the 'paths' problem, where paths of size 'n by 2' are constructed using '2 by 1' rectangles. The red Cuisenaire rods can be used quite effectively, and this can provide me with an equipment-based approach of the type that I find useful because the learners are presented with a practical approach from which they can later make abstractions.

The ways of constructing a '4 by 2' path are shown in Figure 7.2, and can be matched with the results for the four-step problem.

V V V V   V V H H   V H H V   H H V V   H H H H

Figure 7.2 Constructing a '4 by 2' path using '2 by 1' rectangles

The number of ways of getting up 'n' steps and the number of arrangements for 'n by 2' paths both produce the Fibonacci sequence.

Once the Fibonacci numbers have been achieved, the sequence provides opportunities for developing a range of skills and already an important teaching strategy has been used. This is that the starter task has created a spread within the class, and as different children complete this initial task I can suggest a sequence of other tasks in order to encourage the students to engage with mathematics. What is important is that we are not working with isolated skills outside of any context, for now the context is the Fibonacci sequence, and we are going to explore this sequence of numbers further.

The following is a list of follow up tasks that I can draw upon and suggest to different students as they complete the initial starter.

1 Coding the results from the 'paths' problem in terms of H and V – this provides opportunities for attempting to prove completeness.
2 Taking the Fibonacci numbers up to the twentieth (or whatever) term – this provides opportunities for addition.
3 Exploring other patterns in these numbers, e.g. with any three numbers what happens when the outside two are multiplied together and the square of the middle number is subtracted – there are a lot of tasks of this type which provide opportunities for multiplying and classifying.
4 Extending the sequence backwards – this provides opportunities for working with negative numbers.
5 Producing 'five-cell Fibonacci' sets of numbers (see pp. 67–8) – this provides opportunities for working with fractions, negative numbers and negative fractions and for writing formulae.
6 Dividing successive terms by each other ($2 \div 3$, $3 \div 5$, $5 \div 8$ etc.) – this provides opportunities for using calculators to convert fractions to decimals, exploring the idea of a limit, graphing results, considering reciprocals when the calculation is reversed ($3 \div 2$, $5 \div 3$, $8 \div 5$ etc.).

Further work on the Golden Ratio can open up a number of other explorations. For the past few years I have always made a point of telling the class's art teacher when I am planning to embark upon the Fibonacci module and this has resulted in useful cross-curricular links.

7 Looking at the Fibonacci in different modulos (thus in Mod 4 the sequence starting 1 1 continues 1 1 2 3 1 0 1 1 . . .) – this provides opportunities for exploring structures beyond the scope of the present National Curriculum document.

The process of planning for development from a simple starter can be applied to all areas of the curriculum. In doing so we as teachers can take control and can use our responsibilities in imaginative and creative ways that are not being determined either by politicians or writers of textbooks. I find the process of engaging with the planning and structuring of extended modules of work a way of keeping my approaches to teaching fresh and it is therefore a process of renewal.

Of course, this takes time and energy but by looking at where a large amount of teachers' energy is often spent I think that a shift of emphasis can create the space required for such planning. For instance, instead of collecting books in every week and becoming a 'ticker' of lots of little questions, I find a more purposeful use of my time is to collect completed modules of work every three or so weeks and then write a lengthy (50–100 word) comment. I monitor progress throughout the course of a module and part of this monitoring process is about having conversations with individuals or small groups of students. During such conversations I can make all kinds of decisions about when it is useful to move somebody on, I can confirm with another student that they understand what they are doing or I can provide an alternative task to another student who may be struggling to understand an idea.

Responses and feedback

To exemplify in greater detail the types of responses that are possible I shall describe working with a Year 8 mixed-ability group on the Fibonacci module and what I learned as a result.

My anecdote is about learning a variety of skills within the context of a broader problem. Some of the learnt skills were ones that I intended would be worked on, but there were others that I hadn't bargained for.

> Although I have a good idea of where the work is going to lead it is important that other avenues are open for exploration. It is important because I want the learners to have opportunities to develop a task and not always feel that they are only responding to developments that I am able to suggest to them.

We had been doing work based upon the Fibonacci sequence and, having generated the notion of the sequence through the 'paths' approach, I suggested a variety of problems for the children to work on. One such problem I called 'five-cell Fibonacci'.

> I made a clear decision that I wanted to use this particular problem so that the Fibonacci numbers would be generated. There is a debate about how much guidance to give and how much free reign pupils should be encouraged to use, and this particular problem is a fruitful one in order to consider this issue. If I hadn't specified that reflections were to be included in the set of results, the Fibonacci numbers may well not be generated. This then would change the nature of the way that I am able to generate further tasks. However, because I wanted the Fibonacci numbers to be generated initially by the pupils, I chose to state the conditions

at the outset. There will be many other opportunities for the students to take similar types of decisions at other times.

The children worked in twos or threes and each produced lists of five numbers using the Fibonacci method. Having arrived at a list of five numbers, the idea was that one person passed the first and the last number in the list to someone else, who then has to calculate the missing three numbers in the sequence.

> Here the pupils are setting up and solving problems by themselves, I feel that this is different from me defining the problems and then giving the pupils a set of problems from a textbook. By asking them to devise their own problems I am also trying to get them to become ever more independent learners.

The eventual aim was for them to find a way of calculating these numbers other than by trial and improvement.

Three children eventually came to me with a rule that if you add the first and the last numbers together and then divide by three you arrive at the middle number in the sequence. I asked them to write a formula for this if the first number was 'f' and the last number was 'l'. This they were able to do and we then had a conversation about how they could write other formulae for determining the second and fourth numbers in terms of 'f' and 'l'. In order to convince themselves that these formulae held true for other than positive whole numbers, I suggested that they devise some sequences using fractions, then negative values and then negative fractions. Later they came back to me stating that their formulae hadn't worked out using negative values. This then provided me with an excellent opportunity to work with them on the manipulation of negative and positive values. The context for manipulating formulae and checking them continued to be the five-cell Fibonacci problem.

By the end of the lesson we had had further conversations about subtracting negative values and adding negative values. Interestingly all three or four of the separate conversations that we had together took at most 10 minutes and possibly less, and after each conversation the learners reassumed ownership of the problem and worked on it because they were wrapped up inside it and *wanted* to understand what was happening. I would not claim that these three children are now fully conversant with the notion of adding and subtracting negative numbers. However, I am pleased that they have had some real exposure to working with them and know that I shall be able to build upon such interactions the next time that such a concept occurs.

Sharing ideas

Recently a teacher in my department who had not taught a Year 8 group for some years asked me how he might develop the Fibonacci work, whereupon I described to him the anecdote above. At first his reaction was one of being very unsure about the appropriateness of the idea, in fact he thought that the task would have been too difficult for his students to engage with. I was fortunate enough to have kept hold of one of the books of the students mentioned earlier and a photocopy of the work produced provided us with a set of potential teacher notes. The teacher's reaction at the end of his following lesson with his Year 8 group was . . . full of smiles!

This strategy of using copies of past pieces of student's work is one that can be used to good effect to share ideas with colleagues.

Developing other modules

The strategies described above can be applied to most if not all of the mathematics curriculum. I am keen to develop a whole range of starters that tackle the content 'head-on', and one of the most important parts of the process of turning a starter into a module that can encompass various concepts is to have an idea of further tasks that can be set once certain students have shown that they have achieved a good understanding of the initial starter. Below are two further such 'story lines'.

Cuisenaire – fractions – decimals

My first story line starts with Cuisenaire rods. Students are given two rods each of the following colours: white, red, light green, pink, yellow and dark green. The initial task is to find all the possible 'fractions' that can be constructed using this set of rods. Therefore white on red is $\frac{1}{2}$, light green on red is $\frac{3}{2}$ etc. (Figure 7.3).

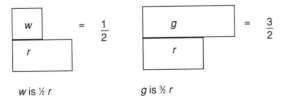

Figure 7.3 Constructing 'fractions' using Cuisenaire rods

Subsequent tasks could include:
– change all the fractions into decimals;
– on a square dot co-ordinate grid record all the decimal equivalents using a mixture of mental and calculator methods – using a 2 cm square dot grid

the actual dots can become the decimal points (with denominators on the horizontal axis and numerators on the vertical axis, as shown in Figure 7.4);

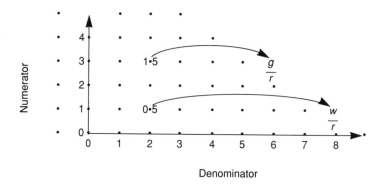

Figure 7.4 Using a square dot co-ordinate grid to record decimal equivalents

- predict decimal results for values outside the range of results gained from the Cuisenaire rods;
- find all the decimal answers on the grid that have answers of 0.5, 1.5;
- write lists of the original fractions that have decimal results of 0.5;
- measure the angles of the lines from the horizontal;
- compare previous results with the 'tan' key.

As a result of working on tasks such as these there is potential for students to engage with content ideas such as fractions, decimals, recurring and terminating decimals, equivalent fractions, graphs, gradients, angle, tangents and reciprocals. At the same time students are exploring ideas by developing and applying process skills such as being systematic, ordering information, pattern spotting, predicting results, specialising, generalising and bringing a spirit of enquiry into their mathematics.

A further key feature is the way that students are encouraged to communicate what they have done and what they have learnt. In doing this they have further opportunities to recognise connections between fractions and decimals and also to transfer such concepts across another context.

Multi-Link – Volume – Dimensions – Surface Area

My next starter is to issue all the students with twenty-four multi-link cubes and ask them to make and record on isometric paper as many cuboids ('boxes') as they can find (Figure 7.5). Subsequent tasks could include:

- write the dimensions of each cuboid;
- calculate the surface area of each cuboid;

– show that all the possible cuboids have been found;
– write a formula for surface area;
– consider minimum surface area using non-integer values;
– find some cylinders with the same volume.

An analysis will reveal that there are opportunities for the development of various content and process skills.

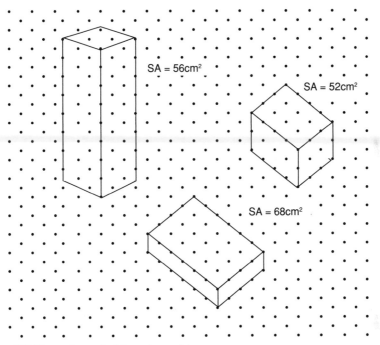

SA = 56cm²

SA = 52cm²

SA = 68cm²

Figure 7.5 Recording cuboids on isometric paper

Resource books such as ATM's *Points of Departure* (Books 1, 2, 3 and 4) provide a wealth of ideas for starter tasks for both teachers and students to subsequently develop.

Sometimes a starter task has sufficient potential and degrees of openness to enable learners to develop their mathematical thinking where the role of the teacher is more of a questioning one. Questions which ask the learner 'what they have done, what they are doing and what they going to do?' are intended to cause the learner to take more responsibility for the course they are steering.

NOTE

Points of Departure can be obtained from the Association of Teachers of Mathematics, 7 Shaftesbury Street, Derby DE3 8YB.

REFERENCE

HMI (1985) *Mathematics from 5 to 16*, London: HMSO.

Part III

How do we know our students are learning and understanding?

Just because pupils are apparently working on mathematics, there is no guarantee that this is also a sign that they are learning or understanding. In Chapter 8 John Mason suggests that correct answers do not imply understanding of what the question is about, nor do they suggest understanding of the concepts being assessed. He describes different levels of understanding and suggests that the way individual pupils respond to a question can be a key to the level of understanding each pupil has reached.

In Chapter 9 the authors explore how elements of classroom experience can be singled out for closer inspection and examine different perspectives on the mathematics curriculum in order to allow the reader to consider how pupils learning can be engaged through the acquisition of the mathematical tools required on leaving school. Through observation of how pupils acquire and use these tools, evidence of learning can emerge.

Chapter 8

Assessing what sense pupils make of mathematics

John Mason

WHAT ARE PUPILS ATTENDING TO?

The problem given in Figure 8.1 came home from school in the hands of 7-year-old Lydia. The problem shown is the first of three, the others having a tricycle and a car respectively, but with the questions otherwise identical. Lydia asked me to help her because 'I don't know what to do'. I asked her to start reading to me. She got to 2 + 2 + 2 + 2 and said, 'Is it eight?' I replied, 'What do you think?' She said in a tentative tone of voice, 'eight'. She skipped over the 'Instead . . .' and went on to '4 groups of 2'.

There are 2 wheels on the bicycle
1   On 4 bicycles there are 2 + 2 + 2 + 2 = 8 wheels
    Instead of ADDING equal groups you can MULTIPLY.
    Write
2   4 groups of 2 = 8
3   4 × 2 = 8
4   4 multiplied by 2 = 8
5   4 times 2 = 8
6   How many wheels are there on 7 bicycles? 14
7   How many wheels are there on (a) 6 bicycles? 12
    (b) 10 bicycles? 20

Figure 8.1 Multiplication tasks: counting in twos

'What does that mean?' she asked.
'What does 4 groups of 2 mean?' I asked her.
'Eight?'

I pointed to the bicycle and asked her what that was doing there. She didn't know. She went on to 4 × 2, then asked, 'What is "multiplied"?' I watched her carry on, using her fingers to do seven bicycles, and in response to my raised eyebrows she did it again. The last bicycle question she did quickly. 'Is that all there is?' She set to, head down, pencil tightly gripped. She worked through the bicycles, the tricycles and the cars. Each question was tackled in turn.

What did she make of the task? What did the author intend her to make of it? I suspect that she was meant to see that the operation of multiplication is signalled and denoted in a variety of ways, and that repeated addition is the same as multiplication. Did she? I doubt it. She looked at me in amazement when I asked her what it was about, as if to say, 'It's just a bunch of questions, Dad (you fool!).'

I conclude that it is not easy to point people in the direction of seeing the general in the particular, the sameness in different events (in this case, the same structure in different settings). Yet 'seeing the general in the particular' is one of the root processes in mathematics, and probably in every discipline. Indeed, different disciplines might be characterised by the features of situations which are attended to, and the ways in which generality is perceived in particularity (Mason 1984b).

The question 'What is going on inside their heads?' is endemic to teaching. At its heart lies a tension arising from what Brousseau (1984) calls the didactic contract. This tension arises between pupils and teachers in the following way. The pupils know that the teacher is looking to them to behave in a particular way. The teacher wishes the pupils to behave in a particular way as a result of, or even as a manifestation of, their understanding of the concepts or the topic. The more explicit the teacher is about the specific behaviour being sought, the more readily the pupils can provide that sought-after behaviour, but simply by producing the behaviour and not as a manifestation of their understanding. Tension arises because the pupils are seeking the behaviour and expect the teacher to be explicit about that behaviour, whereas the teacher is in the bind that the more explicit she is, the less effective the teaching. The question then arises as to how it might be possible to make positive use of the didactic tension rather than descending into a negative spiral in which the teacher is more and more explicit about the sought behaviour and the students more and more mechanical in their production of that behaviour. In reflecting on this question, I have over the years made a number of self-evident but for me potent observations.

Observation 1   I can't *do* the learning for my students.

Gattegno (1971) elaborates on this theme based on his memorable book title, *The Subordination of Teaching to Learning*. If I stop trying to do the learning for students, what are the implications? The ancient expression 'there is no royal road to geometry' has for 2,000 years applied more generally to learning mathematics, yet for 2,000 years teachers have struggled to find the educator's stone!

Observation 2   Students bring to class a rich experience of making sense in the past. Which of these powers do I particularly need to evoke in a given topic?

The expression 'starting where the students are' has unfortunately become a cliché, often meaning little more than not assuming the students know very much, whereas it could focus attention on helping pupils to use their undoubted powers effectively. Gattegno offers the challenging suggestion that 'only awareness is educable', and I take this assertion to encompass my question as a special case. My question then becomes, 'How do I evoke pupils' sense-making powers, and how do I help them work on their awareness?' Some people take Gattegno's expression to extremes, refusing to tell students anything on the grounds that it is useless unless the students discover it for themselves. Telling people facts is not in itself useless, indeed it is often essential, but the critical factor is how students go about making sense of what they are told as well as of what they discover.

Observation 3   The result of making sense seems generally to consist of two elements: articulate stories which explain or account for a variety of situations; manipulative skills which are the subjects of examination questions.

The didactic tension leads to emphasis on manipulative skills, and on the conveyance-container metaphor for teaching. Students are 'given' skills, they try to 'get the point' of the lesson, they do or do not have a 'grip' on the concepts and so on. It is interesting that in any discipline the development of techniques or skills for answering certain kinds of questions arises as the result of people observing a similarity or commonality to a whole range of questions, thus making it worthwhile to try to find a common solution. The common solution is then taught to students as a technique, but in the process what is known is transformed, by a process which Chevellard (1985) calls the didactic transposition, into instruction. The immense amount of construal which is required in order to reach a perception of commonality is not often shared with students, who are simply 'given' the skills without any reference to, or appreciation of, the original or underlying questions.

Observation 4   Because as teachers we are engaged in enculturating the younger generation, there is a tendency to move rapidly from a quick glimpse of an idea to succinct, manipulable, (symbolic) recordings – definitions, technical terms, major results.

As a culture we put great emphasis on the written expression of what people experience or think about. Some pupils have been recorded as saying that school is a series of events to be written about by pupils; thus writing becomes an aim or purpose of school rather than merely one manifestation of making sense.

Observation 5   The push to written records, and to manipulating symbols and technical terms, is due to a teacher's wish for pupils to automate procedures so that they can manifest the desired behaviour. These procedures are both particular, in the sense of being topic based, and general or heuristic, in the sense of being thinking skills which are used throughout a particular discipline.

Reflection on these observations suggests that between *seeing*, in the sense of a vague and fuzzy glimpse, and *saying*, in the sense of striving for succinct verbal expression, and between manipulating examples and formulating articulate stories lies the domain of mental imagery as source for and agent of the act of verbalizing (see Mason 1986a for elaboration). Furthermore, although the act of trying to express in words on paper is helpful for clarifying one's ideas, it is often difficult to write what cannot yet be said. Thus it makes sense to spend time trying to contact any mental imagery that is involved or associated with the topic, trying to express verbally to oneself and to colleagues and only then trying to record or express ideas in pictures and words. Written records may go through many different drafts before becoming succinct and formal. The triad of seeing, saying and recording is a useful reminder that each contributes to the growth of understanding, and that a too rapid push to written records which omits the opportunity to modify, or to try to express oneself verbally, may be so demanding as to block progress, and even to turn the pupil against the particular topic.

It is generally considered good practice to invite pupils to carry out exercises, in the hope that this will literally 'exercise' their growing technical, manipulative skills and give them access to the abstract ideas underlying the technique. There is, however, a good deal more hope than structure in such an approach. Whenever we get stuck on a problem or find some statement too abstract or general, we search in our experience for an example with which we are familiar. In other words, we turn to entities which are for us confidently manipulable, so that we can try to interpret the unfamiliar in a more familiar context. The act of manipulating, interpreting and exploring are more than simply doing exercises, because we are trying to get a sense of what the person is talking about.

In order to 'get a sense' we summon up various forms of imagery connected with past experience of similar situations. If we are given assistance by the speaker in the form of pauses, during which we can try out our examples or ponder examples provided by the speaker in which our attention is drawn to the features salient for the speaker, then by this suitable stressing and ignoring we can be assisted to re-experience the generality which we first heard. If we have opportunity to try to express this generality for ourselves, then we begin to bring to articulation the vague sense that was germinating while working on the illustrative examples. Once we become familiar with, and confident with, manipulating the succinct expressions of the generality, we have new entities which might themselves be employed in later topics as illustrative examples of further ideas. It is convenient to display this

process of making sense, of construing, as a helix in which the move
ment from confident manipulation through imagery and the processes of
specializing and generalizing in order to 'get a sense of' to expressing and
articulating the general principles in an increasingly succinct form, are seen
as one complete turn around the helix (Figure 8.2). When we get into
difficulty with something that someone is saying, we tend to move back
down the helix through our images and through sufficient turns so that we
find something confident that we can use as an example. We then retrace
steps up the helix to try to re-express the generality for ourselves.

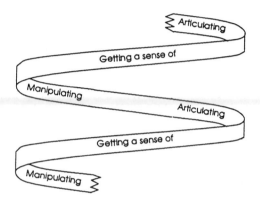

Figure 8.2 The process of making sense

TEACHING AND ASSESSING

One thing a teacher can do is to work explicitly with pupils on the question
of how you make sense in the particular discipline – in my case mathematics.
Thus I need to evoke imagery, to learn to be explicit and precise about the
imagery which I have inside me and from which I speak, to be explicit about
the processes and methods of specializing and generalizing which pertain to
my discipline, and to work explicitly with students on exposing and weaving
together into stories the fragments of their experience which they recall.

Activity of teaching

What would I like students to achieve at the end of a topic or course? I
would like students to have 'seen' connections, to have experienced some
sort of integration or crystallization of disparate experiences which are
subsumed under some general concept. I would like them to have 'gained a
sense of' some coherence of a topic and how the techniques, technical terms
and 'facts' fit together. I would like them to 'be articulate' about the meaning

of various technical terms, of how standard and novel examples illustrate the ideas of the topic (see Michener 1978 for elaboration); I would like them to be articulate about their own story of what the topic is about and what sort of questions it answers or deals with. I would like them to get to the point of employing succinct articulations confidently in the future as components or examples or tools in new topics.

These aims are teacher aims. Does 'subordination of teaching to learning' and 'starting where the pupils are' mean that my aims should be the same as the students' aims? I suggest not. Students quite naturally often wish to minimize their effort, and many are reluctant to stand out from their peer group. The didactic tension comes into play. But the aims I have outlined here are aims connected with making sense, not with showing off or with making extra effort. Consequently, bearing in mind my initial assumption about students wanting to make sense of the world, my aims and students' aims are at least confluent.

The wishes outlined contain automated skills, general impressions and articulate stories, experience and familiarity with examples and more generally with the effect of specializing and generalizing in this particular topic area. The extent to which pupils succeed in all of these aims will depend not only on the teaching style adopted, but on a host of other factors including:

- predisposition/interest/involvement in problematic questions at the heart of the topic;
- peer group attitude to learning;
- teacher attitude to learning and teaching, interest, commitment etc.;
- facility with assumed automated skills;
- the extent to which pupils' *own* powers are evoked and employed in the teaching and learning;
- the extent to which pupils share the teacher's goals.

These are some of the factors which make up the didactic situation (Brousseau 1984). With so many influences it is clear that there can be no royal road to learning or to teaching. Suggestions – such as reconstruction and listening, pausing, attending to the spiral through manipulating, getting a sense, articulating, attending to the back and forth flow between particular and general – are merely fragments of an ethos or *Weltanschauung*. They are devices intended to promote a perspective, and do not comprise a 'method'. Words are the results of attempts to draw distinctions which teachers have found useful, because in the midst of an event suddenly becoming aware of the distinction reminds them that there may be some aspects they may have neglected or some alternative ways of engaging pupils and evoking their powers. In other words, Gattegno's assertion holds equally for students *and* teachers: 'Only awareness is educable.'

Assessment

Consider topics such as density, the Norman invasion, solving triangles, *Macbeth* or any other that comes to mind. I submit that the nature and purpose of formal education is to facilitate movement of attention to and fro between particularities and generalities. In other words, it is to become aware of, and articulate about, patterns or generalities which encompass a variety of contexts and situations (Mason 1984b). (Note this same movement in the use of particular examples like density and *Macbeth* in order to indicate the general.) Successful pupils can move from the particular to the general, and from the general to the particular. Pupils who are process-aware (but not necessarily articulate about it) quite naturally evoke both movements *automatically* as appropriate. In some situations pupils can operate only *reflexively* in the sense that they can employ both movements appropriately when reminded, but not always without being reminded. In some situations pupils can only *react* to explicit suggestions. They need specific help in invoking fundamental thinking processes which they have already used in order to learn to walk and talk, but which for some reasons are not employed in the particular lesson. The triad of reactive, reflexive and automatic helps some teachers to recognize differences in pupil responses that might otherwise have been overlooked, and thus enables them to extend pupils appropriately.

Movement from explicit and detailed work employing thinking processes (and thus developing and refining them) through reflexively triggering off processes by a word or gesture to automatic invocation is subtle. It can be assisted by the use of explicit vocabulary, but words can also become superficial jargon. Mason (1984a, 1986b) elaborates the tension between words as superficial jargon and as precise technical terms, and suggests techniques for developing and maintaining richness and meaning for didactic frameworks.

The six levels of performance shown in Figure 8.3 are based on an analysis of the particular-general movement, together with a distinction between being able to give an *account* of what a topic is about and being able to *account for* various features or anomalies that appear in the topic. The six levels provide both a basis for designing assessment and a technique for helping pupils make sense of a topic for themselves – in short, they allow the pupils to construe and verify their own meanings. An overall picture of the six levels is given in Figure 8.3, which can usefully be read from right to left as a flow from the functional to the perceptive, from left to right as an unfolding of the essence into the functional, or as levels developing clockwise from bottom right round to top right.

Most examinations test facility at level 1 and level 2 with respect to techniques like solving equations. Rarely are pupils called upon to show what they can do at higher levels. Similarly, pupils are frequently put to

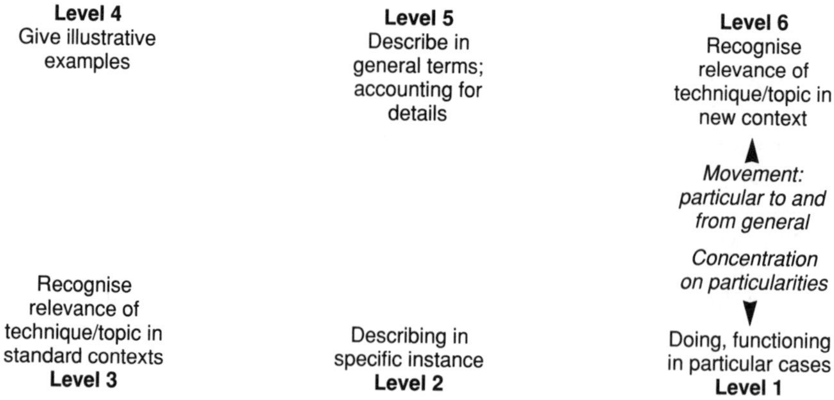

Level 4	Level 5	Level 6
Give illustrative examples	Describe in general terms; accounting for details	Recognise relevance of technique/topic in new context

▲
Movement: particular to and from general

Concentration on particularities

Level 3	Level 2	Level 1
Recognise relevance of technique/topic in standard contexts	Describing in specific instance	▼ Doing, functioning in particular cases

Figure 8.3 Six levels of mathematics processes

work on sets of exercises which are intended to develop facility at level 1 or 2. Rarely are they encouraged to give their own account of a topic, or to account for how topics fit together. Yet it is in the act of explaining to others ('you only really learn when you have to teach it') that most people really make a topic their own by constructing their own story of how all the details fit together.

Levels 1 to 3: giving an account of (describing)

Level 1   Doing specific calculations, functioning with certain practical apparatus (e.g. add fractions of a particular type; make measurements; read tabular data; find a solution to a given pair of equations; find the reflection of a point in a line . . .).

Recalling specific aspects of a topic, and specific technical terms (e.g. fractions can be added, multiplied, compared; equations sometimes have solutions and sometimes not . . .).

Level 2   Giving an account of how a technique is carried out on an example in your own words; describing several contexts in which it is relevant (e.g. you multiply these together and add those . . .; you measure perpendicularly here . . .; fractions arise as parts or shares of a whole . . .).

Giving a coherent account of options, in relation to a specific example (e.g. fractions can be compared by subtracting or by dividing . . .).

Giving a coherent account of what a group did, in specific terms (e.g. we tried this and this, we noticed that . . .).

Level 3   Recognizing the relevance of a technique or topic/idea in standard contexts (e.g. if two-thirds of a team have flu . . . – recognize fractions; two kilos of coffee and one kilo of tea cost . . . – recognize simultaneous equations).

Levels 4 to 6: accounting for (explaining)

Level 4   Giving illustrative examples (standard and own) of generalisations drawn from a topic, or of relationships between relevant ideas (e.g. the simplest denominator is not always the product – give an example; sometimes simultaneous equations have no solutions – give an example).

Identifying what particular examples have in common and how they illustrate aspects of the technique or topic (e.g. what does $5/6 + 1/8 = 23/24$ illustrate about adding fractions?; when this point is reflected in this line, and its image reflected in the same line, you get back to the starting point illustrating the general fact that . . .).

Level 5   Describing in general terms how a technique is carried out; to account for anomalies, special cases, particular aspects of the technique (e.g. to add two fractions you . . .; simultaneous equations with no solution arise because . . .; a triangle reflected in a line cannot be translated and rotated back to its original position – because . . .).

Level 6   Recognizing the relevance of a technique or topic in new contexts. Connecting a topic coherently with other mathematical topics (e.g. fractions are one way to represent and manipulate certain kinds of numbers . . .; reflections are examples of transformations . . .).

The six levels are intended to suggest ways of structuring tasks for pupils which will provide impetus and opportunity for them to make ideas their own, as well as providing a format for assessment of content. The proposed format includes assessment of the major mathematical processes – specialising, generalising and convincing. Other processes such as the use of, and switching between, representations will arise in the context of particular mathematical topics. Problem solving and investigational work could be assessed using the same format, in which pupils are called upon to report (orally or in written form) on their own work and the work of their group at the various levels.

REFERENCES

Brousseau, G. (1984) 'The crucial role of the didactic contract in the analysis and construction of situations in teaching and learning mathematics', in H-G. Steiner (ed.) *The Theory of Mathematics Education*, Occasional Paper 54, Bielefeld, IDM.

Chevellard, Y. (1985) *La Transposition Didactique*, Grenoble: La Pensée Sauvage.

Gattegno, C. (1971) *What We Owe Children: The Subordination of Teaching to Learning*, London: Routledge.

Mason, J. (1984a) 'Towards one possible discipline for mathematics education', in H-G. Steiner (ed.) *The Theory of Mathematics Education*, Occasional Paper 54, Bielefeld, IDM.

—— (1984b) 'What do we really want students to learn?', *Teaching at a Distance* 25: 4–11.

—— (1986a) 'I is for imagery and imagination', *The Investigator* 9: 8–9.

—— (1986b) 'Challenge for change: to stay alive every teacher must become a researcher', *Mathematics Teaching: Challenges for Change*, AAMT 11th Biennial Conference Proceedings, pp. 9–30.

Michener, E. (1978) 'Understanding understanding mathematics', *Cognitive Science* 2: 361–83.

Chapter 9

Ways of seeing

Laurinda Brown, Dave Hewitt and John Mason

Seeing comes before words. The child looks and recognises before it can speak . . . It is seeing which establishes our place in the surrounding world; we explain that world with words . . . We only see what we look at. To look is an act of choice. As a result of this act, what we see is brought within our reach.

(Berger 1973: 7, 8)

What was it you noticed when you first worked in a classroom with another teacher? Did you focus on what the pupils were doing? On what the teacher was doing? Were you interested in the mathematical content of the lesson or what the pupils were learning about? What common errors were made? Were you most concerned with your own interaction with those pupils you worked with?

It is impossible to focus on all the differing aspects of classroom life at the same time, but it is possible to make an act of choice about what to look out for. Such a way of seeing we shall call a filter. For instance, you might be interested in how teachers and pupils use questions within the learning process and use this filter to help you to collect particular examples which you can then reflect on to allow you to work on your own use of questions. Over time you may explore classrooms from many different points of view.

Similarly, how are you going to enrich your view of the mathematics curriculum? What thoughts go through your mind as you prepare to teach a topic to a class? You might naturally concentrate on the mathematical content – making sure you know it yourself so as to be ready to tell others about it. Perhaps you are more concerned with establishing different ways of working such as using discussion? You do need to start from your own strengths and perspectives but what other ways of seeing the mathematics curriculum are there?

Mathematics in the National Curriculum (DES 1991) is one way of defining the mathematical concepts, skills and processes which pupils might learn. What happens as you prepare to teach it? There is some assistance with this question within the *Mathematics Non-Statutory Guidance* (DES

1989), the *Mathematics Programmes of Study, INSET for Key Stages 3 and 4 file* (NCC 1992) and *Mathematics Counts* (the Cockcroft Report, DES 1982), in that different models are offered which give filters for planning lessons. Examples of these models are Figure 9.1 and Table 9.1, taken from

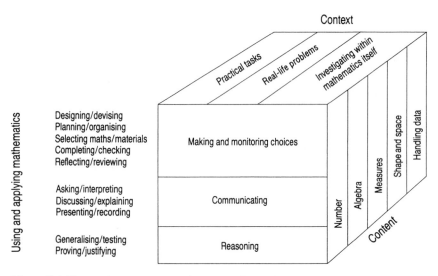

Figure 9.1 The context, content and process dimensions of mathematics teaching

Mathematics Programmes of Study, INSET for Key Stages 3 and 4 file (NCC 1992), and the following, taken from *Mathematics Counts* (the Cockcroft Report, DES 1982):

Mathematics teaching at all levels should include opportunities for:
– exposition by the teacher;
– discussion between teacher and pupils and between pupils themselves;
– appropriate practical work;
– consolidation and practice of fundamental skills and routines;
– problem solving, including the application of mathematics to everyday situations;
– investigational work.

(para. 243)

Either of these models could be used as a checklist in the planning of lessons to ensure a rich and varied set of learning experiences. The purpose of the filters is to provide a basis for designing activities for lessons, together with a detailed sense of the links between, and uses of, various mathematical concepts.

The following sections describe three more filters which you could use to help plan your lessons. They are not mutually exclusive and, indeed, the

Table 9.1 A summary of the National Curriculum requirements

Pupils should be:

Making and monitoring choices

Designing	•	designing/devising a mathematical task
Planning	•	working methodically
	•	checking for sufficient information
	•	recording findings systematically
	•	using 'trial and improvement' methods
	•	using alternative approaches
Selecting	•	selecting appropriate mathematics
	•	selecting appropriate materials and resources
Completing	•	carrying through a mathematical task to a successful conclusion
	•	checking results and considering whether they are sensible
	•	presenting alternative solutions
Reflecting	•	looking back and reviewing progress

Communicating in mathematics

Interpreting	•	interpreting mathematical information presented in oral, written or visual forms
Discussing	•	describing and explaining work being done
Presenting	•	recording findings systematically
	•	presenting findings in oral, written or visual forms

Reasoning

Generalising	•	making and testing predictions, statements, generalisations, hypotheses
Proving	•	defining and reasoning with some precision
	•	using examples to test statements or definitions
	•	following a chain of mathematical reasoning
	•	proving and disproving

purpose of offering them is not to be definitive. The teaching that takes place is a manifestation of each teacher's perspective on the nature of mathematics and of how it is learned. Thus you need to be flexible and broaden your ideas, confronting and considering again and again the basic questions such as:

– what is mathematics?
– what constitutes mathematical thinking?
– what skills do I want my pupils to develop?
– what is the best way for me to help my pupils?

CULTURAL INDUCTION

This way of viewing the curriculum is based on the work of Alan Bishop (1986), who experienced and studied in some detail the challenges of teaching and learning mathematics in a culture very different from his own. There were necessarily differences to be considered but reflecting on the similarities led him to suggest the following six cultural activities which draw heavily on, or are essential to, mathematics and which are critical to each individual in order to be adequately inducted into the culture.

Counting

There are various types of counting:

- using parts of the body as names;
- using counters and abstract names;
- using names alone;

but counting is a composite act. An archetypal mathematical question is 'How many . . .?' as in 'In how many different ways . . .?' Many mathematical techniques amount to clever ways for counting things and many definitions are about when two things are to be considered as different.

Locating

Finding your way around, locating yourself in space, orientation and spatial awareness, all spawn specific mathematical ideas to enable precise calculation, communication and manipulation of ideas.

Measuring

Comparison is the essence of measuring, developing from simple distinctions such as colour or blood type, through relative scales like temperature to absolute scales like length and weight.

Designing

Artistic design is often intensely mathematical, e.g. pottery and fabric decoration, tiles and frieze patterns, Neolithic stone carving. Tools intended for use also involve considerable design care, and often require specific mathematical ideas.

Playing

Games have been part of human activity since long before recorded history, and most games have a mathematical basis which goes beyond the simple ideas of following rules and the working out of consequences.

Explaining

Explaining and the related process of predicting are activities which lift human cognition above merely experiencing the environment and responding to it. Searching and questioning are basic human urges, as are attempting to convince others and attempting to control or at least to prepare for future events.

How does any topic currently taught contribute to these aspects of culture? How might other topics or activities not currently taught similarly contribute? To what aspects of modern culture do pupils need induction?

It would seem possible to view the curriculum through these headings within any one culture or to use the headings within a multicultural environment as a device for enrichment.

MATHEMATICAL TOOLS

This way of viewing the curriculum considers the entitlement of each and every child to achieve familiarity and facility in the use of the mathematical tools available in the society at the present time. It can be seen as teaching 'that' through the use of 'this', where the focus for the teacher is on preparing tasks which need to be supported by various tools. Initially the pupil would have worked on problems with the aid of the tool and, in the process, learned how the tool works and what it can do. Eventually the question would be 'when tackling a problem does the child reach for the tool without being told to do so?'

> The car is a tool although not necessarily a mathematical one. In the 'Your driving test' booklet the advice is not to worry if you make a mistake whilst on test, for this will not automatically mean a failure. What is being looked for is an ability to control the vehicle, confidence, thought for other road users and, to me most importantly, a position from which the candidate will improve. Is this a criteria for having learned how to learn? What I was in fact given was a licence to take care of my own progress.
>
> (Brown 1992: 23)

The image generated, then, is that each child would have obtained a 'licence to use unaided' some or all of a particular set of tools on leaving school. Anita Straker's (1987) Presidential address to the Mathematical Association develops this idea based on a discussion with one of the authors, and John Mason's (1992) article in *Micromath*, 'Geometric tools', explores the idea further.

One example facilitating such a view would be the setting up of an information technology (IT) policy within a school. The National

Curriculum makes explicit which content-free programs, such as databases and spreadsheets, should be used by every pupil. The IT policy would recognise the cross-curricular nature of these tools and, through negotiation, a particular department might agree to be responsible for the initial introduction of each pupil to that program within a context within their specialism. Each department would then be aware that each pupil has previously used the program and, machine availability willing, can plan to make further use of the tool.

The range of mathematical tools would, however, be wider than just computer applications. Inevitably, in a rapidly changing world, any listing of mathematical tools would be expected to grow and develop, so it seems worthwhile to group a proposed listing of such tools in some way. Here is one possible list.

Instruments:	*Hand-held calculators:*	*Counting:*
ruler	numerical	counters
protractor (180°)	scientific	Cuisenaire rods
protractor (360°)	graphical	multibase blocks
compasses	algebraic	abacus
. . .	. . .	. . .

Programming languages:	*Content-free software:*	*Content-support software:*
LOGO	spreadsheet	graph plotter
BASIC	database (creation and interrogation)	geometrical drawing (Euclidean and transformation)
. . .	. . .	. . .

Perhaps, before reading on, you might like to think about the following two questions.

1 What changes you would make to the list – additions and deletions?
2 In the examples provided by the statements of attainment in the National Curriculum there are times when tools are used to explore the mathematical content. Find a statement of attainment which is not exemplified by use of a tool and think of one or more tools which, in being used to investigate particular problems, would be likely to bring someone to work on that content.

ESSENCES

This way of viewing the curriculum considers that if pupils are to make sense of their mathematics lessons then they need to be able to connect these experiences with what they already know. The expression 'starting from where the pupils are' and the cry for relevance are but two of the many versions of the same sentiment. Mathematics lessons can truly start from where the pupils are by attending to root mathematical experiences or essences, evoking and building on them to engage with the desired mathematical content.

Rather than give a list of essences, the following is an activity which might help you to seek them out for yourself or with others. As the important part of the activity is the negotiation of meaning, each individual or group of teachers would be expected to generate a different set of essences. It is in the act of communicating with others that we organise our own thinking, as we are forced to clarify and to make precise for ourself as much as for colleagues. We would like you to work on the activity before reading on so that you can compare your ideas with those given as an example.

Stage 1   Choose something in mathematics (topics, skills, processes, . . .) which you consider to be essential for pupils to learn. You can decide the age of the pupils you have in mind and the level of the mathematics.

Stage 2   Suppose someone has a poor understanding of what you have chosen. Write down three things you could work on in order to help them improve their understanding of this.

Stage 3   Decide on one of these and commit yourself to it. You cannot change your mind later on.
    Go to stage 2.

At each stage, something is being split up and three more fundamental things are considered. As you repeat this process, you may find it hard to keep splitting up each thing you choose. However, it is surprising what relatively fundamental things can be split, so do not give up easily. The task continues until you have arrived at some unsplittables, those things which you feel cannot be broken down any more. If you are doing this activity in a group, then it is at this point that you could share the lists you have produced and the thoughts that went into them. Each person's unsplittables could be considered by the group to see whether they could, in fact, be split further, and a final list could be agreed by the whole group. It is these unsplittables that are the essences.

An example of what one person produced within a group when they had chosen the starting point of Pythagoras is as follows.

Pythagoras
>   Squares and roots
>   Addition
>   Areas

>   *Squares and roots*
>>   Area
>>   Calculators
>>   Multiplication

>>   *Area*
>>>   Multiplication
>>>   Measuring
>>>   Counting

>>>   *Multiplication*
>>>>   Numbers
>>>>   Tables
>>>>   Multiple adding

>>>>   *Numbers*
>>>>>   Names
>>>>>   Order
>>>>>   Patterns

>>>>>   *Order*
>>>>>>   Value
>>>>>>   Greater/smaller
>>>>>>   More/less

>>>>>>   *Greater/smaller*
>>>>>>>   same/different

Same/different was not felt to be splittable and consequently was viewed as an essence.

Such mathematical essences form the basis of much of the mathematics curriculum. In fact the content of the curriculum can be viewed as a collection of different manifestations of essences. For example, 'same/different' is concerned with:

- classifying and naming;
- equivalent fractions;
- factorising and multiplying out brackets;
- arithmetic;
- manipulation of algebraic expressions;
- spotting patterns;
- conjecturing;
- links between decimals, fractions and percentages;
- properties of shapes . . .

Furthermore, there are connections with what the pupils already know since they have had experience throughout their lives of same/different in doing activities such as:

- developing meaning for words in their first language;
- verb endings in their first language;
- recognising particular people even though they might be wearing different clothes;
- naming things and people . . .

It may be that a different starting point for the activity and different routes through it still lead to the same essences. It is our view that the whole mathematics curriculum is based on remarkably few essences.

Another commonly discovered essence is 'inverse', which is concerned with:

- addition – subtraction;
- multiplication – division;
- squaring – square roots;
- powers – logarithms;
- manipulation of equations;
- symmetry;
- trigonometry . . .

The corresponding connections with the pupils' previous experiences are through:

- putting on, and taking off, clothes;
- opening and closing doors;
- turning a tap on and off;
- looking from one part of the room to another, and back again . . .

By working to elaborate for oneself the root essences from which mathematics derives, it is possible both to evoke pupils' inherent mathematical awarenesses and to draw their attention to connections and underlying principles which they may not have noticed for themselves. Tony Gardiner in his book *Recurring Themes in School Mathematics* (1992) develops this principle through a number of themes.

So what is important is that each of us continue to develop our own ways of seeing the mathematics curriculum, using the ideas of others and our own observations. Our filters continue to change and develop over time as we continue to work on our skills and awarenesses as teachers, but earlier perspectives become integrated into what becomes our current style. Different filters dominate our attention at different times, even to the extent that one seems to be more fundamental than the others. By holding on to the notion of 'filter', it may be possible to achieve more depth and richness in one's way of seeing than if a single view is allowed to dominate. What other ways of seeing the mathematics curriculum, which you have found useful in your work, would you want to add to this list?

REFERENCES

Berger, J. (1973) *Ways of Seeing*, Harmondsworth: British Broadcasting Corporation and Penguin Books.

Bishop, A. (1986) 'Mathematics education as cultural induction', *Nieuwe Wiskrant*, October: 27–32.

Brown, L. (1992) 'Perspectives and techniques', *Mathematics Teaching* 139: 23.

DES (1982) *Mathematics Counts* (the Cockcroft Report), London: HMSO, paragraph 243.

—— (1989) *Mathematics Non-Statutory Guidance*, London: HMSO.

—— (1991) *Mathematics in the National Curriculum*, London: HMSO.

Gardiner, T. (1992) *Recurring Themes in School Mathematics*, Birmingham: UK Mathematics Foundation.

Mason, J. (1992) 'Geometrical tools', *Micromath* 8 (3): 24.

NCC (1992) *Mathematics Programmes of Study, INSET for Key Stages 3 and 4 file*, York: NCC.

Straker, A. (1987) 'The challenge to change, presidential address', *Mathematical Gazette*: 193.

Part IV

How is learning mathematics influenced by social and cultural factors?

Should mathematics be culture free?

Should social and environmental issues be integrated into the teaching of mathematics?

In the next four chapters the argument for integration is put in terms of the effect on valuing pupils of all cultures, on being aware of gender bias and on indicating the value of mathematical understanding in examining issues that affect or will affect the lives of all pupils.

In Chapter 10, Stephen Lerman argues for placing multicultural mathematics firmly in the curriculum and offering it so that pupils are aware of the strong history of a subject that has been developed and explored by numerous cultures, not all of them Eurocentric. In Chapter 11, David Urquhart and Graeme Balfour describe how they used information about the AIDS epidemic to teach data handling within the cross-curricular framework of health education. This is followed by Brian Hudson's consideration of how pupils' interest in mathematics can be developed through issues in which they have both experience and interest, which can be explored through a cross-curricular framework and which will therefore stimulate pupils' understanding of the need for mathematics in society.

In Chapter 13, Leone Burton evaluates the mathematics curriculum in terms of entitlement and equality of opportunity and of outcome, thus bringing together the debates highlighted in the previous three chapters.

Chapter 10

Critical/humanistic mathematics education

A role for history?

Stephen Lerman

Example 1: 35 x 23

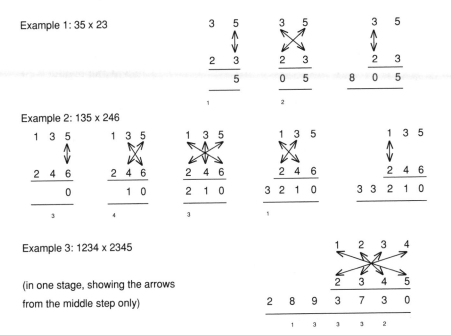

Example 2: 135 x 246

Example 3: 1234 x 2345

(in one stage, showing the arrows
from the middle step only)

Figure 10.1 The stages of multiplication

According to Swami Tirthaji (1965), the method of multiplication that is described here (Figure 10.1) dates back at least to Vedic sutras from 1200 BC and possibly as far back as 3000 BC. This is controversial though, and other historians believe it to be much more recent. The multiplication is always of pairs of single digit numbers, in some cases one pair, in other cases more than one pair, the outcomes of which are added together in the patterns shown by the arrows. The first two examples show the stages of the multiplication separated. In practice the figures are written once and the calculation done in one stage, as shown here in Example 3 of the figure.

This method continues in a similar way for larger numbers. It enables long multiplication to be carried out on one line, uses patterns that are visually appealing and has many other potentially interesting aspects which are left to the reader to imagine and investigate. Tirthaji's book describes short methods of carrying out long division and also for extracting roots.

There are a number of features of this topic in the history of mathematics that I wish to highlight in order to generalise them.

1 It is a useful and interesting piece of mathematics in its own right. It draws on visual symmetry for the performance of an algorithm, and therefore might be easier to remember than the usual one, and the symmetry extends to deal with larger numbers. It can be done in one line, which looks impressive, and that can be attractive to young learners of mathematics.

2 It originates from a part of the world with a rich and ancient culture, one that was 'developed' long before the present so-called developed world. That culture was interested in mathematics and some of the products of that interest have become essential parts of the mathematics used and taught around the world.

3 It opens up possibilities for study of how it has come about that we have what has been called a 'Eurocentric' view of what is mathematics, and its history, and that this mathematics has been exported as 'the way it is' around the world.

I shall return to these points, and expand upon them, later.

It will have become clear that the aspects of this topic which have been highlighted reveal my concern with a particular perspective on mathematics and on mathematics education. I see mathematics as a creative human endeavour, growing, changing and fallible. Mathematics has high social status and analyses of issues and their solutions in mathematical language serve as an important tool in mystifying and reifying knowledge, making people feel powerless to participate in and criticise authority. I am suggesting that in mathematics education we can and should empower pupils (and ourselves!) to question and criticise, and an important element in this is the history of mathematics. (For further elaboration of these ideas see, for example, Lerman, 1986, 1989a, b, 1990.) There are, of course, other more commonly held views of the nature of mathematics and consequently the purpose and function of school mathematics as can be seen, for example, in the recent debate that has been taking place in *Mathematics in School*. Tooley (1990) suggested that his interest as a teacher was in children's 'achievement', measured in particular by GCSE success, and he claimed that multicultural mathematics, and in particular the history of mathematics, plays no positive part in this at all.

In reply, Bailey and Shan (1991) pointed out that the aims for mathematics education, and education in general, are wider than merely passing GCSE, and that in any case achievement levels are related in complex ways to culture, including ethnicity, gender and class. They argued that the rather simplistic conjectures that Tooley put forward to explain who does well in school mathematics and why, did not take account of this complexity. I refer to this debate not only because of its relevance to this chapter but also because it illustrates well how beliefs about the nature and purpose of mathematics and its teaching and learning determine one's perspective on different aspects of the curriculum.

I am not simply arguing for multicultural mathematics through historical examples. Many topics that have been introduced under this umbrella have served quite the opposite function to that intended by teachers. They can be extremely patronising and, although not intentionally, can make other peoples appear backward and primitive; they can embarrass children from ethnic minorities instead of engaging their interest; they can appear to be trivial and outside of the mainstream and are consequently devalued; and, as they are not part of the examined syllabus in school mathematics, they are seen by children to be unimportant. On this last point, those who determined the final form of the National Curriculum for mathematics have to take the responsibility for setting into legislative stone the anti-progressive view that because some multicultural mathematics is patronising and because antiracist mathematics is problematic they should be excluded completely. I am suggesting that multicultural mathematics has to be challenging and empowering, forming a part of a mathematics curriculum with values that are made explicit and are in a quite different direction to the hidden values perpetuated by the National Curriculum, and the history of mathematics can play a significant part in such a critical/humanistic mathematics curriculum.

To pursue the points highlighted above in relation to Vedic methods of long multiplication, and in the framework of the educational values I have identified here, the following should be considered.

1 (continued) Mathematics topics must be mainstream: they must be things that pupils need to know in school and that they can use. That way, pupils will value what they learn and perhaps become interested in the wider implications of the topic. Pupils from an ethnic group whose culture has produced the piece of mathematics are more likely to feel valued than when, for example, the method of construction of grass huts is described, or the geometrical patterns in traditional crafts. In these latter examples, pupils may feel that their culture is being made to appear primitive and backward, even though this is not the intention of the teacher. Other topics that are also valuable in this context are: the triangle usually called after Pascal but known to the Chinese several centuries earlier; and the generalisation of the properties of a right-angled triangle.

2 (continued) The history of mathematics can show that other peoples were

'developed' long before people in this country, and can lead pupils to ask how it is that we receive the impression that these peoples are backward. Colonialism and racism can then be put into a perspective that enables a challenge and critique of British and other imperialism. The Hindu zero and the Persian algebraists are also useful topics in this context.

3 (continued) The most commonly read histories of mathematics perpetuate the image that useful and powerful mathematics has been developed by white, male Europeans, and that the period of history before the Greeks and between the Greeks and the Renaissance were fallow periods. This is challenged more fully in Bernal (1987) and Joseph (1991). History, where it appears in the mathematics classroom, is usually of the 'Napier was a Scottish mathematician' kind, whereas it may be surprising to pupils to find that sophisticated mathematical methods were being used in India so long ago. This surprise can be drawn upon to enable pupils to make that challenge to unconsciously transmitted images.

This brings me to two further important aspects of how the history of mathematics can empower students: studying history through which pupils can learn mathematical ideas, and 'imaginary' histories of mathematics.

Negative numbers have a rich and varied history. They appear to have been better understood by the Babylonians of 1500 BC than by many eminent British mathematicians of the late eighteenth and early nineteenth century. We continue to teach primary children that you can't do '3 minus 5' and secondary pupils that you can after all, and that it is really just a matter of different directions of shifts on the number line, or debits and credits. Negative numbers did not appear in order to deal with banking, nor with sub-zero temperatures. A study of the history of negative numbers, *as history*, may well have the effect of enabling pupils to work with them comfortably, in a more successful way than our present methods, as well as having many other side benefits (Arcavi *et al.* 1982). This may also be true for teaching the fundamentals of the calculus through history. Our usual methods do not generally succeed in giving pupils an awareness of the powerful ideas, such as infinitesimals, and limits, and the metaphor of motion, that occur in the calculus.

My final point concerns other conceptions of mathematical ideas. Imagine that Aristotle was a Hopi Indian (following Whorf 1956), for whom, for example, 'ten days' is different from 'ten men' because the latter can be seen whereas the former has to take place over time, i.e. the former is an ordinal ten and the latter a cardinal. Logic and mathematics would look very different indeed. Further examination of Hopi conceptions of space and time could lead us to construct mathematical and logical ideas that would be appropriate to that world view. I am suggesting that studying 'imaginary' or what would be better termed 'potential' histories of mathematics can suggest to pupils that there is no necessity to the concepts we call mathematical

knowledge; they are the result of this particular set of historical circumstances, actually dominant through hegemony. In his work in Mozambique
(some of which unfortunately borders rather too closely on the dangers
mentioned in point 1 above) Gerdes (e.g. 1985) has encouraged students to
conjecture that African mathematicians could well have developed
Pythagoras' Theorem before Greek times, but that ways of recording ideas
would not have enabled that information to have been perpetuated. This
demonstrates the force of potential histories of mathematics – they may
indeed be as 'actual' as the more well-known ones (for another well-
developed example, see Bloor 1986).

CONCLUSION

In this chapter I have briefly argued that studying the history of mathematics
as history, in the ways suggested, can play a significant part in an empowering
critical/humanist mathematics education. I have made explicit the particular
perspective of the nature of mathematics in which I have framed these
arguments, and have suggested elsewhere (1989c) that the range of possibilities that are engendered by this paradigm are a strong support for it.

This chapter is theoretical, rather than being based on particular classroom
experiences, but I believe that there are many teachers engaged in work of
the kind described here, in their classrooms.

REFERENCES

Arcavi, A., Bruckheimer, M. and Ben-Zvi, R. (1982) 'Maybe a mathematics teacher
    can benefit from the study of the history of mathematics', *For The Learning of
    Mathematics* 3 (1): 30–7.
Bailey, P. and Shan, S. J. (1991) 'Mathematics for a multicultural society, under-
    achievement and the National Curriculum', *Mathematics in School* 20 (2): 20–1.
Bernal, M. (1987) *Black Athena – The Egyptian Origin of Greek Civilisation*,
    London: Free Association Books.
Bloor, D. (1986) *Knowledge and Social Imagery*, London: Routledge.
Gerdes, P. (1985) 'Conditions and strategies for emancipatory mathematics edu-
    cation in undeveloped countries', *For The Learning of Mathematics* 5 (1):
    15–20.
Joseph, G. (1991) *The Crest of the Peacock*, London: Tauris.
Lerman, S. (1986) 'Alternative views of the nature of mathematics and their possible
    influence on the teaching of mathematics', PhD thesis, King's College, London.
——— (1989a) 'A social view of mathematics: implications for mathematics education',
    in C. Keitel (ed.) *Mathematics, Education and Society*, Science and Technology
    Education, Document Series No. 35, UNESCO Division of Science, Technical
    and Environmental Education, Paris, pp. 42–4.
——— (1989b) 'Investigations, where to now?', in P. Ernest (ed.) *Mathematics
    Teaching: The State of the Art*, London: Falmer Press, pp. 73–80.
——— (1989c) 'Constructivism, mathematics and mathematics education', *Educational
    Studies in Mathematics* 20: 211–23.

—— (1990) 'Alternative perspectives of the nature of mathematics and their influence on the teaching of mathematics', *British Educational Research Journal* 16 (1): 53–61.

Tirthaji, Sri B. K. (1965) *Vedic Mathematics*, Delhi: Motilal Banarsidass.

Tooley, J. (1990) 'Multicultural mathematics, underachievement and the National Curriculum', *Mathematics in School* 19 (2): 10–11.

Whorf, B. (1956) *Language, Thought and Reality*, Cambridge, MA: MIT Press.

Chapter 11

Maths aids: pastoral topics through maths

A case study

David Urquhart and Graeme Balfour

In this chapter we shall consider some of the work undertaken with a group of Year 10 during timetable maths periods. One of the first activities was to establish the current level of understanding amongst the pupils concerning the HIV/AIDS epidemic. Particular emphasis was placed on information of a statistical nature, although all contributions had some relevance and were valued. We discussed when the current epidemic began, rates of increase, the number of people with AIDS or HIV in the United Kingdom, the number of new cases per year and so on. All data was taken from original sources such as *AIDS-UK* (Health Education Authority (HEA) 1990) and *The HIV News Review* (Terrence Higgins Trust). It was considered important to use as much data as possible from unadulterated sources; this is not a contrived classroom example but a real-life problem! It gave the exercise an authority and allowed practice in extracting appropriate data from these original sources, a non-trivial mathematical skill.

One of the major pieces of work to involve the students in an understanding of the growth of the epidemic was a modelling exercise using historical data. We took the pupils back to 1982, and told them of a strange new illness that seemed to have surfaced. Three people had been reported to have acquired the illness by that year. The pupils were told that they were responsible for forward planning of health facilities and had to monitor the illnesses. What did they think would happen in 1983? The pupils made their estimate and the actual figure for that year was revealed. In this way we worked forward until 1990, plotting the new cases each year. As the exercise progressed, the pupils made use of the yearly differentials and the rate of increase to help refine their forecasting. Note that these techniques require an understanding in practice of second-order differences. Changes in increase rates were discussed and possible reasons put forward. For example, a significant fall in the rate of increase in 1988 could be due to the result of increased awareness and education in the early 1980s. This takes the built-in time delay in the development of AIDS into consideration. The graph of actual cases is shown in Figure 11.1.

Having got to 1990 the pupils had discovered how the epidemic had

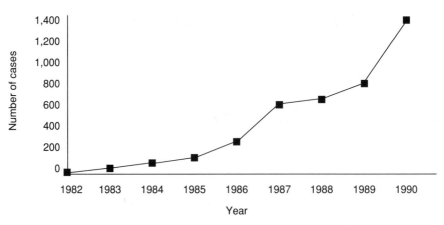

Figure 11.1 Yearly AIDS cases

grown in numerical terms. They then used this knowledge to predict ahead to 1995, again concentrating on new AIDS cases per year. The importance of forecasting was discussed and their predictions compared with the official projection contained in the Cox report in 1987 and the Day report in 1989 (see HEA 1990). The fact that there were differences in the predictions was due not only to the pupils having access to the most recent data available, making them arguably more 'accurate', but also on differing assumptions of growth rates. This then led to a consideration of what factors might lead to an increase in growth rate, and what factors might bring it down. Suggestions for the suppression of the infection rate ranged from free needle exchange schemes for injecting drug users to free condom machines in all public spaces. Much importance was also placed on increasing the level of public awareness and the need for more education.

It is evident from a consideration of recent AIDS data that it is a changing disease. A quote from the HEA acted as a stimulus to investigating these changes.

> Provided the observed behaviour changes among homosexual men can be sustained, the future pattern of the epidemic will largely depend on transmission in the injecting drug use and heterosexual contact categories.
>
> (HEA 1990)

Going back over the same published data the group now concentrated on the growth of the epidemic through heterosexual contact. Year by year figures of new AIDS cases in this particular subset resulted in a near exponential curve (Figure 11.2). The pupils were asked to come up with a mathematically derived curve using figures shown in Figure 11.3. Once this mathematical model of the heterosexual epidemic had been found it could be used to predict ahead, assuming constant growth rates. The first reported case of

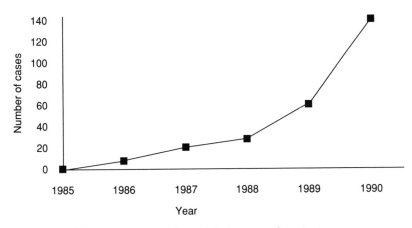

Figure 11.2 AIDS cases per year through heterosexual contact

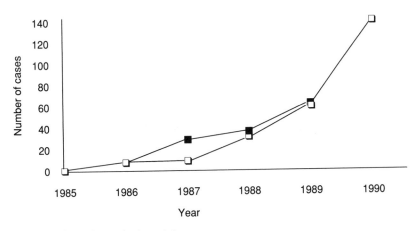

Figure 11.3 A mathematical model

AIDS through heterosexual contact in the United Kingdom occurred in 1985 when there were three cases. Using this base figure and the best fit annual increase rate of 2.155 in the mathematical model, a projected figure of new cases for 1995 was found to be 6,480. The spreadsheet and resulting graph are shown in Figure 11.4. The power of the mathematics to illuminate the reality of the threat was plain, the figures for recent years paling into insignificance.

We had looked at the growth of all cases of AIDS and we had then focused in on the growth through heterosexual contact. While this told us about the growing numbers affected, it did not give us much information about the

	A	B	C	D
1	YEAR	NO. OF CASES	INCREASE FACTOR	MODEL
2	1985	3		3
3	1986	7	2.333333333	6.465
4	1987	25	3.571428571	13.932075
5	1988	33	1.32	30.0236216
6	1989	67	2.03030303	64.7009046
7	1990	138	2.0597011493	139.430449
8	1991			300.472618
9	1992			647.518493
10	1993			1395.40235
11	1994			3007.09207
12	1995			6480.28341

(a)

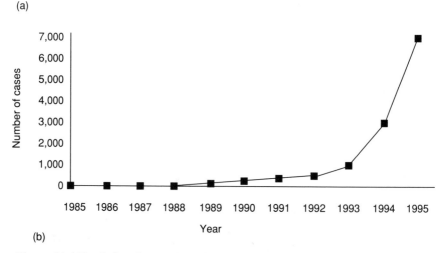

(b)

Figure 11.4 Predicting the number of AIDS cases through heterosexual contact:
(a) spreadsheet; (b) mathematical model using an increase factor of 2.155

changing nature of the epidemic and who it was affecting. It would be useful
to see whether all risk behavioural groups were behaving in the same way.
We could do this by breaking down the data by transmission route and then
comparing figures over time. For example, the pupils found that in
November 1987, 3.7 per cent of people with AIDS had acquired it through
heterosexual contact. The corresponding figure for the most recent accounting period, September 1990–February 1991, was 10.1 per cent, a sizeable
increase which tells us much about the metamorphosis of the epidemic. Of
course we must be careful that we understand the limitation, and the
validity, of bandying about seemingly simplistic numerical information. At
the same time there are opportunities here to do some positive work on the

use and misuse of statistics, their graphical representations and the question-able intention of much of the reported data concerning HIV/AIDS.

> The limitations of public education can be used by politicians and busi-nessmen for mass deception which is largely possible, not because data is withheld, but because the public is not sufficiently educated to fully understand it.
>
> (Stripp 1991)

What became clear during this project was the wealth of other HIV/AIDS issues which continued to present themselves for investigation. Valid work, from both a mathematical and pastoral perspective, could consider, for example, the study of global rates of infection, women with AIDS, young peoples' attitudes towards AIDS, the Uganda epidemic – where one in three of the population is estimated to be infected with HIV – and so on.

Although such sophisticated maths activities are not possible with pupils of all abilities, there is still a wealth of opportunity to be found in the use of HIV/AIDS data. For example, a forecasting exercise done with a group of Year 9 showed up a number of weaknesses in their understanding of percentages. The pupils were to use their own knowledge of the epidemic to establish risk activity categories and then predict the percentage of total cases for each of these categories. In doing this they quickly discovered that the sum of the percentages had to be a hundred and that if the estimate for one category was changed then at least one other must be altered in order to compensate. This enabled discussion about the interdependency of the percentages themselves and their corresponding sectors in the pie chart derived from those percentages.

We have thus extolled the virtues of mathematics work in the context of HIV/AIDS and have demonstrated some of the rich and varied mathematical activities which are possible when working in this way. It is vital, however, that those interested in attempting such work are aware of the implications of doing so. First of all, it is crucial that teachers do not concentrate solely on mathematical aspects of the topic, even if only mathematics time is being used. Whenever pupils exhibit confusion or concern about an aspect of HIV/AIDS, teachers must be able to provide sensitive responses to these worries and allay anxieties, if such HIV/AIDS education is not to do more harm than good. For example, one pupil expressed fear of ever having sex in case he 'got AIDS'. This required immediate and effective counselling if he were not to think of 'sex' as dangerous and something to be avoided under all circumstances. For teachers to be responsive to this type of situation it is necessary that they not only be well informed on the subject matter but also have the ability to deal effectively with issues which may be highly sensitive, personal or controversial. This includes, of course, such things as use of language. For example, we should talk about people *living with AIDS* rather than victims *dying of AIDS*, discuss *risk activities* rather than *risk groups* and avoid moralistic terms such as 'blame' or 'innocence'. Topics which may come into discussion are likely to be subject to the school's sex education policy and if these are inappropriately dealt with parental wrath may be unleashed, in stark contrast to more commonplace topics of study in mathematics lessons. It is well worth considering which teachers are likely to respond favourably and do justice to this topic.

> HMI criticised schools for avoiding controversial issues if they could. Perhaps they should avoid them. If teachers are given no opportunities to develop their own knowledge of the issues, to explore techniques for handling controversial issues, or most important of all, for examining their own attitudes, they are wise to leave well alone.
>
> (Brown 1990)

A further consideration is that of assessment of the completed work. HMI (1991) report that the assessment of Ma1, if attempted, was one of the greatest sources of difficulty to teachers, as was the assessment of group work and discussion. Our experience suggests that assessment of work of this type is far from straightforward and begs the question: if the use and application of mathematics in a meaningful context demands excessive amounts of already precious time to assess, will anyone ever attempt it? Certainly, the National Curriculum defined in terms of assessable ATs does little to encourage us. Further, the current GCSE coursework criteria prohibits the inclusion of any part of this type of work which is not directly mathematical in nature, and is most suited to the more common 'pattern and generalisation' type of investigation.

Although this was a small-scale project and there are limitations to the conclusions that we can make, we believe that the exercise was a valid and successful contribution to both mathematics and HIV/AIDS education and is certainly worthy of further development. By bringing PSHE from its timetable ghetto into the realm of the core curriculum not only is its status enhanced but mathematics may be seen as a socially relevant tool. The pupils increased their understanding of social issues while exercising their mathematical and technological abilities on live data.

SUMMARY

Health Education is to be implemented as a cross-curricular theme in the National Curriculum and in particular has been mapped to ATs concerning data handling in mathematics (DES 1990). It is therefore our responsibility as teachers of mathematics to consider how aspects of Health Education and data handling may be included in the mathematics classroom.

With the government having stated a preference for a cross-curricular delivery of PSHE, we must consider the intentions of this 'preference'. Is it an attempt to convince all teachers that they are responsible for the pastoral curriculum or is it instead perpetuating the devalued role of pastoral studies in the curriculum by making it subservient to the dominant academic disciplines?

> experience of this sort of permeation approach does not necessarily lead one to be optimistic about it. Normally whatever is being permeated actually just trickles away.
>
> (Brown 1990)

For example, if sex education were taught as reproduction in biology or family relationships in religion, then much of the loaded sensitive nature of PSHE would be defused and the moral overtones of much of this work would be lost. Is this the intention?

Whatever the answer, it is up to us to capture the initiative and consider the recommendations as an opportunity to develop a more integrated curriculum.

> if educational reform has reduced curriculum choice and strengthened central control, it has not prescribed specific teaching-learning strategies directly (although statutory testing may make it more difficult for teachers to embark on radical change to their teaching methods). Whatever obstacles the National Curriculum creates, there could still be room for a personal and social education which mobilises the whole school and not just the PSE teacher. In the end the school will have to choose.
>
> (Brown 1990)

Grasping the nettle of pastoral education through mathematics would enable mathematical topics to be taught within a meaningful context, as has been deemed desirable in the mathematics National Curriculum. It would allow us to include, for example, the controversial yet vital area of HIV/AIDS education, where 'education is the only vaccine' (Osborne 1990). Stears and Clift (1990) have suggested that the most favourable situation in terms of covering the scientific, moral and personal issues raised by HIV/AIDS is a co-ordinated approach across science, religious education and a personal, social and health education course. However, their study found that this particular combination of contexts occurred in only 4.4 per cent of schools. We would go further and suggest that HIV/AIDS education would take place not only in these four contexts but across the whole curriculum, and in particular within mathematics. To do otherwise would be lost opportunity.

> Locating topics and themes related to AIDS, sexuality and relationships within mainstream subjects has another obvious justification besides that of exploiting a valuable stimulus to curiosity and learning. This is that young people are entitled to be equipped to make sense of the rapidly

growing and many sided areas of learning that are being generated by work on HIV/AIDS.

(Beattie 1990)

Following on from this Beattie suggests that work can be done in areas such as

> statistics of chance of risk, indices of relative risk, histograms and pie charts, modelling of the spread of HIV/AIDS; rates, ratios and time series in morbidity and mortality figures.

Work recently done with groups of pupils in Northumberland Park Community School, a north London comprehensive, placed particular emphasis on the use of a computer spreadsheet in the handling of data concerning the AIDS epidemic. If we are to genuinely educate about mathematics and AIDS, we must pose some questions about AIDS which require the use of mathematical skills to help us find answers. As the Centre for Mathematical Education (1990) point out, it is very difficult to handle data unless there is some purpose in collecting that data. There must be some initial question which provides the impetus to collect the data and that initial question must then be used as the main criterion for sorting out all the other stages of the data handling process: what information to collect, how to record it, how to process it, how to represent it and how to interpret the final results.

What is important here is the way in which the data concerning AIDS is handled. The data could be used merely to facilitate some statistical example, to put that example in a context. While such use may generate a previously unknown fact or two, it is hardly using the data to address burning issues concerning AIDS. It is essential that the context of the problem should be used not only to introduce the mathematics where the mathematics is the primary objective, but that the context should raise a number of issues which require mathematics as a means of addressing the issues. In this way mathematics is seen as a useful tool for answering specific problems, rather than a complex apparatus stuck on top of, and removed from, real life. It would be irresponsible and dangerous for issues such as HIV/AIDS to be used as a prop for a piece of maths work, to be exploited for the requirements of the academic curriculum.

Working in this issue-based way we shall be satisfying particular requirements of the National Curriculum both in mathematics and in health education. The HMI report of mathematics in key stages 1 and 3 (1991) found little classroom attention being paid to Ma1, concerned with using and applying mathematics, and little evidence of cross-curricular work or of common themes. Together with the obvious relevance to Ma5 with its emphasis on handling data, the opportunities presented by study of the HIV/AIDS epidemic in the mathematics classroom can be seen to be extensive. As Cockcroft (1982) pointed out, mathematics teaching all too often is not about anything. We should therefore inject meaning into our teaching and this meaning must be personal.

> It is inconceivable that children in general will be able to utilize mathematical tools and concepts unless they feel personally involved in their use; that is unless mathematical concepts become functional tools embedded within children's own cultural environment. At the very least we need to find objects other than sweets, toffees and fruit which it makes sense to undertake symbolic manipulation.
>
> (Noss 1991)

The opportunity is there to make education about something, about something that is so important that it may literally save lives. It seems self-evident that the adoption of HIV/AIDS education throughout the curriculum is now a vital necessity. We cannot frighten young people to change their behaviour, nor can we take refuge in giving them 'enough' information and hoping that they will change overnight. Instead we must put HIV/AIDS education into a context which empowers individuals to make reasoned choices for themselves, based on knowledge.

Each classroom activity that was undertaken considered a particular issue of the HIV/AIDS epidemic. In considering the issue it will be necessary to examine relevent AIDS data. Such examination not only helps form a more enlightened understanding but can also help individuals explore their own prejudices, anxieties and ignorances.

This work was done as part of a PGCE at the Institute of Education. We acknowledge the help and support of Jean Jones, Keith Jones and Dietmar Küchemann and Northumberland Park School.

NOTES

The Health Education Authority, Hamilton House, Mabledon Place, London WC1H 9TX; The Terrence Higgins Trust, 52–54 Grays Inn Road, London WC1X 8JU.

REFERENCES

Beattie, A. (1990) 'Partners in prevention? AIDS, sex education and the National Curriculum', in D. R. Morgan (ed.) *AIDS: A Challenge in Education*, London: Institute of Biology, London and Royal Society of Medicine Services.

Brown, C. (1990) 'Personal and social education: timetable ghetto or whole school practice?', in B. Dufour (ed.) *The New Social Curriculum: A Guide to Cross-curricular Themes*, Cambridge: Cambridge University Press, pp. 34–50.

Centre for Mathematical Education (1990) *Handling Data*, Milton Keynes: Open University Press.

Cockcroft, W. H. (1982) *Mathematics Counts*, London: HMSO.

DES (1990) *Curriculum Matters 5: Health Education*, London: HMSO.

HEA (1990) *AIDS UK*, Issue 8.

HMI (1991) *The Implementation of the Curricular Requirements of the Education Reform Act: Mathematics Key Stages 1 and 3. A Report by HM Inspectorate on the First Year 1989–90*, London: HMSO.

Noss, R. *The Computer as a Cultural Influence in Mathematical Learning*, in M. Harris (ed.) (1991) *Schools, Mathematics and Work*, London: Falmer.

Osbourne, quotation taken from D. Stears and S. Clift (1990) *A Survey of AIDS Education in Secondary Schools*, AVERT, p. 1.

Stears, D. and Clift, S. (1990) *A Survey of AIDS Education in Secondary Schools*, AVERT.

Stripp, C. (1991) 'Maths, its nature and the curriculum', *Mathematics Teaching* 134: 26.

Chapter 12

Environmental issues in the mathematics classroom

Brian Hudson

A submission was made to the Committee of Inquiry into the Teaching of Mathematics which stated that 'Mathematics lessons in secondary schools are very often not about anything'. Its findings were published in 1982 in *Mathematics Counts*, which is better known as the Cockcroft report. It states the following.

> You collect like terms, or learn the laws of indices, with no perception why anyone needs to do such things. There is excessive preoccupation with a sequence of skills and quite inadequate opportunity to see the skills emerging from the solution of problems. As a consequence of this, school mathematics contains very little incidental information . . . most teachers (mathematics) in no way see this as part of their responsibility when teaching mathematics.
>
> (Cockcroft report 1982: para 462)

This situation was certainly true of many mathematics classrooms at the time that this submission was made, and is still an accurate reflection of many over ten years later. There is much evidence that such a view of mathematics is not only unattractive to very many people but also destructive in terms of interest in and motivation towards the subject as a whole. My own experience of teaching in comprehensive schools and of working with student teachers leads me to believe that one of the most crucial aspects of a teacher's role is to motivate young people's interest in mathematics. I believe that one way in which this can be achieved is by appealing to the pupil's own experience and interests and it is quite clear that many young people have a deep concern for and interest in the environment.

RATIONALE FOR CROSS-CURRICULAR WORK

Mathematics Non-Statutory Guidance from the National Curriculum Council (NCC 1989) provides a rationale for the development of cross-curricular work. Such guidance is particularly relevant to the delivery of Attainment Target 1 (Ma1) 'Using and applying mathematics'. Reference is made to 'the development of a teaching and learning approach in which the uses and applications of mathematics permeate and influence all work in mathematics' and which the National Curriculum requires all schools to address. In justifying the need for such an approach it is noted that 'In life, experiences do not come in separate packages . . . mathematical experiences present themselves alongside others'. It is further noted that 'mathematics pervades many areas of the curriculum and mathematical activity can contribute significantly to the development of more general skills such as communicating, reasoning and problem-solving'. The cross-curricular potential is highlighted in relation to one particular subject in the following passage, as is the potential beneficial effects upon young people's views of mathematics.

> It is generally well-appreciated that mathematics is needed by pupils to help them understand and to communicate in the sciences . . . similar examples can be found throughout the curriculum, and these opportunities for using mathematics need to be exploited. The application of mathematics in contexts which have relevance and interest is an important means of developing pupils' understanding and appreciation of the subject and of those contexts.
>
> (NCC 1989: F 1.4)

It seems quite clear that the consideration of environmental issues is desirable, necessary and also very relevant to the effective delivery of the National Curriculum in the mathematics classroom. My own experience supports the advice given in the *Mathematics Non-Statutory Guidance* that such an approach is likely to lead to improvements in pupils' motivation and understanding: 'There is abundant evidence that work which is triggered by pupils themselves leads to better motivation and understanding . . . Teachers should have sufficient flexibility built into their schemes to capitalise on pupils' interests.' This view is further supported by the NCC in the guidance provided to support curriculum planning in the documents on *The Whole Curriculum* and *Environmental Education*.

THE WHOLE CURRICULUM

In defining cross-curricular elements the NCC has identified dimensions, skills and themes in *Curriculum Guidance 3, The Whole Curriculum* (NCC 1990a). A number of these have particular relevance to the mathematics classroom. Included within the element of skills are numeracy, problem solving and the use of information technology, which are especially appropriate to the mathematics classroom. Five themes are identified, which it is recognised are by no means exhaustive, amongst which is environmental education. This is defined as being concerned with promoting positive and responsible attitudes towards the environment. In schools it aims to increase pupils' knowledge and understanding of the processes by which environments are shaped; to enable them to recognise both the quality and vulnerability of different environments; and to help them to identify opportunities for protecting and managing the environment.

(NCC 1990a: 6)

ENVIRONMENTAL EDUCATION

Guidance on the implementation of the theme of environmental education is given by the NCC in *Curriculum Guidance 7, Environmental Education* (NCC 1990b). A framework for environmental education is presented and the common characteristics of the cross-curricular themes described as 'the ability to foster discussion of questions of values and beliefs; they add to knowledge and understanding and they rely on practical activities, decision making, and the inter-relationship of the individual in the community' (NCC 1990b: 4). The objectives necessary to develop an environmental curriculum are presented in terms of knowledge, skills and attitudes. Illustrations are provided of the way in which the skills in particular can be developed through environmental education. Those which are of particular relevance to the mathematics classroom are as follows (NCC 1990b: 4).

Numeracy skills

- collecting, classifying and analysing data, e.g. carrying out an (ecological) survey
- interpreting statistics

Problem-solving skills

- identifying causes and consequences of environmental problems
- forming reasoned opinions and developing balanced judgements about environmental issues

Information technology skills

- collecting information and entering it into a database
- simulating an investigation using information technology

Environmental issues

The range of current environmental issues is very wide and the associated data are vast, so there are many different starting points for mathematical activity. For the purposes of this work I have chosen to take a number of issues for consideration as examples of how environmental education might be developed in the mathematics classroom and I have also highlighted recent resources of relevance to this.

Urbanisation

The data in Table 12.1 is included in the *Century Maths Theme Book 'City Living/Getting Around'* (Hudson 1993b), which was sponsored by WWF UK in collaboration with the Mathematics Education Centre at Sheffield Hallam University. The book is aimed at pupils in Years 10 and 11 and could provide suitable material for extended coursework tasks. The activity outlined provides details on the growth of squatter settlements in Peru and in particular the growth of the Pueblos Jovenes squatter settlements in Lima.

Table 12.1 Growth of 'Pueblos Jovenes' (squatter settlements) in Lima

	1961	1969	1977	1979
Number of settlements	192	273	301	432
Population	400,000	760,000	1,130,000	1,510,000

Source: Hudson 1993b: 19, from 'Estudio de caso de Villa el Salvador', 1986, CIDAP

Questions such as 'How many squatter settlements do you think there were in 1990?' or 'How many do you think there will be in the year 2000?' give rise to necessary mathematical activity. For example, one might choose to draw a graph of the data as in Figure 12.1. Joining the points together and continuing the graph enables predictions to be made about the figures not provided in the table, e.g. for 1990 and 2000 (Figure 12.2). It is important that underlying assumptions are made clear and are questioned, e.g. will past trends always be a reliable indicator for the future and upon what conditions is a particular prediction likely to prove accurate?

Similar questions might be posed about the population data and these figures might be compared with population data on Peru and Lima as a whole (Table 12.2). Examples of further questions might include the following.

1 What do you think the population of Peru was in 1990?
2 What do you predict the population of Peru will be in the year 2000?
3 Similarly for Lima?
4 What proportion of the total population of Peru lived in Lima in 1990?
5 What is likely to be the corresponding figure for the year 2000?
6 Is this proportion increasing or decreasing?
7 If it was your job to run the government of Peru what sort of problems could you see for the country and its capital city in the year 2000?
8 How might you begin to plan to solve some of these problems?

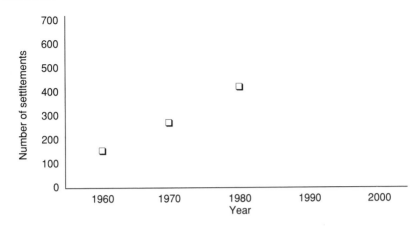

Figure 12.1 The number of squatter settlements

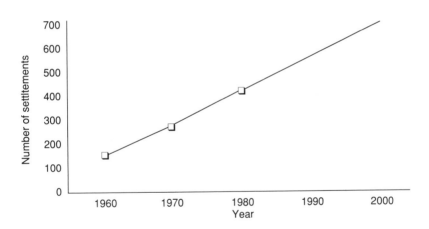

Figure 12.2 Predicting the number of squatter settlements

Table 12.2 Population data – Peru and Lima

	1961	1972	1981
Peru	9,910,000	13,500,000	17,000,000
Lima	1,840,000	3,420,000	4,610,000

Source: Hudson 1993b: 17, from 'Estudio de caso de Villa el Salvador', 1986, CIDAP

In order to begin to answer some of these questions pupils would be required to carry out a range of numerical calculations and/or to draw graphs, thus enabling them to formulate their hypotheses on future trends. They would be required to apply the numeracy skills previously outlined in analysing and interpreting data and also the problem-solving skills in 'forming reasoned opinions and developing balanced judgements about environmental issues'.

Accompanying the text is a datafile on the world's fifty largest cities enabling comparisons to be made between predictions for 1990 and the actual data contained on the datafile. The data is provided in written form in addition to the disc version which is designed to be used in conjunction with the Logo2000 software and in particular LogoBase. Logo2000 consists of the three integrated microworlds LogoBase, LogoSheet and LogoPlotter, which are respectively a database, a spreadsheet and a graph plotting program. This resource enables pupils to develop and apply their information technology skills in the interrogation of the database and in the utilisation of the numerical and graphical capabilities of the spreadsheet and graph plotter. The use of the computer as a tool in this way is integrated into the resources and a flexible classroom environment involving group work and discussion is encouraged. By providing a variety of classroom activities the materials are designed to provide a flexible framework within which the potential for using a single microcomputer in the classroom is maximised.

The CITIES datafile contains data on quality indicators of life in urban areas as detailed in Table 12.3. The computer database enables the user to interrogate it for details on a particular country by name or groups of countries with certain characteristics, e.g. high or low rates of murders, infant deaths, etc. Statistical functions and graphs can be used to analyse the data further and to make comparisons between particular countries and/or

Table 12.3 The CITIES datafile indicators

Fieldname	
CITY	Name of city
COUNTRY	Name of country
POPULATION	Population of city
MURDERS	Murders per 100,000 people per year
FOODCOSTS	Average percentage of income spent on food
LIVINGSPACE	Average number of persons per room
WATER/ELEC	Percentage of homes with water and electricity
TELEPHONES	Number of telephones per 100 people
SECSCHOOLS	Percentage of children (14–17 years) in secondary school
INFDEATHS	Infant deaths (0–1 years) per 1,000 live births
NOISE	Level of background noise (1–10) (low–high)
TRAFFICFLOW	Average miles per hour in rush hour

Source: Hudson 1993b: 7, from Population Crisis Committee, 1990

groups of countries, e.g. to see how Birmingham, Manchester and London compare with global averages. The datafile can also be ordered on the basis of one field, e.g. noise level, and a print-out or graph obtained. A further datafile is provided with each indicator allocated a score on a basis of 1 to 10 in the way devised by the Population Crisis Committee, thus enabling a grand total to be calculated for each city. Some further investigations into possible correlations are suggested in the example of a pupil page given in Figure 12.3.

The pupils are also encouraged to relate the issues to their own locality by drawing up an action plan for their own environment as illustrated in a further example of a pupil page given in Figure 12.4 (this section follows on from a task involving the calculation of a number of indicators of quality of life and the expression of the results as an overall percentage for the pupil's own town or city).

Investigate these ideas with a partner.

- Illustrate your findings using scatter graphs and lines of best fit.

- Explain any conclusions that you make.

Figure 12.3 A group looking into the idea of correlations–links between some indicators
Source: Hudson 1993b: 13

Share the tasks out in your group.

Set a time to gather all the information and report back.

Use these data to revise the total score for your town or city.

Find the new overall percentage.

● Once you have completed the task:

– Write a report on your findings, showing those indicators which had a low score.

– Explain your methods clearly and how you arrived at the scores.

– Make some recommendations for improving the low scores.

– Share your findings with those from other groups.

– Send a copy of your report and action plan to the city or town council.

● You may find it helpful to make a data file of your own.

Figure 12.4 An action plan for your environment
Source: Hudson 1993b: 11

The activities outlined are particularly relevant in terms of analysing and interpreting data (Ma5 'Handling data') and also in some aspects of number. In addition a range of the mathematical skills and processes outlined in Ma1 'Using and applying mathematics' can be developed and utilised. They also go some way towards raising awareness of the issue of the rapid rate of urbanisation in the Third World. The associated issues of rapid industrialisation (and de-industrialisation in the Western economies), high birth rates, migration from rural to urban areas and survival rates might most usefully be developed in collaboration with a colleague in the geography or humanities department for example. This might be done by the geography teacher developing these issues further once they had been introduced through such activities. Alternatively the activities could be timed by the mathematics teacher to complement more in-depth discussion of the issues initiated by the geography teacher and followed up in the mathematics classroom.

Tropical deforestation

The issue of deforestation provides another rich source of data and endless possibilities for investigation. For example, Table 12.4 contains data on tropical rainforests in Africa, Asia and South America for the years 1980 and 1985. Possible questions as starting points for mathematical activity might include the following.

1 What do you think was the figure for the total area of rainforest for each of these regions in 1990?
2 What do you think the figure will be in the year 2000?
3 What is the rate of loss between 1980 and 1985 for each area as a percentage of the 1980 figure?
4 When would you predict almost complete extinction of the rainforests in each of these regions on current trends?
5 This activity provides an example of the use of some relevant data to provide the starting point for mathematical activity.

Table 12.4 Area of rainforest

Region	Total area of rainforest (thousand hectares)	
	1980	1985
Tropical America	653,926	633,893
Tropical Africa	214,403	207,805
Tropical Asia	291,951	283,038

Source: Lanly 1983

Pollution

An example of a cross-curricular resource is the package produced by WWF UK entitled *Can White Be Green?* (Webster and Hudson 1993). This is a case study of the manufacture of white pigment by Tioxide Europe Limited on the banks of the Humber Estuary. The pack contains classroom activities covering science, geography, mathematics and English and is relevant to the National Curriculum themes of environmental education and economic and industrial understanding.

Data are provided on levels of pollution in industrial and sewage discharges to the Humber in various sampling sections of the estuary and at specific water quality sampling sites. These are provided in the form of datafiles for the spreadsheet Schema and the pupils are encouraged to use the software to analyse the data and to represent them graphically.

Style:	Plain		
Cell:	C11	Plain	◈Enter ◇Edit ◇Macro
Block:	C11XC19		☐Text mode ☐Mouse inserts ☐ OK

		Suspended	Cadmium	Chromium
4				
5	Suspended sediments – milli g/litre			
6	Heavy metals – micro g/litre			
7	SOURCE: Working Paper 7– Environmental Pollution,			
8	1990,University of Hull			
9	Sampling section	Suspended	Cadmium	Chromium
10		sediments		
11	above Beal	0.000	unknown	unknown
12	above Long Drax	45.577	unknown	unknown
13	Beal to Boothferry Br.	85.287	unknown	unknown
14	above Rawcliffe Br.	0.000	unknown	unknown
15	Boothferry to Blacktoft	1017.817	0.015	0.077
16	above Keadby	56.814	0.005	0.021
17	Blacktoft to Brough	124.125	0.004	0.026
18	Brough to Salt End	441.026	0.141	0.859
19	Saltend to Spurn	1157.100	0.078	2.353
20				

Figure 12.5 A sample screen from the Schema spreadsheet
Source: Webster and Hudson 1993

The key enquiry is to answer the question 'Is the Humber polluted?' and 'If so, by what?'

Energy

A further resource sponsored by WWF UK has been produced in collaboration with the Mathematics Education Centre at Sheffield Hallam University on the theme of energy. As part of this resource datafiles are provided on global energy consumption for the major countries of the world. This data covers coal, gas, electricity and petrol consumption for a number of years between 1950 and 1988. Further datafiles are available providing this same data per head of population and also providing data on the various sources of electricity production, e.g. hydro, thermal, geothermal and nuclear. Datafiles are provided for the spreadsheet Schema and also for the database Key Plus. Pupils are encouraged to explore the datafiles for trends over time and to make predictions on this basis. They are also encouraged to explore the differences between levels of energy consumption between groups of countries, e.g. the mismatch between the levels of consumption in the developed countries of the northern hemisphere and in the developing countries in the south. Of particular relevance to recent debates on the future energy needs of the United Kingdom is the data contained in Table 12.5 which is included in the pack.

Table 12.5 Electricity production

66 per cent of energy produced is used to supply heat
Less than 10 per cent of uses must be in the form of electricity, e.g. lighting, television, motors and appliances etc.
40 per cent of primary energy is lost as waste heat when it is converted to electricity or being delivered to the user

Source: Hudson 1993c, from *Friends of the Earth*, 1985

Endangered species/population growth

The study of endangered species raises considerable potential for using mathematics to analyse and predict future trends. The example given in Figure 12.6 is taken from *Green Maths (KS4)* (Hudson 1993a).

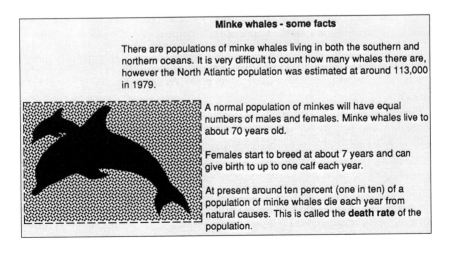

Minke whales - some facts

There are populations of minke whales living in both the southern and northern oceans. It is very difficult to count how many whales there are, however the North Atlantic population was estimated at around 113,000 in 1979.

A normal population of minkes will have equal numbers of males and females. Minke whales live to about 70 years old.

Females start to breed at about 7 years and can give birth to up to one calf each year.

At present around ten percent (one in ten) of a population of minke whales die each year from natural causes. This is called the **death rate** of the population.

How does the size of a population of whales grow?

Simple growth

A calculator or spreadsheet program will make your investigation much faster.

• The box above contains some information on minke whales.

• Use the information to make a rule for working out how many births there will be each year in a population of 1000 minke whales. This is the birth rate.

Write an explanation of how you made up your rule. What assumptions did you have to make?

• Investigate how the size of this population of 1000 grows during the course of a few decades.

Use the rule for birth rate that you have made, along with the information above on the death rate.

Figure 12.6 Should we allow whales to be hunted?
Source: T. Steeg, in Hudson 1993a

CONCLUSION

By investigating the data related to such environmental issues it is clear that pupils can be successful in meeting the requirements of the Mathematics National Curriculum especially in relation to 'Number', 'Handling data' and 'Using and applying mathematics'. The consideration of such issues has potential for a greater degree of collaboration with teachers from other subject areas who might develop some of the issues raised in the mathematics classroom further and who could also be a source of support for mathematics teachers in dealing with some of these issues themselves for the first time.

My own experience of working with student teachers is of a generally high level of awareness of such issues and of a wish to incorporate these into the mathematics classroom. The difficulties encountered in the past have often been associated with a lack of appropriate resources and readily accessible data rather than an unwillingness to tackle such issues. These difficulties have been recognised by those involved in curriculum development and much support has been given to this process in recent years, by WWF UK in particular.

Finally I would argue for a whole school approach to environmental education and regard my role as a teacher as involving the education of the whole child. In adopting such an approach I would expect that I would be more likely to achieve my objectives as a mathematics teacher given the greater level of interest, motivation and understanding on the part of the pupils. At the same time I would be contributing to their personal development and helping to prepare them for their future role as citizens in an increasingly complex and interdependent world.

REFERENCES AND CLASSROOM RESOURCES

Cockcroft, W. H. (1982) *Mathematics Counts*, London: HMSO.

Hudson, B. (ed.) (1993a) *Green Teacher Resources, Green Maths (KS4)*.

—— (1993b) *Century Maths Theme Book 'City Living/Getting Around'*, Cheltenham: Stanley Thornes.

—— (1993c) *Energy (Mathematics Supplement)*, Sheffield: WWF/Sheffield Hallam University.

Hudson, B. and Rouncefield, M. (1993a) *Century Maths Focus Book Handling Data Y10/11 Core*, Cheltenham: Stanley Thornes.

—— and—— (1993b) *Century Maths Focus Book Handling Data Y10/11 Extension*, Cheltenham: Stanley Thornes.

Lanly, J. P. (1983) 'Assessment of the forest resources of the tropics', *Forestry Abstracts* 44.

NCC (1989) *Mathematics Non-Statutory Guidance*, York: NCC.

NCC (1990a) *Curriculum Guidance 3, The Whole Curriculum*, York: NCC.

NCC (1990b) *Curriculum Guidance 7, Environmental Education*, York: NCC.

Webster, K. and Hudson, B. (1993) *Can White Be Green?*, WWF UK.

Chapter 13

Evaluating an 'entitlement curriculum'

Mathematics for all?

Leone Burton

There are a number of ways of approaching an evaluation of curriculum. We can use a checklist of items without which we feel any published curriculum is deficient. We can look at outputs by examining achievement levels, and/or achievement by particular groups. We can do an in-depth study of particular classrooms. All of these approaches provide us with information, although, as with all research, in each case that information has been filtered through the value system of the initiator of the search. I want to make my value position clear and then construct a theoretical model of the curriculum, and the mathematics curriculum in particular, which can be used to ask questions about entitlement and equality, of opportunity and of outcome.

In choosing to focus upon 'mathematics for all' I am placing myself firmly against the implicit, and sometimes explicit, beliefs and practices that mathematics is an esoteric discipline, available only to those few who are born with a special aptitude and whose knowledge base mystifies the majority of those who encounter it. I not only acknowledge that mathematical practices are used by everybody in their daily lives but that the style of thinking that we recognise as mathematical is necessary to everyday functioning. Thus we all make conjectures, test them using such means as classifying, enumerating, ordering and embedding, build them into generalisations and even sometimes set out to attempt that most mathematical of all strategies, proving. I am proposing that mathematics itself is a powerful language which provides access to ways of viewing the world through number, shape, algebra, measures and statistics (including probabilistic notions) that are informative and creative. Like spoken language, it has its own 'semantics' and its use opens the way to thinking about the world mathematically, that is processing information in a particular way to obtain certain kinds of outcomes. Most people can and do use it as a natural part of their daily living. I therefore have an obligation to share my understanding of how mathematics and the process through which it is learned and taught manage to disempower the majority and mystify the discipline.

In terms of 'entitlement', it seems to me that we must ask what it is to which learners are being told they are entitled. It is a narrow conception that views 'the curriculum' simply as a syllabus. Were we to do that, we would have to agree that a nationwide curriculum in mathematics has existed for a very long time in the form of widely used texts series. These have been criticised by Philip Davis and Reuben Hersh (1981: 282) for the style in which they are presented, which is authoritative and formal, with the human-ness removed by the failure to show, or allow the learner to experience, the struggle for meaning. They say:

> The presentation in textbooks is often 'backward'. The discovery process is eliminated from the description and is not documented After the theorem and its proof have been worked out . . . the whole verbal and symbolic presentation is rearranged, polished and reorganized according to the canons of the logico-deductive method. The aesthetics of the craft demand this. Historical precedents – the Greek tradition – demand it. It is also true that the economics of the book business demand maximum information in minimum space. Mathematics tends to achieve this with a vengeance. Brevity is the soul of mathematical brilliance or wit. Fuller explanations are regarded as tedious.

It is the failure to engage learners in mathematics which has led to the current situation where most young people do not enjoy or achieve well in mathematics and, at the end of compulsory schooling, where females not only achieve less well than males in terms of assessable results but have measurably poorer attitudes towards mathematics. Far from being empowered by their mathematics learning, such pupils' self-image has been distorted.

> While not making equal outcomes a direct goal, we are not satisfied with the current imbalances in both entries and results in public examinations at 16+ and 18+ . . . particularly in such central subjects as mathematics, English, sciences and modern languages.
>
> (Stobart *et al.* 1992)

The statutory National Curriculum is, however, articulated as a syllabus in that it is presented as a content list with one attainment target being identified in process terms but listed as statements of attainment and four other attainment targets listing knowledge and skills. In terms of curricular experience this is a limited view and one which is reminiscent of the textual mathematical experiences to which reference has already been made. We have evidence dating back into the latter years of the nineteenth century that such a syllabus view of mathematics is inefficient to learning, as it mystifies many learners with its limitations in terms of *their* experience and understanding. When mystification makes mathematics inaccessible, entitlement to its power is denied. We have all watched young people struggling to remember the rule to apply in particular circumstances when their commonsense enables them to produce a correct answer once they are released from the reproductive 'school' behaviour.

If a syllabus view of curriculum is insufficient, what is missing? Learning cannot take place without learners, and learners bring to the classroom a rich resource of experience, understandings, expectations and so on. The style with which the learners are encouraged to encounter the content of the lesson will result in different outcomes for different individuals, part of the excitement as well as the challenge of teaching. So the pedagogic context within which the content is met, experienced and 'understood' is a necess-ary component of the curriculum. The norm of mathematics classrooms, however, has always been individualised instruction, whether within class-based lessons or with using workcards or workbooks. This places math-ematics within a certain set of expectations which encourages a view of learning the subject that emphasises speed and competition and supports the presentation of rules by which 'right' answers can be achieved quickly but not necessarily with comprehension. The underlying view of math-ematics is of a discipline which consists of 'objective' knowledge and given, prescribed methods which must be understood and practised. There is nothing here about entitlement. On the contrary, mathematics is perceived as 'belonging' to a minority who impose upon its learning their own behavioural norms.

The curriculum suggestions contained in the *Mathematics Non-Statutory Guidance* to the National Curriculum do suggest a broader, more question-ing, pupil-driven curriculum. Unfortunately, this message contradicts that of the statutory instrument and its influence is consequently diminished. Most unacceptable of all, however, is the separation of evaluation and assessment of mathematics learning from the syllabus and learning questions which set up the conditions for attainment. Pupils, teachers and other interested parties make judgements about educational outcomes at all times. A necessary part of learning is the self- and other-evaluation which accom-panies this process. Externalising evaluation, and labelling it as 'assessment', separates it from the curriculum to which it is attached and introduces assessment-led teaching which has proved, in the past, to be destructive to so many. The movement away from this state of affairs, towards a component of classroom-based 'coursework', has been constructive and challenging for learners precisely because it involved them in deliberate reflection and self-evaluation which made their learning more meaningful.

I am suggesting, therefore, a model of the mathematical curriculum which a teacher can use to plan for coherent and broad learning. Three choices must be made: of syllabus content, of classroom experiences or pedagogical 'style' and of evaluative (or assessment) techniques. Effective curriculum planning provides evidence that the teacher, in deciding the 'what' of the lesson, has also considered the 'how' and given thought to asking 'what will constitute evidence of attainment?' These three decisions then lock together into experiences which provide a learner with the structures necessary to make effective use of classroom experiences.

How does this view of the curriculum affect 'entitlement'? Coherence and interrelatedness are not noticeably curricular concepts which promote the learning of one constituency only. On the contrary, considering what we know about how females like to learn and the areas in which they achieve, learning success reinforces the notion that an 'entitlement curriculum' is one which is both accessible and meaningful to all learners. Making the curriculum accessible imposes a discipline on the teacher of asking why and how the chosen syllabus content relates to the experience, understanding and skills of the learner group. Developing meaning imposes a discipline on learners of engaging with the offered activity and developing questions out of which new knowledge and skills might be generated. An effective learning style to encourage this process is one in which pupils work collaboratively, listening to each other's alternative views, choosing a question and method which seem most productive to their enquiry, and pursuing that question without fear of dead-ends, in a reflective spirit.

This style is one encountered, for example, in language learning, and encouraged by recent approaches to language and literature teaching, as well as in personal and social education. It is rarely seen in the mathematics classroom where the public image of mathematics, its objectivity, certainty, formality, utility and absolutism, encourages a didactic approach to the content, competition between learners and a consequent dependency between learner and teacher. It runs counter to a view of mathematical knowledge as being socially negotiable, depending upon the sharing of perspectives which requires teachers and learners to consider the nature of mathematics and what it means to know mathematics.

In evaluating the curriculum, therefore, we can ask a number of questions which expose the underlying educational philosophy of the classroom and the assumptions of teachers and learners about the nature of mathematical learning.

- Is the learning of mathematics a process of induction into a secret society which plays a particular kind of game as in formal, deductive classrooms, or a process of ascribing and negotiating meaning, setting boundaries and examining their implications, making and testing conjectures, as in a collaborative classroom?
- Does the geography of the classroom reflect delivery of knowledge and skills by a teacher who 'owns' the content, or has the locus of control shifted to groups of pupils engaged upon mathematical enquiries which provoke interpretation and reinterpretation of their knowledge and skills?
- Is the classroom inactive, focused on the production, by the teacher, of items of knowledge or skills where questioning is the sole technique to locate knowledge, or does it demand active engagement with the representation

of a mathematical knowledge which is personal and fluid, provoking the exchange of interpretation between learners and the engaging of teachers and learners in dialogue to locate meaning?
- Are the pupils' knowledge, skills and understanding of mathematics externally assessed by tests constructed upon reproduceability, or do they undertake regular self-, paired-, group- and teacher-evaluation to track the growth of their understanding and match that against personal, class and social expectations in a manner which accords personal and interpersonal respect and ownership?

Mathematics is one example, of many, of disciplines which are socially construed where, far from consisting of indisputable truths, the knowledge base is socially interpretable and negotiable. David Bloor (1991: 110) gives four examples of

> variation in mathematical thought each of which can be traced back to social causes. They are (i) variation in the broad cognitive style of mathematics; (ii) variation in the framework of associations, relationships, uses, analogies, and the metaphysical implications attributed to mathematics; (iii) variations in the meanings attached to computations and symbolic manipulations; (iv) variation in rigour and the type of reasoning which is held to prove a conclusion.

He also devotes a chapter (Chapter 7) to a fifth source of 'variation in the content and use of those basic operations of thought which are held to be self-evident logical truths' (1991: 110). Perhaps for a non-mathematical audience the most surprising of his examples is the discussion of whether or not 'one' is a number and the shifting response to this question from different societies at different times.

The process of coming to learn mathematics, then, is not dependent upon acquiring knowledge and skills fixed throughout time but depends upon utilising the skills of interpretation and negotiation of meaning. This style of learning requires pupils to be active and autonomous in their pursuit of personal understanding as they work together, asking questions of each other, challenging, offering convincing arguments and reflecting upon their growing comprehension. The result of this process might not necessarily be 'objective' mathematics in the sense of mathematical 'truths' but is socially constructed mathematics understood and applying within the terms of reference of the group which has derived it. Because 'ownership' is so powerful for learning, it is a small step to take from 'locally' negotiated understanding to societally acceptable understanding. Such a learning environment leads to an evaluation system which requires the learner to report, explain, relate, predict and question without an emphasis on knowledge reproduction or timed tests. The skills that are required to operate in a classroom of this kind are more noticeable among females than among males. Males in the mathematics classroom tend to be demanding and to dominate teachers and other students, frequently harassing any female students who attempt to engage with the lesson. Females, on the other hand, respond positively to opportunities to collaborate, to focus together on a mathematical challenge, organising themselves, supporting each other and negotiating as they go. They use their language skills to share, exchange, report and challenge each other and they report positively on the results.

Meaning in mathematics is, therefore, open to negotiation and so, ultimately, are the conditions in the mathematics classroom which must reflect this fundamental paradigmatic shift. Refusing to acknowledge the degree to which meaning in mathematics is negotiable is one way of retaining its mystery and power and keeping control over who joins the ranks of the select. I am not suggesting that this is a conscious process. However, in most societies, the decisions about what mathematics is accorded importance are most likely to be made by white males or by those who have accepted their terms of reference, the status quo, the power distribution, the norms of behaviour within the mathematical community. These people are then in a position to exercise considerable power over the learning experiences of all pupils. It seems reasonable to predict that their choices and emphases will reflect their interests and I have no reason to believe that these interests are necessarily the same for all learners. It is equally reasonable, it seems to me, to expect that the introduction of the interests of different groups might lead to differently emphasised areas of mathematics, or different interpretations of mathematics.

With this shift in mathematical philosophy from the objective and absolute to the socially negotiated and the personal, the teacher is faced with the necessity of shifting her pedagogy from the transmissive and didactic to the transformational and interactive. To make the changes that are necessary to support mathematics for all requires teachers to work together at the complex issues affecting the learning of mathematics in their classrooms. These include responses to the questions already mentioned about the nature of mathematics and what it means to know some mathematics. They also include questions of the contextualisation of mathematics, so-called 'real' mathematics, the place of mathematical modelling, the role of intuition, imagination and creativity in mathematics. They demand thought about personal, compared with public, knowledge and its evaluation, about informal as compared with formal knowledge and its evaluation. Most of all they require a reconsideration of how mathematics is learned so that the focus moves away from the individual onto the group.

I wish to stress that we can make changes. Let us start with ways of affecting the syllabus.

1 We can broaden the content to include aspects of mathematics which have been of interest to other cultures. An example might be the methods of

Vedic arithmetic which, in George Joseph's words, 'provide an original and refreshing approach to subjects which are often dismissed as mechanical and tedious' but also provide 'new insights . . . into the scope and strength of place-value number systems such as ours' (1991: 244).

2 We must also ensure that the mathematics which is already included in the syllabus is correctly referenced so that we accord respect to all the communities that have contributed to our present mathematical knowledge state; for example, the theorem we know as Pythagoras' theorem has a history which dates back to Old Babylonia during the period from the fourteenth to the eleventh century BC.

3 We can humanise the mathematical story by including, with our teaching, references to and information about the people who have used mathematics in the past. We can display a poster about a mathematical woman and her work alongside the poster about a mathematical man.

4 We can invite into our classrooms those who are currently using mathematics so that learners can meet and question people for whom mathematics is a necessary part of their work. In doing this, we can ensure that we deliberately counter the masculine image of mathematics by, for example, inviting as many, if not more, mathematical women to visit the classroom as men.

My assumption is that just as different societies and different times have found different aspects of mathematics interesting, exciting, creative or productive, so pupils will relate to or be excited by mathematics construed in different ways, or focusing on different styles of interpretation. It is not equal treatment unless these possibilities are part of curriculum entitlement.

With respect to the pedagogy of mathematics, I have already drawn attention to the impact on their learning of pupils working together to negotiate meaning. We have growing evidence that this style of learning is highly effective for females and certainly preferred by them. A curriculum which reifies individualistic knowledge gained in a competitive environment is, therefore, working against the interests of many pupils in the classroom. Additionally, a curriculum which encourages a creative and innovative approach to mathematics, personalising its use and stressing its informality, is more likely to have broad appeal because of the space that it creates for individual interpretation. By introducing a mathematical curriculum which is challenge instead of knowledge based we remove the conditions with which competitive behaviour thrives to capture the attention of the teacher, or to capture other scarce resources such as the computer. Groups of learners look inwards to the group to generate understanding and become less aware of the dynamics of the rest of the classroom. As teachers, we need to reinforce this collaborative style and ensure that the rules of classroom behaviour include no sanctioning of sexual or racial harassment.

When we come to consider assessment we become even more aware of the pressure to maintain styles of testing and examination which are inconsistent with the shifting pedagogy and with the socially constructive philosophy underlying it. In the United Kingdom the limited introduction of a minimum of 20 per cent coursework as a required component of the 16+ examination in mathematics has positively affected the performance of females. This is so interesting, and controversial in the light of pressure to return to 100 per cent unseen written examinations, that interest has been expressed in a European-wide study of differentiation and assessment style in the secondary school. It is unreasonable to continue with assessment styles which have emerged through historical accident when there is evidence that these are part of discriminatory practices affecting pupil performance in mathematics.

In recording his conclusions on the results of introducing assessment innovations in the Netherlands, Jan de Lange Jzn (1987: 260) wrote the following.

1 Girls perform less well than boys on restricted-time written tests.
2 Girls perform more or less the same as boys on oral-tasks or take-home tasks.
3 From the above, one is tempted to advise more oral and take-home tasks in order to offer girls fairer chances.
4 Oral-test results have a somewhat higher correlation with restricted-time written test results than do take-home tasks.
5 Students perform best with take-home tasks. The constructive and productive aspect seems to offer students a fair chance to show their abilities (creativity, reflection, etc.). Positive testing is at its optimum in this way . . .

We started our explorative study on alternative tasks because of the fact that the restricted-time written tests as carried out by the teachers did not meet the intentions and goals of Mathematics A . . . [which] is strongly process-oriented; the mathematization process needs time to develop, time to reflect, time to generate creative and constructive thoughts. These 'higher' goals are not easily operationalized with timed tests.

(1987: 260)

It can only be regretted that the oral examination disappeared years ago. The introduction of the Math A curriculum makes it necessary to reconsider oral examinations, not in the last place to offer girls better opportunities.

(1987: 265)

Except for one primary programme, of which I am proud to be part-author (Kerslake *et al.* 1990), which sets up group work in a classroom predicated upon learner enquiries, the traditional mode of teaching mathematics has been through texts at every level. Concern which is expressed in many different countries provides ample evidence that such an approach to mathematics in school leads to disaffection and disablement.

To engage in a mathematics for all learners requires us to listen to what they are telling us about their experiences and actively to change those experiences so that the learner is empowered. Learning anything is difficult; perhaps learning mathematics is particularly so, although I do not believe that. Sanitising it into bite-size pieces which appear easy and enjoyable is not the answer. That usually trivialises the content and the learner. Let us acknowledge that learning is difficult but it is not the difficulty which constitutes an obstacle. On the contrary, everybody manages to achieve control over their family language long before they enter formal schooling. This is probably the greatest learning challenge a person has to face and they do so without any formal teaching. The skills that they demonstrate in the process, such as classifying, ordering, enumerating, conjecturing and testing are mathematical thinking skills. If we can remember and learn from that, we can construct classrooms which provide learning challenges and which validate the means of meeting learning challenges rather than reifying their arbitrary content. In such classrooms, while the learner is engaged upon a lifelong journey of development, he or she is empowered to make choices and decisions in a social context which celebrates individual differences but also interdependence. Such a climate, I feel sure, would not only benefit mathematics. It would also provide a more realistic learning experience for all young people, nurturing their entitlement to a mathematics which, like language, is an integral part of their world.

REFERENCES

Bloor, D. (1991) *Knowledge and Social Imagery*, London: University of Chicago Press.

Davis, P. and Hersh, R. (1981) *The Mathematical Experience*, Harmondsworth: Penguin.

de Lange Jzn, J. (1987) *Mathematics Insight and Meaning*, Utrecht: OW & OC.

Joseph, G. G. (1991) *The Crest of the Peacock*, London: Tauris.

Kerslake, D. *et al.* (1990) *HBJ Mathematics*, London: Harcourt, Brace, Jovanovich.

Stobart, G. *et al.* (1992) 'Gender bias in examinations: how equal are the opportunities', *British Educational Research Journal* 18 (3), August.

Part V

What drives the curriculum?

The introduction of new technology into mathematics has recently been the source of much debate. Or has it? In Chapter 14 Costel Harnasz suggests the phenomenon is not so recent by highlighting the debates that occurred when the slide rule was first introduced. He draws parallels to the current debates about calculators 'rotting the brain' or making pupils idle and ridding mathematics of its rigour. The debate is then brought up to date in the subsequent chapters; Janet Duffin writes about a large-scale calculator project undertaken in primary schools in which she contests the above statements by describing the development of pupils' facility with number concepts. Kenneth Ruthven's chapter explores the use of supercalculators in secondary schools and argues for changes in the curriculum and the way it is examined to take account of the skills that may be rendered redundant because of the technology now readily and cheaply available. Ronnie Goldstein echoes these sentiments in his description of the impact of computers and calculators and conjectures what the mathematics curriculum in the future might look like.

Chapter 14

Do you need to know how it works?

Costel Harnasz

What can a dispute that occurred in seventeenth-century England over who invented the circular slide rule offer students and teachers today? The slide rule has all but disappeared – it is difficult to come across one these days. More often than not they have become something like a family heirloom, or an object of curiosity, because the knowledge of how to operate it has, like grandfather, passed away.

However, they once had their heydey, and it is really quite astonishing and interesting to reflect on how quickly the slide rule disappeared from the scene. Within the space of a few years they had been ousted by the arrival of the electronic calculator. Astonishing, because they had been continually refined and modified and in use for so long. Interesting because some of the arguments that arose in connection with the silicon-chip-based pretender echoed those being voiced some 350 years before.

But first, some background. What is a slide rule? It is a pair of rules, each with its own scale, fitted in such a way that the scale of one slides along the scale of the other. In its simplest form it can be used for adding and subtracting, as shown in Figure 14.1. In fact, two ordinary rulers can be used to perform the calculation in this way. Suppose we wished to add together 5 and 2.5. Scale A is moved until its zero is opposite 2.5 on scale B. We then look along scale until we come to 5 and find the number that lies opposite on scale B, in this case 7.5. Of course, we could add any number to 2.5 in this way, and perhaps invent a cursor to move along the scales to make the readings easier. The inverse operation, subtraction, is the addition operation performed in reverse.

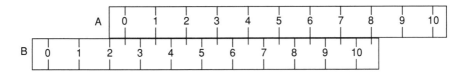

Figure 14.1

Now normally discussion about slide rules brings the operations of multiplication and division into mind. We do not usually need a device or instrument of this sort to do simple additions and subtractions – although it can have its use as a teaching aid if it is thought of as two moveable number lines. But I shall leave that to be explored in the classroom.

Now it may come as a surprise that multiplication can be carried out by using a slide rule. Or at least there is usually acknowledged to be some element of mystery about this. But take Figure 14.2. Here are two scales, maybe made on paper or thin card, with the marks on each of them placed at intervals of equal length. To multiply 10 by 1,000 you set them up as shown in Figure 14.3, reading the answer 10,000 on the bottom scale, opposite the 1,000 of the upper one, which has had its '1' placed adjacent to the '10' mark as shown.

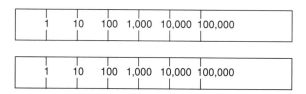

Figure 14.2

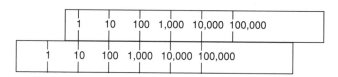

Figure 14.3

This is fine if you want to confine yourself to multiplying and dividing these powers of ten, but what is needed is a way of marking the numbers between 1 and 10, 10 and 100, and so on. And in fact, this is the basis of an investigation in *Starting Points* by Banwell *et al.* (1986) and from *The School Mathematics Project Book 2* (SMP 1969) from which the following quotation is taken.

Advances in scientific achievement have always resulted in a demand for ways of speeding up the arithmetical work associated with problems. Galileo's invention of the telescope, for example, produced more accurate measurements of the large distances involved in astronomy. These more accurate measurements resulted in more arithmetical work; consequently it was no coincidence that, in the early seventeenth century, John Napier pioneered a new technique for calculation at the same time as Galileo was observing the movements of the moon and planets.

We shall approach the problem in the way that Napier did.

(SMP 1969: 176)

I have chosen this extract for a variety of reasons. First, because it begins to offer suggestions as to what motivates mathematical developments and this one in particular. Second, because it illustrates the style and content of a text that seems to have disappeared, a kind of reflection of the present day in which, as has been pointed out, only 'two people are mentioned by name in the National Curriculum' (Cheshire County Council 1992).

You may have heard of or seen 'Napier's bones' (Figure 14.4), maybe it is one of those phrases that just sticks in the mind and comes up at intervals in quizzes and bad puns. Napier's bones are in fact one of several computational aids which he invented. They consisted of the columns of a multiplication table inscribed onto rods. These are then aligned, choosing the appropriate ones for the calculation being performed, in such a way that the 'partial products' are readily obtained and displayed in a fashion which makes adding them up straightforward. In a sense it is a little like a partly mechanised form of long multiplication.

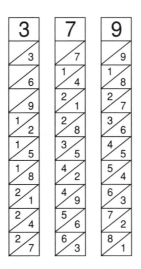

Figure 14.4 Example of Napier's rods (or bones) set up to show multiplication by 379

But Napier achieved greatest fame for his invention of logarithms. Looking back at the scales for multiplying powers of 10 it can be seen that the task of multiplying two numbers can be changed to the simpler method of addition – in this case it turns out to be adding the number of zeros. Ten does not have to be adhered to as a basis; for example, if we work with another geometric progression as illustrated in Figure 14.5, i.e. where the common ratio is now 2, it can readily be seen that if any two numbers in the upper sequence, e.g. 4 and 8, are multiplied, their product (in this case, 32) is to be found above the sum of 2 and 3 in the bottom line. When the sequence is written as in Figure 14.6 it can be seen that it works because

$$4 \times 8 = 2^2 \times 2^3 = 2^5 = 32,$$

i.e. powers of two are added and this is the basis of his discovery. Napier coined the word logarithm from Greek words meaning 'ratio-number'.

...	¼	½	1	2	4	8	16	32	128	...
	-2	-1	0	1	2	3	4	5	6	

Figure 14.5

...	¼	½	1	2	4	8	16	32	128	...
	2^{-2}	2^{-1}	2^0	2^1	2^2	2^3	2^4	2^5	2^6	

Figure 14.6

Although I have used pictures and scales to aid an understanding of logarithms, and have discussed slide rules from the beginning of the chapter, the invention of the slide rule actually followed that of the logarithm. A number of school texts up to the 1970s which dealt with this topic also precede their description of logarithms by a discussion of the slide rule. Napier's description of logarithms was published in 1614, in Latin, with the title *Mirifici Logarithmorum Canonis Descriptio*. This is interesting, for until that time he had become widely known for having written (in English) a religious Protestant treatise that appeared in 1594, and this suggests that he was trying to reach a more learned and possibly international audience with his mathematical work. Another date for the time line is that Elizabeth I had died in the intervening period, in 1603, ushering in the Stuart era.

What happened next is history! The time was ripe for this new invention to sweep across Europe. It was clear that logarithms were something different and that they held the promise for greatly facilitating certain calculations. This was no more keenly felt than by Henry Briggs, Professor of Geometry at Gresham College in London. He read the description and decided that he just had to meet Napier in person. He made the long and difficult journey to Napier's home in Scotland in the summer of 1615 and an account of their first meeting upon Briggs' arrival at Napier's house 'where almost one quarter of an hour was spent, each beholding the other almost with admiration before one word was spoke' is given in Fauvel and Gray (1987). This illustrates the very human dimension involved, of two people collaborating closely together. How this is in contrast to the commonly held notion of mathematics as being discovered (or invented) by the mathematician working on his or her own! However, their time together was fruitful, the practical working details of logarithms were 'debugged' and soon knowledge of them spread rapidly. They had a use in navigation as the world was being opened up, and on the continent, Kepler, who was reshaping the universe, was so moved when he read a copy of Napier's book that he dedicated his next work to him.

A turning point was reached in which cultures clashed. An old order was changing. Michael Mästlin, Kepler's old astronomy teacher, was rather distrustful of logarithms. He made two points: first, that mathematicians should not be using these new tables if they did not know or understand how they had been constructed, because if the calculations worked in specific cases there was no certainty that they would always do so. Further, in a delicious turn of phrase he told Kepler, 'it is not seemly for any professor of mathematics to be childishly pleased about any shortening of the calculations' (Open University 1987). We can still hear this today, in the form of children being unable to do 'long' multiplication or division. I am not sure if the abacus engendered such sentiments, but a debate was started which continued to rumble through the centuries to surface a couple of decades ago when logarithm tables were being displaced by calculators. This tension between mathematical education practice and technical innovation can even occur within advances in the same technology. Witness the reconsideration of what 'curve sketching' means with the availability of cheap and powerful programmable graphics calculators. More recently, the same sort of reaction has occurred with the use of computers in mathematics, making us queasy about what can constitute a proof, as happened when the four-colour map problem recently finally surrendered to programming power.

However, returning to the early seventeenth century, a key advocate and proponent of logarithms at that time was Edmund Gunter, who in addition to lecturing at Gresham College also invented and modified a number of mathematical instruments of the period. He was the first to mark out the new logarithms onto a ruler – using a pair of dividers to transfer the distances along the ruler and so make handy, usable multiplications. This was the first step towards the slide rule.

However, another mathematician of the time, William Oughtred, found this new logarithmic rule rather awkward to use, and he took two such scales and put them next to each other so that they could slide and perform the kind of operation observed in Figures 14.2–14.3. So was born the slide rule.

But soon came the dispute; for Oughtred had also devised another form of slide rule in which circles of different sizes were each marked with a logarithmic scale joined at the centre so that they could rotate. He called them his 'circles of proportion'. Again, multiplication was carried out by adding a length on one scale to a length marked on the other. But it was a former pupil of his, Richard Delamain, who had a description of a similar instrument, published in 1630. An argument broke out between them over who had been the first to invent the circular slide rule. Who were these men that had this unseemly argument? After all, it is not the sort of behaviour that is usually associated with mathematicians! Oughtred was a clergyman of private means, and a key figure of the time. He had written a book entitled *Clavis Mathematicae*, or *Key to Mathematics*, which helped spread the notion of working with algebraic symbols. It was one of the books that Isaac Newton used when an undergraduate at Cambridge. He was also an influential teacher whom many students sought, for instance Christopher Wren had been among his pupils. Less is known about the younger man. Delamain had started off as a joiner but by attending the Gresham lectures and mixing with learned men he acquired enough knowledge to become a 'teacher of practical mathematics'. He eventually became wealthy and successful from the sales of his mathematical instruments and handbooks.

As a result of the rivalry surrounding this priority claim there is a body of writing that gives an insight into the atmosphere of the mathematical community of the day and of the changing relationship between mathematics and society, and also of the issues of the teaching of mathematics. Oughtred took the view that one should understand the theory behind the mathematical instruments that were being used.

> The true way of Art is not by instruments but by demonstration. The use of instruments is indeed excellent if a man be an artist but contemptible being opposed to Art.
>
> (Cajori 1916: 88)

Delamain took the opposite view, stating

> for no-one to know the use of a Mathematical Instrument, except he knows the cause of its operation, is somewhat too strict, which would keep many from affecting the Art, because they see nothing but obscure propositions, and perplex and intricated demonstrations before their eyes.
>
> (ibid.: 90)

So here are two clearly contrasting views about the use of mathematical instruments. Oughtred favouring theoretical understanding and Delamain saying it was not necessary.

Oughtred said that certain teachers (with perhaps Delamain in mind) made their pupils 'only doers of tricks and as it were, jugglers' (Cajori 1916: 88). This comment too, perhaps, has a resonance today when pupils are using calculators and they display an answer that may be hopelessly out, but by accepting what the display says draw the thought from teachers that 'they don't really understand what they are doing'. Delamain was quick to defend himself from these words of criticism as

> they are touching, and pernitious, by too much derogating from many, and glancing upon many noble personages, with too grosse, if not too base an attribute, in terming them doers of tricks, as it were to juggle.
>
> (Cajori 1916: 89)

You can imagine what the young wealthy scholars were asking of Delamain: 'look, I'm not interested in how it works, just tell me what to do.'

Perhaps Oughtred was a little put out by Delamain's success. There was a commercial side to this, too. The technology for making the instruments of the time, sundials, quadrants and so on, was being used in London, and there was money to be made.

In fact, at the heart of the matter is the way they differed in their attitude to the teaching of mathematics. Delamain said that pupils could start with the instruments straight away even if they did not understand the reasoning behind them. Besides, gentlemen did not want to learn very much mathematics, just what was necessary for their work, being the management of estates, the navy, trade or administration, all of which were coming to require some skill in the subject. Oughtred, however, emphasised the need for rigorous thinking.

There remains the paradox that Oughtred, in his student days and subsequently, had invented sundials, planispheres and various types of slide rules, so why did he discourage the use of instruments in teaching mathematics to beginners? On the face of it, his espoused pedagogy goes against the story of his own intellectual development. But then, he had a passion for the subject while a student at Cambridge, at a time when it had no particular emphasis. Therefore he would have really tried to work things out for himself, and besides, it is known that he took a delight in assisting his fellow students.

Meanwhile, the realm of England was undergoing upheaval. Society was changing and there was an attack on established forms of learning. Mathematics could not continue to exist as a pure body of knowledge, but was becoming useful to society in a way that hadn't been seen before. The general instability led to the civil war which was about to take place, during which Delamain perished and the first King Charles was beheaded. Oughtred himself managed to escape sequestration and died fifteen years later, in 1660, near Guildford where he had been this clergyman with an avid interest in mathematics.

So, at the end of the day, who had the right approach, Oughtred or Delamain? Perhaps they can stand as metaphors, not just for the issues concerning the employment of new technologies today, but in the current 'return to traditional methods of teaching' debate. Isaac Newton made sundials, windmills and a clock in his childhood. Would we stop or encourage such activities?

Perhaps then we can consider a balance between the two. Of developing that kind of awareness when the time is right to be concrete and practical, but being sensitive to the moment when it is appropriate and fruitful to enter an abstract realm, and develop insight.

REFERENCES

Banwell, C. S., Saunders, K. D. and Tahta, D. S. (1986) *Starting Points*, Diss: Tarquin Publications.

Cajori, F. (1916) *William Oughtred – a Great Seventeenth Century Teacher of Mathematics*, Chicago: Open Court.

Cheshire County Council (1992) *Mathematics Guidelines*, Cheshire: Cheshire County Council.

Fauvel, J. and Gray, J. (eds) (1987) *The History of Mathematics: a Reader*, London: Macmillan.

Open University (1987) *The Renaissance of Mathematical Sciences in Britain – Unit 6 of the Open University History of Mathematics Course*, Milton Keynes: Open University Press.

SMP (1969) *School Mathematics Project, Book 2*, Cambridge: Cambridge University Press.

Chapter 15

Mathematics for the 1990s

A calculator-aware number curriculum

Janet Duffin

I was fascinated to read, in a recent issue of *Mathematics Teaching*, about Viggo Hartz's closing lecture at last year's ATM Conference. The paragraph which stands out most in my mind is the one in which he said:

> I am about to lead a project over the next three years aimed at giving up entirely the teaching of written algorithms for the four rules. We feel sure that giving children a pocket calculator as soon as they start school, and concentrating more on mental calculation, will give them greater competence.

In the same paragraph he also said: 'In Denmark we do not carry out experiments in school, we do development work.'

These two excerpts from his talk go right to the heart of work I have been doing in this country during the past four and a half years. First, because his description of what he is going to do in the next three years sums up so clearly and simply the spirit of the project I have been evaluating since January 1987. Second, because his comment about Denmark suddenly illuminated for me a possible reason why it has not always been easy for teachers in this country to accept the terms of the project.

THE BACKGROUND

The Calculator-Aware Number (CAN) project was set up in September 1986 with aims similar to those described by Viggo Hartz for Danish children. The project guidelines asked participating teachers not to teach the standard algorithms. Instead they were asked to develop mental facility alongside calculator use. At that stage no predictions were made about the outcome in terms of pupils' number competence, thoughts were rather on seeking a curriculum more appropriate to a calculator age than the current one.

The rationale behind the guidelines for the project came from a survey of practice in primary classrooms (Shuard 1986) together with evidence from surveys of number practice in adult life (Sewell 1982). The former found that heavy concentration on the standard algorithms in schools was not matched by adult practice.

In the first place the project was seen only as curriculum development, and initiators and participants alike were unprepared for the dramatic changes which occurred amongst children and their teachers – except for those teachers who had, before the project came into being, already changed their teaching style in mathematics to fit more closely developments in practice in other areas of the primary curriculum.

Partly, perhaps, because they could no longer put the emphasis on the teaching and practice of the standard algorithms which had been common before the start of the project (80 per cent of the total time spent on number competence in primary schools in England and Wales, the survey found), teachers were forced into listening to and observing their children in a way they had not done before in mathematics. A new teaching style began to emerge, one in which the teacher became less prescriptive, more an enabler and a facilitator, whose responsibility it then became to provide an environment in which the children would be free to develop their own strategies and thinking.

Children began to demonstrate the power of their thinking, partly because of this new approach on the part of their teachers, partly because of the kind of activities they were experiencing – more open-ended and investigatory than before. And out of these changes there also emerged the looked-for changes in the curriculum. It seems likely that these occurred mainly because of the freedom the calculator gave for exploration of numbers. This, alongside the new activities and new teacher attitudes, enabled such concepts as decimals and negative numbers to be encountered earlier than had hitherto been usual. The new way of working also began to make teachers question the standard ways of approaching some topics and concepts. Children's experience of place value, for example, was radically altered because of calculator use, as was their introduction to the idea of a negative number.

Perhaps because the new way of working was one which was already established in other areas of the curriculum for many primary teachers, difficulties encountered during the first three years of the project appeared largely, though not entirely, amongst those teachers for whom the change was revolutionary rather than developmental. But when the first children in the project got to within two years of secondary transfer, some teachers began to have doubts about the ban on the standard algorithms. They felt these would be expected by the secondary schools and that, without them, their children might be disadvantaged.

AUTONOMY AND AUTHORITY

It was at this stage that other questions, too, began to arise: questions about presentation, about refinement of children's methods to make them acceptable for later stages. Even in schools where hitherto the ban had presented no problems or queries, participants began to wonder whether these children should meet the standard algorithms before transferring to the secondary school and, if so, how this could be done within the project's original guidelines and within the teaching style which had evolved.

Almost since its beginning, an important element in the project has been the recognition that it is about autonomy: for the teacher, for the children, for the advisory teacher and for the evaluator. Everyone has been learning about their role in the project from their experience within it. So some teachers have been thinking of ways to handle the problem of what to do about children's diverse methods in an environment in which, they fear, standard methods may be expected. Others have a different view.

Sharing of methods amongst children has become common in CAN classrooms. Now some began to ask why, if it is appropriate for children to 'share' ideas and methods, it is not also appropriate for teachers to contribute their standard method. Nick James,[1] after visits to several CAN schools, recognised the dilemma some teachers find themselves in. He had this to say:

> The teacher has to learn to give children autonomy. Instead of the teacher being the authority in the classroom, a climate must be created in which everyone's opinions have value and if teachers contribute their method before child autonomy is established, that method will be seen as authoritative and therefore to be accepted by all.

He went on to say that holding back on the part of the teacher can be very hard to learn.

EXPERIMENTATION OR DEVELOPMENT?

This is still an unresolved dilemma for some teachers and it is on this point that I find myself returning to Viggo Hartz's statement about not experimenting in Danish schools. Is it possible, I ask myself, that the dilemma stems from a feeling amongst some teachers that we are conducting experiments on the children and that is not acceptable? If we could be sure in England as they appear to be in Denmark that what is being done is developmental work rather than experimentation, it might be easier to overcome the misgivings of genuinely doubting teachers.

Another aspect of this problem has recently arisen from the outcome of a questionnaire distributed to all participants with the idea that participant evaluation should be part of the autonomy which permeates the whole project.

The questionnaire, after a few questions related to factual information required to help with any analysis of the results, was composed mainly from comment and opinions expressed over the years by participants and others about the project. It was designed to ascertain attitudes of participants to such things as the algorithms; the children's and their own attitudes to the project; concerns felt about such things as secondary transfer; parental attitudes; dissemination; children's knowledge of numbers facts; their strategies and their recording procedures, to name a few of the items contained in it.

A small case study was undertaken of nine late returns with the idea that a 'pilot' survey might bring out issues more difficult to discern in the larger study. I was quite startled by one thing which emerged from this sample. Amongst the nine respondents there were four who believed that the standard algorithms were still essential to the primary curriculum. These same four respondents also believed that, while the project had been beneficial to the able and the average children, it was not for the less able.

This was interesting, for one of the things which had emerged from talk with teachers, particularly those who were not sure of the wisdom of refraining from teaching algorithms; was that they felt that the standard algorithms were necessary for those children who did not find it easy to develop their own methods. Such children might be able to calculate reasonably competently in their heads and use a calculator when that proved difficult, but they could not devise a competent and economical way of recording a calculation. For example, some less able children could not find a method for subtraction which would always work; some appear to be unable to move on from equal additions to finding a suitable method for multiplication.

There is no doubt that one of the concerns of teachers in every region has been about the need for all children to be able to refine their methods to produce a written procedure which would be acceptable at the secondary stage. The belief of some teachers appears to be that where children fail to devise a satisfactory method for themselves they must be taught the standard methods.

For me this belief raises a very big question about the success of these standard methods in the community at large, judging by several recent reports used to castigate teachers and teaching methods. I find myself wondering about the usefulness of giving the standard procedures to those who have failed to devise their own because there is so much evidence that the less able – and some of the more able too – have never been able to remember them either in school or after they have left. It is an issue which must be debated both inside and outside the project.

But it is not on this aspect that I want to concentrate in this chapter. What I should like to do instead is to look at two examples of children's methods, both of which have something to tell us about the developmental nature of children's learning when it is given the opportunity to demonstrate itself through a teaching style which is prepared to await that development.

Some early subtraction methods

From a mixed group of 7 yr olds:

$$135 - 72 = 63$$

First I take 70 away from 100.
That leaves me with 30
Then I add the other 30 back.
That makes. 60.
Then I take 2 from 5 that left 3
so the answer is 63.

TWO LESS ABLE
CHILDREN AT 9 YRS

$$72 - 58 = 14$$
$$70 - 50 = 20$$
$$2 - 8 = -6$$
$$20 - 6 = 14$$

90 - 36 = 56

First I did 90 take away 30 and that come to 60 and then
I did 0 - 6 and that came to -6 and then I added 60
and that come to 54.

$$96 - 34 = 62$$
$$96 - 10 = 86$$
$$86 - 10 = 76$$
$$76 - 60 = 66$$
$$66 - 4 = 62$$

(364 - 47)

$$60 - 40 = 20 ,, add 4 = 24 , take 7 = 17 , add 300 = 317.$$

First I did 61 - 20 and that came to 41 then I did 41 - 8 and it
came to 33.   (61 - 28)

Addition and Subtraction of larger numbers

TWO CHILDREN EXPLAINING THEIR SUBTRACTIONS

765 + 143 + 289 = 1197
700 + 100 + 200 = 1000
60 + 40 + 80 = 180
5 + 3 + 9 = 17

1. 31 - 17

7 AND 8 IS 15. 15 AND 15 IS 30,
30 AND 1 IS 31, SO THE ANSWER
IS 8 + 15 + 1 = 24

x 356 + 1 + 65
356 + 100 = 8456
8456 + 65 = 8516

Q : WHY DO YOU START WITH 7 AND 8 ?

A : BECAUSE IT MAKES 15 AND 15 IS
HALF OF 30

$$8.333 - 165 = 168$$
$$300 - 100 = 200$$
$$30 - 60 = -30$$
$$3 - 5 = -2$$
$$200 - 30 = 170$$
$$170 - 2 = 168$$

2. 32 - 19

FIRST I THOUGHT I'D USE TILLICH
BLOCKS AND THEN I THOUGHT I
SHOULD DO IT IN MY HEAD. I
PRETENDED THE 32 WAS 30 AND
THE 19 WAS 20. 20 FROM 30
IS 10 SO THE ANSWER IS
3 MORE.

5534 + 3164
5534 - 3100 = 2434
2434 - 64 = 2370

Figure 15.1

DEVELOPMENT OF A SUBTRACTION METHOD

On a visit to a CAN school during the first year of the project I was shown a piece of work done by a 6/7 year old.

$$
\begin{array}{r}
427 \\
-259 \\
\hline
232 \\
\hline
\end{array}
$$

(and written at the side: But the real answer is 168.) I asked the child about this. Unfortunately it had been done a few weeks previously and he had forgotten why he wrote that.

I gave him another to do. This time he wrote down

$$
\begin{array}{r}
524 \\
-278 \\
\hline
-354 \\
\hline
\end{array}
$$

I pointed out that this was a different kind of answer from the one he had given before. His reply was 'Oh, I didn't know about negative numbers then', but he was still not able to explain much more about his answer.

I tried him on a two digit question: 74−38. He told me

70 take away 30 is 40
4 take away 8 is −4
so the answer is 44

Before he gave me his final answer I thought he was on to a valid way to subtract and I was disappointed with his reply. I took it no further that day. When I returned the following term he was satisfactorily applying a correct procedure with both two and three digit subtractions. His way of recording was as above except that his answer would now be 36.

I considered the stages through which his development seemed to have gone.

First a strategy of subtracting the smaller digit from the larger for each column, a method which did not give him the answer which his own internal logic told him was the right answer. I wondered where the conflicting logic of always taking the smaller from the larger came from. On another occasion with another child I thought I had seen the reason why: at the concrete stage of encountering subtraction, children always 'take away a smaller number' of objects from those they have in front of them. And even if originally they meet other manifestations of subtraction this seems to be the one which persists when the concrete is overtaken by recording the process. It is comparatively easy to think of ways in which calculator use could undermine this early perception.

Replaced by a strategy which had a different consistency: if you start by taking the top digit from the bottom digit then you must do that for all digits, which would account for the '−' in front of the answer in the second presentation.

Via an intermediate stage, when operating with the negative numbers produced is not yet fully established, leading on to a competent algorithm which can handle the negative numbers sometimes generated. It is perhaps interesting to note here that, while most CAN children who use this method write it out as above, in some work done under the Wiskobas scheme[2] children in the Netherlands write this method as follows:

$$
\begin{array}{r}
437 \\
-289 \\
\hline
252 \\
\hline
148
\end{array}
$$

Many CAN children seem to calculate from the left instead of from the right as in the standard methods. I was puzzled about why this should be until I spoke with another child who had told me about his way of adding 27 and 46: 20 and 40 are 60, 7 and 6 are 13, so the answer is 73. Asked what he had used to help him to do this, he got out sets of ten connected cubes and individual cubes and, after laying them out in front of me, he picked up the tens cubes first. On being shown that, it seemed obvious that one would pick up the bigger pieces of equipment first. In the abstract it is not so obvious because we are so tied to the standard ways of calculating.

So it appears that by being given the freedom to develop and mature without interference children can come to a compact and elegant method for a process which standard procedures previously denied to all those except the ones who were always prone to devising their own methods. The big difference is that previously, as I know from work with undergraduates, there was a tendency for these self-devised methods to be kept hidden for fear of censure. Now they can be made public they are more likely to spread amongst those who may not be able to devise a competent method for themselves.

TWO WAYS TOWARDS PLACE VALUE UNDERSTANDING

My other example demonstrates that ways towards understanding may not be the same for all children. I was with a group of children who were doubling. One girl told me that she had got as far as 512. She said she had done up to 64 in her head and remembered 128 because she had done it last week but that the other two she had done on her calculator. I asked her if she thought she could do the next one in her head. She was doubtful but a boy sitting near said: 'It'll be ten hundred and twenty-four and the next one will be two thousand and forty-eight.' I asked him to key his numbers into his calculator. He showed me 200048. Meanwhile the girl had got there by doing it on her calculator and told me correctly what the number was. They compared their displays and were nonplussed.

I was not able to follow up this episode but it interested me greatly that these two children both had some understanding of place value and both had some deficiency in their ability to handle the processes they were working with. The boy was more competent mentally and could translate from hundreds to thousands accurately, but he did not know how to record his answer correctly; the girl failed to do the mental calculation but could read correctly the answers her calculator gave her. In a classroom which recognises the right of children to develop towards competence through their own efforts and in their own way, such examples are likely to occur often and suggest that a preconceived view of a 'correct' way towards mastery of a procedure may not be conducive to maximum achievement for all children.

So besides my initial reasons for starting by quoting from Viggo Hartz's article I am also delighted to find that there are other countries now looking at similar things to ourselves.[3] Denmark, the Netherlands and Australia are three countries where I know these developments are taking place.

It will be interesting to see if similar problems to those we have been encountering arise in these other projects. We may then be in a better position to determine whether problems are unique to this country or occur similarly for other countries. Either way we are likely to be better equipped to see how to overcome those common problems which do arise.

Nevertheless, in spite of our difficulties I still believe this is a development for the future and I hope that those teachers willing and able to take on board the ideas, philosophy and practice of the CAN project will be able to go on from strength to strength showing us that English children are not so innumerate as some in the community tend to believe them to be.

NOTES

1 Nick James worked in mathematics education at the Open University for a number of years.
2 The Wiskobas scheme was a developmental project in the Netherlands and the method used by Dutch children can be found in the proceedings of the 1988 Annual Conference of the Psychology of Mathematics Education group.
3 Projects similar to CAN have been started in both Tasmania and Victoria, Australia. Two linked projects were launched in the Netherlands about a year ago, one university based, the other in school.

REFERENCES

Fitzgerald, T. (1985) *New Technology and Mathematics in Employment*, London: DES.

Sewell, B. (1982) *Uses of Mathematics by Adults in Daily Life*, ACAE.

Shuard, H. (1986) *Mathematics Today and Tomorrow*, London: Longmans.

Chapter 16

Supercalculators and the secondary mathematics curriculum

Kenneth Ruthven

THE SUPERCALCULATOR AS A PERSONAL TECHNOLOGY

During the 1980s the advent of cheap portable calculators created the changed technological conditions within which a radical rethinking of the primary mathematics curriculum could take place. This rethinking centred on the development of the Calculator-Aware Number curriculum (Shuard *et al.* 1991; see also Chapter 15). Now, a new generation of 'supercalculators' (Shumway 1988, 1990; Waits and Demana 1988; Ruthven 1990a, 1992a, b; Burrill 1992; Dick 1992) seems set to provoke a similar intellectual revolution in secondary mathematics over the 1990s.

Although technical innovation will continue relentlessly, notably through the convergence of the scientific calculator with the palmtop computer, the main characteristics of the supercalculator are already clear. It is an essentially algebraic device, combining (and increasingly integrating) facilities for representing and transforming mathematical relationships expressed in numeric, graphic and symbolic forms.

To illustrate the facilities of a typical supercalculator, consider the popular 'maxbox' problem (HMI 1985: 27): this concerns the volume of an open box created from a square piece of card, with identical smaller square pieces cut from each corner, as shown in Figure 16.1. To explore this situation, the supercalculator user can enter into the machine an algebraic formula relating the volume of the box to the size of the cut. With the calculating utilities, this formula can be evaluated for a given cut, solved for a given volume and maximised, as shown in Figure 16.2. With the graphing utilities, the formula can be plotted, a cursor moved on the resulting curve and the extreme value located, as shown in Figure 16.3. With the symbol-manipulating utilities, the formula can be expanded, simplified, differentiated and the resulting quadratic solved, as shown in Figure 16.4.

In future supercalculators we can expect numeric and graphic representations to be 'linked' to the symbolic (Kaput 1989). In such a system, any standard operation on a symbolic expression is associated with a corre-

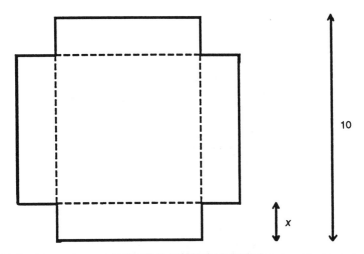

Figure 16.1 The net of an open box, created by cutting an identical small square piece (of side *x*) from each corner of a square piece of card (of side 10). The 'maxbox' problem is to examine the relationship between the size of the cut and the volume of the resulting box; in particular, to find the maximum volume achievable

sponding transformation in a numeric table and graph plot. As an illustration, Figure 16.5 shows the three representations of a simple linear equation before and after a symbolic operation to rearrange terms, emphasising the invariance of the solution under this operation.

Of course, similar facilities are available on computers, often in more sophisticated forms. But the significance of the supercalculator is that it can become a genuinely personal tool for individual students in a way that the classroom computer cannot. The supercalculator is cheap, portable and readily available. A class set of supercalculators for individual use is comparable in cost to a single classroom computer: already, many students are choosing to provide their own supercalculator in preference to a conventional scientific calculator. The supercalculator is portable, travelling with its owner and available for use beyond (as well as within) the mathematics classroom. Consequently, whereas student opportunity to use the classroom computer is usually limited, and subject to the control (and often the initiative) of the teacher, access to the supercalculator can be unrestricted – chosen and controlled by students themselves.

Early experience in a pilot project (Ruthven 1992a) has shown the significant impact on students of such unrestricted access to supercalculators. Although the initial period of familiarisation could be frustrating for students at times, knowing that the resource would be available when wanted was a powerful incentive to learn to use it; and this learning could take place

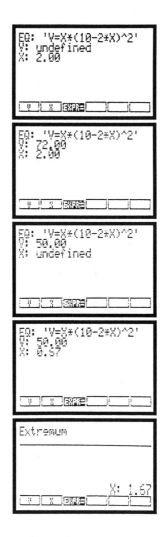

Figure 16.2 A sequence of five screens recording a numeric analysis of the 'maxbox' problem on a supercalculator. The small boxes at the foot of each screen show a 'pop-up menu' of the different variables involved. Keys located immediately below the screen correspond to each box and allow variables to be selected easily. On the first screen, *V* is declared an unknown and *X* assigned a value of 2; the second screen shows the result of instructing the supercalculator to evaluate *V*. On the third screen, *X* is declared an unknown and *V* assigned a value of 50; the fourth screen shows the first solution for *X* located by the supercalculator. The fifth screen shows the result of instructing the supercalculator to locate an extreme value

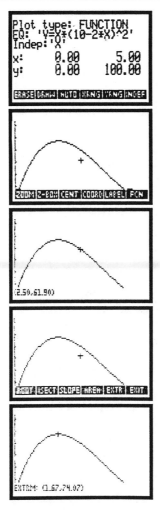

Figure 16.3 A sequence of five screens recording a graphic analysis of the 'maxbox' problem on a supercalculator. The small boxes at the foot of each screen show a 'pop-up menu' of commands likely to be particularly useful at each stage. On the first screen, appropriate ranges are chosen for each axis using the XRNG and YRNG commands (the AUTO command will automatically select an appropriate *y* range). The previous graph is erased using the ERASE command and the DRAW command is used to produce the graph on the second screen. The COORD command is selected so as to display the co-ordinates of the cursor (marked as +) as it moves under key (or 'tracker ball') control, as shown on the third screen. On the fourth screen, the menu is restored and the command EXTR selected to locate the maximum value, as shown on the fifth screen. Other commands shown in the menu have the following functions: the ROOT command moves the cursor to successive root positions; SLOPE calculates the gradient of the graph at the cursor position; AREA calculates areas under a marked section of the graph

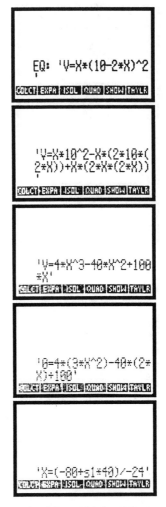

Figure 16.4 A sequence of five screens recording a symbolic analysis of the 'maxbox' problem on a supercalculator. The EXPAN command is used to expand the formula, creating the second screen. The COLCT command is then used to simplify to the result shown on the third screen. Application of the differentiation command (from the main keyboard) produces the quadratic equation on the fourth screen; then the QUAD command is used to solve it, as shown on the fifth screen (where a + or − sign can be substituted for s1)

more privately, spontaneously and informally than with a classroom microcomputer. Students quickly became proficient in using the calculating and graphing facilities provided by their supercalculators, incorporating them confidently into their mathematical practice.

The performance of a sample of project students was compared with that

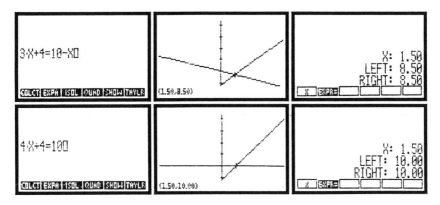

Figure 16.5 Two sets of three screens corresponding to symbolic, graphic and numeric representations of a linear equation. The first row shows the symbolic representation, followed by graphic and numeric representations highlighting its solution. The second row shows the result of some symbolic manipulation (to collect terms in *x* on one side of the equation), followed by the corresponding graphic and numeric representations. Note how this illustrates the invariance of the solution under these manipulations

of an equivalent group without access to graphing technology (Ruthven 1990b). Students were asked to tackle a set of tasks involving the reverse process to that automated by the supercalculator; providing a symbolic description of a given graph. Although both groups employed predominantly the same type of strategy, the performance of the project group was markedly superior, both in recognising a graph as being of a particular type and then in exploiting salient information to arrive at a precise symbolic description, as illustrated in Figure 16.6.

The supercalculator, then, might be described as an 'appropriate' technology (Dunn 1978), 'intermediate' in cost and power between traditional (pen and paper) and advanced (computer) technology (Schumacher 1973), and 'convivial' in the way that it can be easily used, by anybody, as often or as seldom as desired, for the accomplishment of a purpose chosen by the user (Illich 1973).

MATHEMATICAL REASONING AND THE SUPERCALCULATOR

When teachers and students start to work with a supercalculator, they continue to employ mathematical concepts and strategies which they have already established. A supercalculator utility may simply be used to check a result gained by a more traditional procedure. More productively, it may be used as a rapid, reliable and less taxing substitute for such a procedure: evaluating an expression, graphing a function, solving an equation or

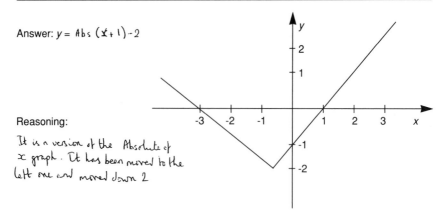

Answer: $y = Abs\,(x + 1) - 2$

Reasoning:

It is a version of the Absolute of
x graph. It has been moved to the
left one and moved down 2

Figure 16.6 Solution of a 'reverse' problem. The student recognises the general form of the graph and recalls a corresponding symbolisation; then analyses the relationship of the given graph to the standard form in transformational terms, and makes appropriate refinements to the symbolisation

simplifying an expression. In other respects, however, the mathematical strategies of such users tend to remain traditional.

But, as familiarity and fluency with the supercalculator increase, novel concepts and strategies may emerge. The strategic idea of trial-and-improve is one important instance: this involves the progressive refinement of guesses in the light of evidence generated by the supercalculator. For example, to calculate how many years it would take a sum of £1,000 invested at 1 per cent compound interest to double in value, a user might carry out the sequence of calculations shown in Figure 16.7, analysing successive results systematically in order to home in on a solution.

```
'1000.00*1.01^100'
2,704.81
'1000.00*1.01^50'
1,644.63
'1000.00*1.01^70'
2,006.76
'1000.00*1.01^69'
1,986.89
```

Figure 16.7 A numeric trial-and-improve strategy. The supercalculator screen shows a sequence (from top to bottom) of trial calculations aimed at finding the number of years that it takes for £1,000 to double in value when invested at 1 per cent compound interest. The first guess of a hundred years produces a figure that is substantially too high. The second guess of fifty years gives a result that is too low, but closer to the desired value. The next guess, of seventy years, is chosen to be between the preceding two, but closer to the lower value: this produces an answer only slightly too high. Finally, sixty-nine is tested, but gives an answer slightly too low. The problem is now solved

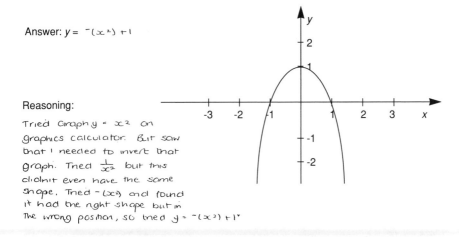

Answer: $y = ^-(x^2) + 1$

Reasoning:

Tried Graph $y = x^2$ on graphics calculator. But saw that I needed to invert that graph. Tried $\frac{1}{x^2}$ but this didn't even have the same shape. Tried $-(x^2)$ and found it had the right shape but in the wrong position, so tried $y = ^-(x^2) + 1$"

Figure 16.8 A graphic trial-and-improve strategy. The student is working on one of the 'reverse' problems already referred to. The standard graphic form is recognised and the corresponding symbolisation recalled. The student recognises the graphic inversion and the need for a corresponding symbolic transformation. Graphic feedback shows clearly that the initial conjecture is inappropriate; and then that the revised conjecture is almost correct. To complete the solution the student then identifies a transformation which will shift the graph into the desired position and the corresponding symbolic modification

Figure 16.8 illustrates how trial-and-improve may use graphic rather than numeric feedback. Here a student gives an account of the experimentation which led to the achievement of a precise symbolisation for a given graph. This points to a second important feature of the supercalculator: the way in which it can support and encourage visual reasoning drawing on graphic representations. Another striking illustration is provided by the argument for the cosine double-angle formula, as recorded by a student in Figure 16.9: this highlights the role of transformational concepts in constructing such chains of reasoning.

Equally, supercalculator utilities may themselves embody novel concepts. An excellent example is the utility which enables the user to 'zoom' in and out on a particular section of a graph. In effect, this creates a new graphic environment for working with ideas of approximation and limit. It supports, for example, a more simple and direct approach to the generalised notion of the gradient of a curve by making it possible to zoom in progressively on a particular neighbourhood of the curve (Tall 1985), as shown in Figure 16.10. This approach is more cognitively direct than the elaborate, and often misunderstood, traditional approach to the idea of gradient through the construction of a secant line tending to the tangent (Orton 1977, 1983).

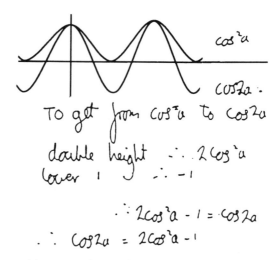

Figure 16.9 A graphic approach to a trigonometric identity. The student notes the correspondence of peaks and troughs on the two graphs and constructs an appropriate sequence of transformations from one to the other, using this to identify a corresponding symbolic relationship

These examples show how the supercalculator makes novel mathematical approaches possible; notably approaches which exploit the numeric or graphic processing capacities of the supercalculator. In particular, when exploring unfamiliar situations and meeting new ideas, it can often be helpful to work directly with a range of examples in numeric or graphic form, before moving to a more generalised symbolic form. This is true both where students are working independently to solve a problem and where their teacher is introducing a new concept to them.

Traditionally, symbolic reasoning has caused great difficulties for many students. One contributory factor has undoubtedly been an undue emphasis on manipulation without concern for wider purpose or meaning. Some see the linking of numeric, graphic and symbolic representations (as described in the opening section) as providing a particularly promising environment for developing understanding of symbolic ideas and techniques (Kaput 1989, 1992). Take, for example, the algebraic concept of equivalence. As shown in Figure 16.11, this can be conceived in distinctively symbolic, graphic and numeric ways: that two expressions can be manipulated to the same symbolic form; that the two expressions have identical graphs; and that whatever value is substituted, the two expressions take the same value. Working with linked multiple representations, then, offers support in developing a particularly rich concept of equivalence, integrating these three perspectives.

Equally, working with a supercalculator entails use of its symbolic language, increasingly convergent with that of standard mathematics.

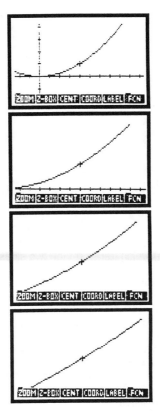

Figure 16.10 A sequence of four screens recording the process of 'zooming in' on a particular neighbourhood of a curve. On the first screen the curve is drawn and the command CENT used to centre the graph on the desired point. The second screen shows the result of applying the ZOOM command, producing a 'magnified' image of the neighbourhood of the point. The third and fourth screens show further 'magnifications'. Note how, as the neighbourhood becomes more and more local to the point, the curve becomes more and more linear, establishing a direct connection with the simpler idea of gradient of a straight line

Experience of this active use of a mathematical symbol system can both increase confidence and competence with using symbolism in other contexts and motivate the exploration of underlying regularities. One vignette (Ruthven 1993) reports how involving students in generating successive terms of sequences on their supercalculator meant that rules had to be formulated in terms of the formal language of the calculator: the language of '+', '×' and 'Ans' (which is the supercalculator symbol for the answer to the preceding calculation). Here, different strategies for finding an iterative rule led to different symbolic formulations of the rule: the terms 2, 4, 8, 16, . . . , for example, producing rules such as Ans + Ans or 2 × Ans; or 2, 4, 10, 28, . . .

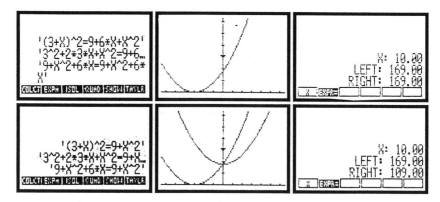

Figure 16.11 Two sets of three screens corresponding to symbolic, graphic and numeric representations of a proposed identity. The first row of screens shows a valid identity. Here the first screen records a sequence of symbolic manipulations (expanding and collecting) which transform the two sides of the identity (as shown in the top line) to exactly equivalent forms (as shown in the bottom line); the symbolic concept of equivalence. (The . . . on the second line indicates that part of the expression is off-screen.) Note that this sequence is exactly the reverse of that sought in a conventional deductive proof! The second screen in the first row illustrates the graphic concept of equivalence: the graphs of the two sides of the identity are indistinguishable. The third screen corresponds to the numeric concept of equivalence: whatever value is substituted, the two sides take the same value. The second row of screens shows the three representations of an invalid identity. In the first screen the two sides cannot be manipulated to the same form; in the second screen their graphs are clearly distinct; and in the third screen they take different values for a given substitution

suggesting rules such as Ans + Ans − 1 + Ans − 1, Ans − 2 + 2 × Ans, as well as 3 × Ans − 2 and Ans + Ans + Ans − 2. This provided the opportunity and experience to discuss the distinction between procedure and product and to develop the idea of the equivalence of symbolic expressions.

RETHINKING THE SECONDARY MATHEMATICS CURRICULUM

The preceding sections have illustrated how supercalculators can support novel mathematical strategies and improve mathematical performance. Such outcomes, however, result not simply from ready access to the machine, but from corresponding changes in the mathematics curriculum to reflect the changed technological context of mathematical thinking and learning. Previous experience demonstrates that a new mathematical tool, even one so readily available as the conventional calculator, may have little influence on the curriculum. Not only may the tool fail to penetrate the classroom, as appeared to be the case for the 22 per cent of secondary students who reported themselves as rarely or never using calculators at school (Foxman *et al*. 1991), but even where the machine is accepted, its use may be largely assimilated to traditional mathematical practices, as described earlier.

There is no reason to believe that the unmediated impact of the supercalculator will be much different. Change in curricula will be informed by technological possibilities, rather than driven by them. In practice, change most often comes about first on a small scale, in the form of thoughtful developments by imaginative teachers and researchers. Only later are some innovations institutionalised on a wider scale through curriculum guidelines, published schemes and assessment procedures.

This concluding section, then, seeks neither to predict nor prescribe, but to bring out some likely central features of a 'supercalculator-aware' secondary mathematics curriculum. There is widespread agreement (Shumway 1990; Bibby 1991; Tall 1992) that the emphasis of such a curriculum should shift away from matters of technique (now increasingly automated by the supercalculator) towards the conceptual issues which underpin intelligent use of mathematics and mathematical technology. And because it is an essentially algebraic device, the supercalculator raises particularly important questions about the algebra component of the curriculum.

In recent years there has been a diminishing emphasis on algebra in the curriculum of most students. Although the Cockcroft report (DES 1982) suggested that 'efforts should be made to discuss some algebraic ideas with all pupils' (p. 141), it concluded that for those of average attainment only 'some simple algebraic work on formulae and equations which involves symbolisation is . . . desirable' (p. 144) and that 'formal algebra is not appropriate for lower-attaining pupils' (p. 141). Some attention to this aspect of algebra was encouraged only for higher-attaining students for whom 'it is . . . hard to achieve the degree of facility in algebraic manipulation required for [advanced] work in mathematics if [they] have not started to develop it before they enter the sixth form' (p. 133).

The influence of success or failure in mathematics on students' educational and employment opportunities has been widely noted; and the particular significance of algebra in this filtering process has been documented (Wolf 1990; Harvey *et al*. 1992). This, of course, is not capricious: it reflects the widespread importance of mathematics in general, and algebra in particular, in many scientific, technical and managerial fields. Nonetheless, this lack of accessibility can be seen as a major barrier to the equalisation of educational and employment opportunities. In the United States, concern about disparities in opportunity has led to the recommendations that all secondary-school students should follow a common core mathematics curriculum including a strong algebra component, and that supercalculators should be available to such students at all times (National Council of Teachers of Mathematics 1989).

In England and Wales, the present National Curriculum in mathematics (DES 1991) now requires some study of algebra for all secondary-school pupils. The three recognised algebra strands correspond closely to the key forms of representation: patterns and relationships to the numeric; formulae, equations and inequalities to the symbolic; and graphical representation to the graphic. The possibilities of operating within each of these representations by, for example, solving equations using numeric and graphic as well as symbolic strategies is recognised, with explicit mention of the use of calculators and computers. In some respects, however, the National Curriculum has not fully grasped the extent of the cognitive and curriculum reorganisation made possible by the supercalculator. An appropriate illustration is through two of the statements of attainment expected of the typical school leaver.

The statement 'Solve simple equations' is given two exemplars: 'Solve: $3x + 4 = 10 - x$' and 'Solve equations such as $x^2 = 5$ and $x^3 = 20$ by "trial and improvement" methods'. Now, of course, such equations are most easily solved using the automatic root-finder of the supercalculator. But while this much diminishes the practical importance of either of the implied methods as a generally appropriate technique for solving equations, the concepts underpinning each remain important. Traditionally, the topic of linear equations has acted as a vehicle for making important ideas about the structure of the number system explicit to students: in a reformed curriculum, the development of such ideas would be a more explicit curriculum goal, and there would be recognition that student experience with symbol-manipulating tools might contribute to its achievement. In the second exemplar, the idea of trial-and-improve itself, and its development into the concept of iteration, would be emphasised, rather than its particular use as a technique for solving equations.

The other significant statement of attainment currently expected of the typical school leaver is 'Use and plot Cartesian coordinates to represent mappings'. With ready access to supercalculator graphing, both the level and form of this statement ought to be revised. While the traditional curriculum is organised around the development of graphing techniques, the supercalculator subverts this approach at a keystroke. But in a reformed curriculum placing more emphasis on graphic ideas and argument in response to new technological possibilities, the idea of what a graph represents assumes greater and earlier importance. Indeed, the present curriculum defers graphic ideas to a surprising extent. Arguably, in a reformed National Curriculum, key graphic ideas (such as knowledge of particular graph forms, solving equations using graphical methods and using transformational ideas to describe relationships between graphs) would all be placed two levels earlier. And the absent idea of graphic zoom would be developed systematically from an early stage.

In the domain of algebra, then, as in arithmetic, calculators are creating the conditions for radical changes in mathematical practice, which, sooner or later, must influence the 'normal' (Kuhn 1962) practice institutionalised in the school mathematics curriculum. Previous experience suggests that the period of transition will be one not only of passionate debate, but of strange ironies. Will the 1990s see classrooms where students use their supercalculators to find the symbolic derivative of an expression and its roots, in order to sketch its graph; just as, in some classrooms of the 1980s, students were being taught to use their calculators to multiply two numbers by using the logarithm and addition keys rather than the multiplication key?

REFERENCES

Bibby, N. (1991) 'Wherefore "plug-and-chug" ', *Mathematical Gazette* 75(471): 40–8.

Burrill, G. (1992) 'The graphing calculator: a tool for change', in J.T. Fey and C.R. Hirsch (eds) *Calculators in Mathematics Education*, Reston,VA: National Council of Teachers of Mathematics.

DES (1982) *Mathematics Counts: Report of the Committee of Inquiry into the Teaching of Mathematics in Schools* (Cockcroft report), London: HMSO.

—— (1991) *Mathematics in the National Curriculum*, London: HMSO.

Dick, T. (1992) 'Super calculators: implications for calculus curriculum, instruction and assessment', in J.T. Fey and C.R. Hirsch (eds) *Calculators in Mathematics Education*, Reston, VA: National Council of Teachers of Mathematics.

Dunn, P. D. (1978) *Appropriate Technology: Technology with a Human Face*, London: Macmillan.

Foxman, D., Ruddock, G., McCallum, G. and Schagen, G. (1991) *APU Mathematics Monitoring (Phase 2)*, Slough: National Foundation for Educational Research.

Harvey, J. G., Waits, B. K. and Demana, F. D. (1992) 'The influence of technology on the teaching and learning of algebra', paper presented at the Seventh International Congress on Mathematical Education, Quebec.

HMI (1985) *Mathematics from 5 to 16*, London: HMSO.

Illich, I. (1973) *Tools For Conviviality*, London: Calder and Boyars.

Kaput, J. J. (1989) 'Linking representations in the symbol systems of algebra', in S. Wagner and K. Kieran (eds) *Research Issues in the Teaching and Learning of Algebra*, New York: Lawrence Erlbaum Associates.

—— (1992) 'Technology and mathematics education', in D.A. Grouws (ed.) *Handbook of Research on Mathematics Teaching and Learning*, New York: Macmillan.

Kuhn, T. (1962) *The Structure of Scientific Revolutions*, Chicago, IL: University of Chicago Press.

National Council of Teachers of Mathematics (1989) *Curriculum and Evaluation Standards for School Mathematics*, Reston, VA: NCTM.

Orton, A. (1977) 'Chords, secants, tangents and elementary calculus', *Mathematics Teaching* 78: 48–9.

—— (1983) 'Students' understanding of differentiation', *Educational Studies in Mathematics* 14(1): 1–18.

Ruthven, K. (1990a) 'Advanced calculators and advanced-level mathematics', *Mathematical Gazette* 75(471): 48–54.

—— (1990b) 'The influence of graphic calculator use on translation from graphic to symbolic forms', *Educational Studies in Mathematics* 21: 431–50.

—— (1992a) *Graphic Calculators in Advanced Mathematics*, Coventry: National

Council for Educational Technology.

—— (1992b) 'Personal technology and classroom change: a British perspective', in J.T. Fey and C.R. Hirsch (eds) *Calculators in Mathematics Education*, Reston, VA: National Council of Teachers of Mathematics.

—— (1993) 'Developing algebra with the supercalculator', *Micromath* 9(1): 23–5.

Schumacher, E. F. (1973) *Small is Beautiful: A Study of Economics as if People Mattered*, London: Blond and Briggs.

Shuard, H., Walsh, A., Goodwin, J. and Worcester, V. (1991) *Calculators, Children and Mathematics*, London: Simon and Schuster.

Shumway, R. (1988) 'Graphics calculators: skills versus concepts', in J. De Lange (ed.) *Senior Secondary Mathematics Education*, Utrecht: OW & OC.

—— (1990) 'Supercalculators and the curriculum', *For the Learning of Mathematics* 10(2): 2–9.

Tall, D. (1985) 'The gradient of a graph', *Mathematics Teaching* 111: 48–52.

—— (1992) Review of 'Mathematica: A system for doing mathematics with a computer', *Micromath* 8(1): 45–6.

Waits, B.K. and Demana, F. (1988) 'How computer graphing can change the teaching and learning of mathematics', in J. De Lange (ed.) *Senior Secondary Mathematics Education*, Utrecht: OW & OC.

Wolf, A. (1990) 'Testing investigations', in P. Dowling and R. Noss (eds) *Mathematics Versus the National Curriculum*, London: Falmer.

Chapter 17

Mathematics education, computers and calculators

The next ten years

Ronnie Goldstein

What will mathematics education be like in ten years time? How will the computer and the calculator have altered what we teach and the way that we teach it? These are difficult questions to answer with any degree of certainty. It is not at all obvious what sort of machines there will be in the twenty-first century, let alone how they will have altered our classrooms. But the use of new technologies raises many issues which should concern mathematics educators across the world. We may not be able to provide final answers but, if we are all aware of the issues, there is a better chance that we will avoid some of the possible pitfalls.

Computers are used advantageously across the whole curriculum in our schools but the link with mathematics has always been a very close and special one. When computers first found their way into classrooms (the first stand-alone micros appeared in the late 1970s) it was always the mathematics department who took charge of them. Even today, many of the teachers concerned with information technology (IT) across the curriculum started their careers in mathematics classrooms. The fundamental connection between mathematics and IT is important. While teachers appreciate that computers can enhance many areas of the curriculum and that they can change the teaching methodologies used across the school, in mathematics there is always a more far-reaching prospect which needs to be addressed: computers and calculators are continually changing the mathematics curriculum itself. The mathematics which society needs changes and the mathematics which is accessible to our students is also different. And with the current rate of technical progress it is not clear from one year to the next what is most appropriate to be included in the curriculum.

MATHEMATICAL SKILLS

Much of mathematics education has always been concerned with the skills and techniques which students need to go about their daily lives and to solve problems. The emphasis which is placed on the teaching of mathematical skills is certainly not constant. The Cockcroft Report (DES 1982) may have reduced this emphasis in the 1980s but the National Curriculum may be strengthening it in the 1990s! Another factor in determining which skills are required at any particular time is the technology available.

There used to be only one way for most people to solve $634 + 2364 + 972$. Some may have had the facility to do it mentally but most of us needed the certainty of setting out the numbers in a vertical column and using the standard written method which we knew would work for all numbers. Mental arithmetic is still a vital means for the relatively simple calculations which we need to do with some degree of spontaneity, but, now that we have pocket calculators, the skill of performing the written algorithm is less valuable.

It is not only in the primary school that the technology is making certain skills redundant Graph plotters[1] and graphic calculators enable students to produce the graph of a function at the touch of a button, and so teachers have to re-think the need for their pupils to practise the skill of drawing graphs manually by constructing tables of values and plotting individual points. Symbol manipulators[2] (or computer algebra systems) are designed to perform many other skills which appear in the traditional mathematics curriculum. The factorisation or simplification of an algebraic expression, the solution of equations and differentiation and integration are all areas of the curriculum which will need to come under very close scrutiny in the near future.

As the technology progresses, more and more of the traditional skills we teach become redundant or, if they do still have a place in the curriculum, they certainly do not need to be practised quite so often. But how do we decide which skills are no longer necessary and which skills are still important? Should our pupils depend on a computer to expand $(x + 1)^2$ or differentiate x^3? If we can decide which skills are still required, how should we teach them with the new technologies that are available to us?

We ought to be able to learn some lessons in these areas by considering the parallels between the use of symbol manipulators within the A level curriculum and four-function calculators with younger children. Developments such as the Calculator-Aware Number (CAN) project[3] have shown that there are very many positive benefits when calculators are integrated into the mathematics curriculum. In particular, many aspects of number arise before the children have had any formal introduction to them. Children naturally stumble upon large numbers, and negative numbers appear on the screen when they key in $3 - 6$. Similarly, decimals cannot be avoided when calculators are readily available. Schools involved with CAN have found that the number curriculum for young children has to be radically reconsidered (see Chapter 15).

When older pupils use symbol manipulators regularly, they will stumble upon new conceptual ideas in similar ways. Perhaps they will meet complex numbers by trying to solve quadratic equations. The order of the curriculum will need to be reconsidered and only experience will properly inform us how the curriculum in secondary schools will need to be set out in the future.

Consider again the impact of the calculator and the possibilities that this suggests for the use of symbol manipulators. If pupils are encouraged not only to exploit the machines when they provide answers but also to use them to generate data and to explore patterns, much more can be achieved. A simple lesson to assist with the understanding of decimal notation is for children to use a calculator to multiply or divide a variety of numbers by ten, or powers of ten, and to make observations on the results. (Of course this activity might be possible without calculators if the products are set out in the conventional way, but the dangers are obvious: some pupils will not be able to complete enough written calculations to see any pattern and, worse still, mistakes will certainly not make the patterns any clearer.)

With symbol manipulators pupils are able to explore algebra in similar ways. For instance, in a very short period of time it is a simple matter to factorise a number of quadratic expressions so that the relationship between the expressions and the factors becomes clear. Alternatively, the roots of quadratic equations can be displayed so that pupils can explore when they are equal, or when they do not exist, or whatever. Calculus is also accessible without the need to have learned too many routine algorithms. The software can be used to differentiate a large number of polynomial expressions so that the rule quickly becomes evident. Integration can be seen to be the reverse process: the area of a curve can be divided into Riemann rectangles and an approximation for the total area can be obtained from the computer, by summation.

But *why* is it true that the differential coefficient of a polynomial is found by reducing the power by one and multiplying by the old power? And *when* is it important to differentiate a polynomial? The computer enables us to explore plenty of data and to see what might be generally true but it is not able to explain results or to contextualise them. (This may not be a simple matter for pupils to understand – see the following section.) When machines which can perform all the necessary routine algorithms are universally available, we shall be able to give these questions far more time in our classrooms. At present the syllabus is very crowded and there are very many routine skills that pupils need to practise. This means that, apart from some token explanations at the start of a new topic which are soon forgotten, there is no time to think analytically or to address the fundamental questions of *why* and *when*. Most importantly, when pupils spend the bulk of their time practising routine skills, there is no space for them to behave like mathematicians.

To summarise this section, we must recognise that machines will make certain mathematical skills redundant and we have to think carefully about which skills these are. Furthermore, we have to decide how to replace the skills which are no longer necessary. The curriculum must be developed so that pupils can concentrate, where possible, on thinking of a different order: symbol manipulators do not understand when or why to apply an algorithm but they will extend the complexity of expressions that can be handled and they will shift the focus of our teaching from training in the execution of mathematical algorithms to conceptual understanding, which may involve the planning and interpretation of these operations.

EXPLANATION AND PROOF

Computers are excellent devices for generating data and so they can be used to display results and to help pupils spot patterns. In the previous section it was stressed that they cannot explain the patterns that they find. However, from the learner's perspective, matters may not always be quite so straightforward. The computer can generate so much data, and so quickly, that the learner may not feel the need for any further analysis.

The following fictional conversation is between a sixth-former (SF) and her mathematics teacher (MT). The sixth-former has been using a graph plotter. She has drawn two graphs on the same screen; one was for the function $\cos 2x$ and the other for $2\cos^2 x - 1$. They appear to coincide and so she is quite sure that the two functions she had entered must have been identical, but her teacher has a pure mathematical bent and she is not convinced so easily.

MT: The two lines on the screen might appear to be on top of one another, but what happens further away from the origin, outside the limits of the small screen?

The sixth-former is not deterred by this.

SF: But I can easily tell the machine that I want to look at a different section of the graph. Look, if I alter the range on the x axis from 100 to 110, the graphs are still the same.

MT: But after you've altered the range, I can still ask the same question. What happens from $x = 1,000$ to $x = 1,010$? You can alter the ranges of both axes as many times as you like, but you won't convince me that it always works. Even if you could, just because the lines look the same on the screen doesn't mean that they are identical. Your knowledge is limited by the accuracy of the machine.

SF: It's the same thing here. I can zoom in on the graph as much as I like and the graphs are always identical. I may not be able to zoom indefinitely, but I certainly can go as far as you want me to. Surely that convinces you that the lines are the same?

MT: No, I'm sorry, calculators and computers simply cannot prove anything. They can verify results with lots of examples, but that's not proof.

SF: 'Lots' is an understatement, isn't it? Supposing I create a spreadsheet with three columns (Table 17.1). I agree with you that the

Table 17.1

a	a^2-1	$(a + 1)(a-1)$
1	0	0
2	3	3
3	8	8
4	15	15
5	24	24
6	35	35
7	48	48
8	63	63
9	80	80
10	99	99

information here is not enough to prove that $a^2-1 = (a + 1)(a-1)$, but I can alter the first column in any way I like and the second and third columns are always identical. If I change the number 1 at the top of the first column to 11, I can show that the identity works for $a = 11$ to $a = 20$. Or, by inserting -57, I can show that it works for $a = -57$ to $a = -48$. I can show that the identity works when $a = 261.479$ or any other awkward number you care to choose. This would convince anybody that it is always true. That's what proof means, you know, convincing people.

MT: Well, I'm not convinced. If someone wants to prove a theorem she has to show it always works. It's not good enough for her to say that she *could* type any numbers into the computer and then the theorem *would* hold for those numbers.

SF: One final example – have you used a dynamic geometry package?[4] It allows you to create points and lines and circles, and then you can draw constructions such as parallel lines or tangents. It's more than a drawing package though, because the computer remembers the mathematics. If you construct the perpendicular bisector of two points and then move one of the points, the perpendicular bisector also moves so that it remains in the correct position. Now, imagine you have a triangle on the screen and then you construct the three perpendicular bisectors of the sides of the triangle. As you can see, the perpendicular bisectors are concurrent (Figure 17.1). You can move the three original points anywhere on the screen and, as long as you don't destroy the triangle by having the three points in line, the perpendicular

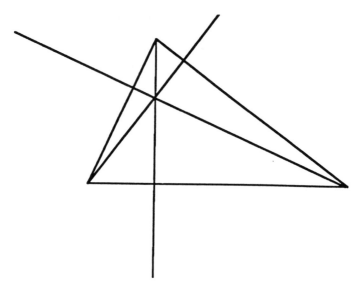

Figure 17.1

> bisectors remain concurrent. The software makes it obvious that it always works. Convinced?
>
> MT: When you drag a point around with your mouse you may think that you're testing all the points on the journey, but the computer is fooling you. It's really drawing several still pictures and, because they're drawn so fast, you think that it's a dynamic model. So you haven't actually tried every position in the plane for each of the points, and you never can. It's just like the spreadsheet – lots of examples don't make a proof.

Proof is not objective; it is not independent of the people concerned, the person writing the proof or the person reading it. Also, the need for any sort of formal proof depends on what the person already knows. A pupil at school must learn to appreciate when a proof is necessary and this is not easy. In the dialogue above, the computer seemed to militate against proof but there will also be many situations where the computer data stimulate the question *why* and pupils are encouraged to explain their results. We need to learn which sort of environments are most likely to be positive in this respect.

Any mathematician, at school or at university, will need to understand the result in concrete terms and at least be convinced of its likelihood before wanting to think in terms of formal rigour. Computers and calculators may not be able to replace the proof required by the pure mathematician, but no one doubts that they can support the exploration which leads to the result in the first place.

MICROWORLDS

The software for existing computers is slowly becoming more compatible and more standardised. It is now quite feasible to work with a spreadsheet and import the final result into a word processor. In some respects, the two applications may also be driven in the same way. For instance, it is likely that there are two or three menu options concerned with filing, printing and editing which have similar functions in the spreadsheet and the word processor. However, progress is slow and limited.

In the future we might be able to consider a more fundamental standardisation of various educational software applications. Rather than working *within* a spreadsheet and then *moving* from there to a word processor, we ought to be in a single, standard environment where the pupil's work is at the centre of all operations. When we need spreadsheet facilities we will be able to call them from the disc, and when we need to do some writing we will load the word processor too. If space permits, we might have several major applications available simultaneously, all in the same window, but, even if this cannot be achieved, the pupil's work should remain fixed while the applications are imported and exported. Today it is the other way around.

A small start has been made in this direction with Logo microworlds.[5] LogoTile and LogoGrid are small pieces of software which enable Logo to be used to cover specific areas of the curriculum. LogoSheet and LogoPlotter provide access to larger applications (a spreadsheet and a graph plotter respectively), but also from within the general purpose Logo language. In the future, these microworlds will be based around Boxer[6] or some other modern derivative of Logo, but today Logo provides the most suitable general environment in which microworlds can be built. The remainder of this section will be used to describe the distinctive features of Logo microworlds and to outline their rationale.

Essentially, Logo microworlds provide a number of extra commands which behave in the same way as all Logo primitives. For example, in LogoTile TILE 8 draws a regular octagon and in LogoPlotter GRAPH 3 $*$:x $*$:x is the command to draw the curve corresponding to $y = 3x^2$. The use of these new commands is not forced in any way. Whilst they exist in the computer's memory they can be used as and when they are needed, just like all Logo commands. Also, users always have the full power of the Logo language available to them, and the new procedures are additional to that power. This means that pupils' work might be integrated with other projects, or their work with the microworlds might be extended by the use of Logo.

Pupils in our schools could be learning Logo in a free and natural way, in full control of their own learning. They might be continually posing problems as well as solving them and the work being done might genuinely belong to the pupils who are producing it. But the nature of the pupils' projects is often not explicitly mathematical. Much of the thinking is mathematical, but it is most likely that the aims of the pupils will be to draw a picture, or write an interactive quiz. Whilst they are writing their programs, the pupils will stumble across many mathematical concepts, skills and processes. They will use symmetry without necessarily studying reflection or rotation formally. They will practise estimation continually. They will generalise, make conjectures, break problems down into more manageable parts and learn to work more systematically. The list of mathematical ideas which are inherent in Logo is a very long one. There are also many aspects of Logo which could provide powerful models for later formal studies. For instance, when pupils learn about variables, it is valuable to be able to refer to the use of inputs to Logo procedures. Pupils who have spent some time working freely with Logo will have been engaged in many mathematical processes. They will have used many mathematical ideas, implicitly if not explicitly, and the seeds will have been sown which will facilitate other important mathematical concepts. Teachers can exploit all this activity and forge the links between Logo and the mathematics by using microworlds. The main purpose of a Logo microworld is to enable the pupils to focus on specific areas of the curriculum or particular computer applications while, at the same time, retaining all the benefits of working freely with Logo.

An association with Logo makes a microworld far more versatile and flexible than an independent program with a similar design. If, for example, a pupil wants to use colour in her tiling design, all the colour commands of Logo are available to her. Periodic tiling designs are likely to prompt pupils to work with procedures. Having all aspects of turtle geometry available will allow the exploration of more complex arrangements of tiles. Working with LogoPlotter enables a pupil to draw one graph in blue on one side of the screen and another in red on the other side. This may seem a trivial benefit, but the facility to use Logo with the graph-plotting tools enables the pupil to follow his or her own challenges.

So it is not only the power of a computer and its associated software which play a fundamental role in determining the way that pupils think and what they think about. The accessibility is also critical. In this section it has been demonstrated how the software might be more friendly and integrated in the future; the next section concentrates on the accessibility of the hardware.

PERSONAL TECHNOLOGIES

In many secondary schools today, pupils have to be transported to a special room before they are able to use a machine. The machines are spread around the perimeter of the room and so the pupils have the stark choice of staring at the screen or at the classroom wall. There is a central table which remains

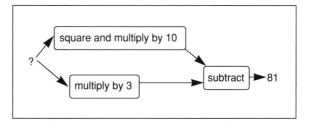

Here is a complex mapping machine.

Which number(s) can be put in so that 81 is the final output?

Figure 17.2

empty and none of the pupils stir from the machines during the entire course of the lesson. The lessons are inevitably 'computer lessons' and the use of the machines may not be properly linked with the mathematics curriculum.

Some departments are more fortunate and there may be one computer on a trolley which can be wheeled into the mathematics classroom when it is required. Better still, one or two desktop computers might even be available permanently in the classroom. This will allow them to be used more appropriately, but it is still most likely to be the teacher who decides when they are needed and how they are used. As suggested earlier, it may often be quite right for the teacher to lead exploratory activities, but in the future we must expect all learners to be equipped with their own lap-tops, and then it will also be natural for pupils to use their machines spontaneously. When pupils own small computers, they will be used in the classroom, in the library, at home, or wherever they are required.

Even though we know that this situation is very likely to be upon us soon, it is very difficult to anticipate how pupils will respond when they always have access to powerful computer applications such as Logo and a spreadsheet. What is clear, however, is that they will need to learn how to make choices. In any particular situation, they will need to decide which application to use and, possibly even more crucially, whether or not it is appropriate to use the machine in the first place. Activities with mapping machines to represent functions are good examples of the need for flexibility (Figure 17.2). Younger pupils tackling this problem will need to use a calculator and try several possibilities and, by systematic trial and improvement, they may arrive at a solution.

input   = 1
output = 7

input   = 10
output = 970

input   = 5
output =

Using a spreadsheet (Table 17.2) will necessarily mean that the pupil's approach is a systematic one. Also, the learners will be starting to think algebraically as they instruct the spreadsheet to print a number in a cell which is equal to a function of a number in a different cell.

Table 17.2

Input	Square	×10	×3	Subtract
1	1	10	3	7
2	4	40	6	34
3	9	90	9	81
4	16	160	12	148
5	25	250	15	235
6	36	360	18	342
7	49	490	21	469
8	64	640	24	616
9	81	810	27	783
10	100	1,000	30	970

If pupils are able to use algebraic notation and they are familiar with Logo, they may be able to write one procedure to represent the function and another to create the table (Table 17.3).

Table 17.3

to f :x	table 1	
op 10 * :x* :x−3 * :x		
end	1	7
	2	34
to table :num	3	81
if :num>10 [stop]	4	148
(print :num f :num)	5	235
table :num + 1	6	342
end	7	469
	8	616
	9	783
	10	970

One solution is already clear but, both with the spreadsheet and with Logo, the pupils will be able to alter the table to find another one. In both cases it is an easy matter to change the starting number for the table or the increment.

Another possibility might be to use a graph plotter and to zoom in on the points where the curve crosses the line $y = 81$ (Figure 17.3).

Finally, if the pupils are in the sixth-form and they have started to learn the calculus, they might want to use a symbol manipulator to find the differential coefficient of $10x^2−3x$, and then the value of x when this differential is equal to zero.

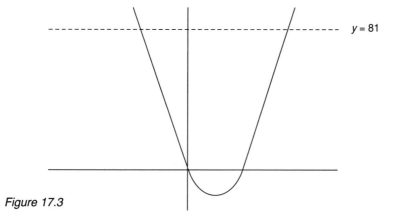

Figure 17.3

When all learners have their own machines they will often need to make their own decisions about appropriate software and, as teachers, we will need to help them to become more independent. Faced with mathematical problems, learners of the future will need to know whether and when to use the computer and which software packages to choose.

Another fundamental issue which we will need to address is how best to organise our classrooms. At present, computers are still relatively scarce and so it is not often feasible to allow pupils to work individually; the resource provision determines the classroom methodology. It is generally recognised that computers can stimulate valuable discussion between groups of pupils and we may need to be very careful not to lose this benefit. Also, there are occasions when a teacher needs to work with a single computer in front of a larger group. Present lap-tops have screens which can only be viewed comfortably from particular angles. Perhaps we will need to keep one or two desktops in each room so that groups of four or five can work profitably. Alternatively, perhaps the technology will improve so that better screen definition is also provided with portable computers.

Personal technology has the capacity to change the pupils' approach to much of their mathematics. It is stating the obvious to say that a learner will be influenced by a machine if he or she always has ready access to it. We already know how pupils who own graphic calculators might use a graphical method rather than symbols to solve a trigonometric identity. They adapt their approaches and their methods to exploit the strengths of the machine. Experience will teach us exactly how pupils will benefit from the freedom to load Logo, spreadsheets, databases, computer algebra systems and dynamic geometry packages whenever they want to use them. What is clear now is that new tools generate new solutions, and when all learners have personal calculators or computers (the distinction between them is becoming increasingly blurred) teachers must expect pupils to adapt their approaches to the curriculum accordingly.

CONCLUSION

This chapter has emphasised that the new technologies will fundamentally alter the mathematics curriculum but that we should be wary not to allow the generation of plenty of data to replace pupils' explanations. Microworlds may be the way to standardise the software interface and access to hardware will be improved dramatically.

The main technological themes in this chapter have been power and accessibility. Computer software is becoming more powerful at an alarming rate, and in the future we should also expect more access, in terms of both the ease of use of the software and the availability of the hardware. These issues have been important since the first computer was used in a school classroom. While it has always been recognised that the larger software applications ought to be both powerful and accessible, in the past it has rarely been possible to achieve both of these features. With the single exception of Logo, we have always had to make difficult choices: we could either use a package which was simple and friendly but was lacking in certain important areas, or one which allowed us to do everything that was necessary but was not designed to be handled by learners.

As increasing quantities of memory become cheaper some aspects of the debate become less critical. For instance, it is beyond doubt that powerful symbol manipulators will soon be available on small machines owned by many students. However, while education is under-funded, we may find that we rely increasingly on the standards of industry and commerce and that educational software will not be as readily available. This is a much more open question and we must hope that we can soon have the microworlds and the dynamic geometry packages which are not of interest outside the world of education as well as the symbol manipulators which industry certainly will promote.

NOTES

1 The most popular graph plotters for computers found in schools today are probably MousePlotter (Shell Centre, Nottingham University) for the Archimedes and Omnigraph (Software Production Associates) for the RM Nimbus.
2 Derive (Soft Warehouse, Honolulu) is available (and affordable) for PCs and there is also a version for one of the Hewlett-Packard calculators. Mathematica (Wolfram Research Ltd, Long Hanborough, Oxon) and Maple (Symbolic Computation Group, University of Waterloo, Ontario, Canada) run on Apple Macintosh and PC machines but they will need to be powerful computers which are probably out of range for most schools in 1993.
3 CAN (Calculator-Aware Number) began as a curriculum development project associated with PrIME. The main emphasis of the work was to give children in primary schools unlimited access to calculators and to encourage free exploration in place of the teaching of formal algorithms.

4 Cabri-géomètre (University of Grenoble) and Geometer's Sketchpad (Key Curriculum Press) both run on the Apple Macintosh and Cabri-géomètre also runs on PC compatibles.

5 A number of mathematical Logo microworlds have been published in the United Kingdom to run with Logotron Logo on Archimedes and BBC computers and with RM Logo on the Nimbus: LogoBase, LogoPlotter and LogoSheet (Logo 2000, Stanley Thornes); LogoGrid and LogoTile (NCET); Locus, Multi, SqGrid, IsoGrid and Buggy (Logo Microworlds, Association of Teachers of Mathematics); 3D Logo and Newton (Longman-Logotron); LogoMetric (to be published).

6 Boxer is the computational environment which may succeed Logo. It is available now, but not yet on machines which schools can afford. For a full description of the software see C. Hoyles and R. Noss (1992) *'Introducing Boxer'*, *Micromath* 8(3).

REFERENCE

DES (1982) *Mathematics Counts, Report of the Committee of Inquiry into the Teaching of Mathematics in Schools*, under the Chairmanship of Dr W. H. Cockcroft, London: HMSO.

Part VI

Can we improve teaching and learning?

In Chapter 18, I examine some tasks teachers can introduce into their lessons to try to increase pupil autonomy; to encourage them to think about what they are learning, how they are learning it and whether they understand what they are learning. These tasks are not necessarily restricted to the mathematics classroom and indeed they have been used as strategies in all areas of the curriculum, but in the chapter here I have attempted to demonstrate the possible effects on learning mathematics.

Chapters 19 and 20 explore ways in which teachers working together can improve the quality of pupils' experience in the classroom. Chapter 19 highlights the fact that 'working together' can encompass many frameworks: a school mathematics department working on a new scheme of work; a support group working either on their own or with outside facilitators such as advisory teachers; funded research projects; and involvement with a publisher who is developing a new mathematics scheme. Laurinda Brown describes the benefits of working in some of these ways and then, in Chapter 20, Sue Burns gives the background to one project in particular, the Nuffield Advanced Level Mathematics Project, explaining how practice has developed and how teacher involvement has enhanced the work of the project.

Chapter 18

Understanding

Michelle Selinger

Many teachers report that they suddenly have the feeling that they are the only person in the classroom who cares whether the pupils can do mathematics or not. In front of them there is a sea of faces waiting for the next instruction. The pupils seem to be saying:

'You are in charge.'
'Give me something to do and I will do it.'
'When I've finished this, you can give me something else to do.'

These teachers are unsure whether it arises because their pupils do not see any point in the mathematical topic or whether it is because they have no interest in mathematics at all. The teachers also believe that this cannot be a productive way to learn mathematics, nor a way to discover the power of the subject. They want their pupils to find out that working on mathematics can be challenging and exciting; that the connections and similarities between different aspects of mathematics can be a constant source of amazement and new insights.

Before reading on, the reader is invited to construct a map of how pupils learn mathematics. This chapter describes some ways teachers have tried to encourage pupils to *want* to learn and to start asking questions about the mathematics they were doing. Their methods are often indirect, relying more on stimulating pupils to reflect on their work than on setting challenging mathematical problems.

TWO FORMS OF UNDERSTANDING

An article by Richard Skemp (1976) outlined two types of understanding, 'instrumental' and 'relational'. Instrumental understanding he described as 'rules without reasons'; $A = L \times B$, $a^2 + b^2 = c^2$, 'borrowing' in subtraction, 'change the side, change the sign'. On the other hand, pupils who had relational understanding would be able to reconstruct forgotten facts and techniques: for example, they would be able to demonstrate, perhaps by means of a diagram of a right-angled triangle on which squares have been constructed on each side, the relationship between the areas of the squares of the three sides. Being able to quote rules like Pythgoras' in parrot fashion does not constitute full understanding and a story of Skemp's highlights this strongly. He tells of a young child returning home from school and reporting that he now knew his four times table. 'Well done,' said his mother, 'so tell me, if there are seven children at a party and they are each given four balloons, how many balloons will there be?' The child looked confused and his face fell as he said to his mother 'But we haven't done balloons yet!'.

Skemp outlines three advantages for teaching instrumental understanding:

1. Within its own context, *instrumental mathematics is usually easier to understand*; sometimes much easier. Some topics, such as multiplying two negative numbers together or dividing by a fractional number, are difficult to understand relationally. 'Minus times minus equals plus' and to divide by a fraction you 'turn it upside down and multiply' are easily remembered rules. If what is wanted is a page of right answers, instrumental mathematics can provide this more quickly and easily.

2. *So the rewards are more immediate and more apparent.* It is nice to get a page of right answers, and we must not under-rate the importance of the feelings of success which pupils get from this . . .

3. Just because less knowledge is involved, *one can often get the right answer more quickly* and reliably by instrumental thinking than relational. This difference is so marked that even relational mathematicians often use instrumental thinking.

(Skemp 1976: 23)

However, he argues that relational understanding can be

more adaptable to new tasks. Recently I was trying to help a boy who had learnt to multiply two decimal fractions together by dropping the decimal point, multiplying as for whole numbers, and re-inserting the decimal point to give the same total number of digits after the decimal point as there were before. This is a handy method if you know why it works. Through no fault of his own, the child did not; and not unreasonably, applied this method to division of decimals. By this method $4.8 \div 0.6$ came to 0.08 . . . He was simply extrapolating from what he already knew. But relational understanding, by knowing not only what method worked but why, would have enabled him to relate the method to the new problem, and possibly adapt the method to new problems. Instrumental understanding necessitates memorising which problems a method works for and which not, and also learning a new method for each new class of problems. So the first advantage of relational mathematics leads to:

2. *It is easier to remember.* There is a seeming paradox here, in that it is certainly harder to learn. It is certainly easier for pupils to learn that 'area of a triangle = $\frac{1}{2}$ base $\times$ height' than to learn why this is so. But they

then have to learn separate rules for triangles, rectangles, parallelograms, trapeziums; whereas relational understanding consists partly in seeing all of these in relation to the area of a rectangle. It is still desirable to know the separate rules, one does not want to have to derive them afresh everytime. But knowing also how they are inter-related enables one to remember them as parts of a connected whole, which is easier.

(Skemp 1976: 23)

It might be thought that pupils would be attracted to relational understanding because it minimises their memory load and so it might provide the key to a way forward in motivating pupils to learn more effectively. But encouraging pupils to learn more relationally can be problematic for both teachers and their pupils; the investment required to make connections is greater than in instrumental learning and the content of the curriculum needs to be considered so that connections can be easily and readily established. The way a teacher works may affect the way their pupils want to learn. A test can be set in such a way that instrumental understanding will not be useful for all of the questions and relational understanding is required in order to make sense of the questions.

MAKING CONNECTIONS

There are several ways in which relational understanding can be developed to help pupils make connections and which can be used to help understand concepts. Pupils can be set a range of tasks; some which will help them increase their understanding of concepts within a topic and some which will encourage them to stand back from their work, view it as a whole and examine the way in which they make sense of new concepts. It is such tasks which include the use of concept maps, matching statements, marking fictitious homework or using metaphors to describe learning which form the focus of this chapter. I have tried several of these and find that although some tasks appear different from normal classroom practice they can be successfully integrated.

Concept Maps

Concept maps present a method of visualising concepts and the relationships between them. Because concept maps are explicit, overt representations of the concepts and relationships we hold, they allow teachers and pupils to exchange views on why a particular relationship is valid, and to recognise missing linkages that suggest a need for further experience. Because they contain externalised expressions of relationships, they are effective tools for highlighting misconceptions.

Concept maps are more than a mere overview, they can be used as tools

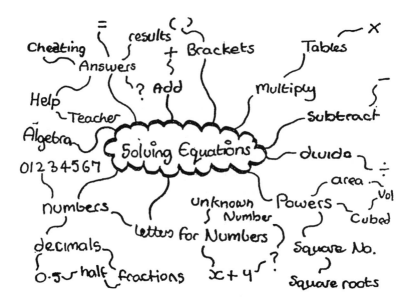

Figure 18.1

for negotiating meanings. They offer a method by which the relationships between concepts can be shared, discussed and negotiated. One of the most important single factors influencing learning is what the learner already knows; consequently many teachers recognise that it is useful to have some idea of what their pupils already know (or misunderstand) before beginning a new topic. By using concept maps with a class, I can be provided with some of the necessary information which will help me decide on a starting point that will involve all my pupils in building from what they know.

One approach I used with concept maps was to select a key idea from a new topic and to then invite pupils to construct a map showing all the concepts and relationships they can link to this key concept (Figure 18.1). At other times, in order to assess the kind and extent of previous learning, I selected ten to fifteen concepts from a new topic of study and asked pupils to construct a concept map using some or all of these concepts, and to add other concepts they think might be relevant. As a further extension, I sometimes ask pupils to construct three or four sentences linking two, three or more of the concepts.

Heather Scott (1991) introduced her pupils to concept maps through the term 'mathematical maps'.

A mathematical map would consist of 'towns' and various connecting routes. The towns could represent a variety of items . . . concepts knowledge, skills or processes. The routes too may be symbolic of many things . . . a connection, a need, or a particular method.

(Scott 1991: 5)

Scott found that pupils' maps 'highlighted understandings and misunderstandings as well as vital gaps in areas of mathematics which would need to be closed for progress to be made'. Pupils were able to add towns and routes as they learnt and made new connections or understood a concept more fully and the teacher's role became that of provider of 'tickets to travel to more towns and upon different routes on the map'.

Once the notion of constructing concept maps has been established with pupils, concept maps can become a tool for them to use when they are faced with a concept they appear to have forgotten. They can be encouraged to try and recreate their understanding by referring back to a concept map constructed earlier or to try to reconstruct their understanding through a new mental concept map. Pupils can delete 'towns' or change their meaning as a result of new learning.

Matching statements

In the task of matching statements, I present pupils with a list of mathematical statements or number names and ask them to sort these in any way they like but to justify the way they have been sorted. For example, this might be a list of fraction names written as numbers and words, decimal names, ratios and percentages. In initial sorts many groups of pupils put the statements into separate sets of fractions, decimals, ratios etc., so I then invite them to sort them in another way. This time some pupils start to group the equivalent fraction with its decimal, percentage and ratio, e.g. three-quarters, $\frac{3}{4}$, 0.75, 75% and 3:4 can be grouped together. I then invite pupils to share their groupings with others and to search for similarities and differences and to point out where they think a grouping may be incorrect. A consensus as to what the correct grouping ought to be must then be reached. As a result of these groupings and re-groupings, pupils who had always seen concepts such as decimals, percentages and fractions as unconnected ways of representing types of numbers can now start to gain insights into the connections that will help them recognise percentages as another way of writing fractions or fractions as another way of writing decimals. In other words their relational understanding will be enhanced.

Marking homework

Another way in which I help pupils to make connections or to see where a misconception has occurred is to give groups a 'fictitious' homework to mark. This might have been compiled from errors made by a class in a previous homework that I have collated and rewritten to ensure anonymity of the authors (and to avoid embarrassment). As a result, I hope that 'cognitive conflict' might occur in which the pupils become aware of their own difficulties through the discussion and arguments that are generated. They see errors they might also have made themselves and they are caused to rethink their understanding in order to make sense of the errors and also to work on the correct solutions. Having to justify and explain will help pupils to make use of and enhance both their relational and their instrumental understanding.

AWARENESS OF LEARNING

Asking pupils to consider how they learn or to think about one new thing they learnt in a lesson can also help them consider the learning process. Below is a transcript of part of an interview I had with two 12-year-old girls about their learning.

MS: When you are doing a problem, do you ask yourself whether you are on the right lines?

LISA: You do, don't you? Because when you're in the middle of something and you're not sure, you do say, 'Am I doing this right?'

MS: Do you ask yourself if you understand?

KATYA: Yes, I suppose so, cos if you don't, you go and ask the teacher and she'll tell you. If you don't think about it, if you don't ask yourself if you understand you wouldn't go and tell the teacher, would you?

MS: Do you learn with a partner or a group of three or four?

LISA: Yes, I learn with a partner.

KATYA: Yes, that might be it, I don't learn when I'm with a group of three or four because everyone starts talking, so you don't get much done.

LISA: I think I learn best when I work with a partner because you have to discuss. It's easier to discuss with two people because you don't have as much argument.

KATYA: I think I like working with a partner best, I don't like working on my own at all.

MS: What do you like best about working with a partner? Say, comparing answers?

LISA: Yes.

MS: Does that help you learn?

KATYA: Yes because you go 'I've got 94 and she's got 93' and then you go 'OK we'll see who's right' and do it again, and it helps you get things right and helps you learn.

MS: Do you learn when you listen to others?

KATYA: Yes, because if they got it right and they're explaining to you then you're learning.

MS: Is it better than a teacher explaining it to you?

LISA: Yes, because they're the same age as you and they use the words that you know. Basically they know all that you know . . . so when they explain it to you . . . it'll be easier to understand.

MS: Does it help if you are shown how to do something?

LISA: Yes, then, because if they talk to you, you might not get it in your head, but if they show it to you, by writing it down or whatever (if you're allowed to do that in your maths book) then you understand it more clearly like dividing a chocolate bar into thirds.

MS: Does repetition help you learn?

KATYA: No, that doesn't help you learn, cos when you're doing your maths book and you've got a whole page of timesing, it doesn't help you learn cos you think 'this is boring', you get about two done in a day.

LISA: It does help with your spellings though, doesn't it? If you do a spelling over and over again you learn how to do it eventually.

MS: Does discussion help you learn?

KATYA: Yes, I think so, because you listen to other people's thoughts about it and then you put them together and you decide I think she's right and you sort of mix them up and see what you get until you think each other's right.

MS: If you are not understanding, does it help trying to work it out for yourself?

LISA: Yes, because if you've not understood something and then you can do it, you feel you've really achieved something and you remember it. You think it's the first time I've achieved that, I've really stuck my teeth into that and you think, I'll remember that one.

MS: Does trying several ways to do a difficult problem help?

LISA: I suppose it does in a way.

KATYA: It means you've learnt the first way, because you think about the first thing you've done and you . . .

LISA: If you've worked out all the ways to do it then you've got more chance of remembering what you had than if you had just learnt one way, you'd have more things in your brain to remember.

Finding out how pupils view mathematical learning can often open the door to their fears and concerns as well as revealing what it is about mathematics that motivates them. Another way of exposing their views is to ask pupils to consider metaphors for learning mathematics. For example, learning mathematics is like . . .

- wondering [*sic*] through a maze
- doing a jigsaw
- climbing a mountain
- a flower blooming
- filling a bucket

I recall a lesson in which I tried to find out about a new set of Year 10 pupils' views of mathematics by introducing the idea of metaphors to describe their learning. Rather than give the pupils the bald statement, I had some cartoons illustrating three or four of these metaphors mounted on card. I gave each group two of the cartoons and asked them to consider the following questions for each one and write a response.

1 In what ways do you agree with this statement?
2 In what ways do you disagree with this statement?
3 Try to think of a time when you felt like this about learning mathematics. Describe the topic you were doing and what you were learning when you felt like this.

The pupils were reluctant to start but once they started talking about each cartoon, the discussion seemed to be very valuable. One girl started to laugh and said, 'my bucket's got a great big hole in it'.

The completed sheets certainly showed depth of thought I had not anticipated and highlighted some of the difficulties they were experiencing particularly in the areas of algebra and loci. Here are some of the responses the pupils gave.

Learning mathematics is like . . . building a wall:

> You add a new brick every lesson, as a brick represents knowledge and cement represents understanding . . . sometimes we have a lot of bricks but no cement to stick them together.
>
> By the time you reach the top of the wall some of the knowledge is forgotten, and where we didn't understand, there may be bricks missing.

. . . being a sponge:

> learning maths is not really like this because when reading a book about maths it goes in one ear and out of the other, but when working something out practically, you thoroughly understand it.
>
> I feel like this when revising for a test.

We all shared the comments and then I invited the class to invent their own metaphors and explain why the metaphor was appropriate. The following are examples of some of the responses. Learning mathematics is like:

> a gold ring . . . because you never think you will get it, but when you do, you can be very proud of it;
> a rock . . . flipping hard;

a tree . . . one minute you are upright and fine, and the next minute, when
the wind blows, you are confused and sad;

a foggy day . . . sometimes it is clear, sometimes it is not;

making a cake . . . when you mix the right things together, the result is
perfect.

This lesson had allowed the pupils to find a way to articulate their feelings
about learning mathematics, to express their difficulties and anxieties as
well as their enjoyment. I think it helped them to become more comfortable
in mathematics lessons because they were more aware of how others felt about
mathematics and realised they were not alone. The metaphors had also
provided the means by which they could describe their learning in the future.
As a teacher I was more aware of how individuals viewed mathematics; I
gained some insight as to whether they viewed mathematics as a collection of
facts and skills to be learned and practiced (instrumental understanding) or
whether they saw it as a collection of inter-related concepts which could be
drawn on when a new concept was introduced to help make sense of it and to
incorporate it into their understanding (relational understanding). I was able
to adapt my teaching style to help individual pupils overcome anxieties which
had been highlighted as a result of the exercise and to work on the idea of
learning mathematics more relationally. It also helped me to discuss and
describe individual ways of learning when the class was working on mathematical activities. I could say to one pupil, 'you are in a maze today, how do
you think you could get out of it?', or to another, 'you're trying to soak up too
much in one go, think about how you could wring out your sponge without
losing what you have learnt so far'. By using metaphors which both the pupils
and I understood, we could talk about their learning. Alternatively pupils
could describe their difficulties to me with a metaphor so that we immediately
had some shared understanding of these difficulties. It offered me an insight
into each pupil's thinking and enabled me to help them find a suitable strategy
to resolve the problem.

SUMMARY

Instead of summarising how I believe these strategies have offered pupils an
opportunity to learn and understand mathematics relationally, I invite the
reader to reflect on how their own concept map of pupil learning could be
reformulated by reading this chapter.

NOTE

Much of the work described in this chapter is based on research undertaken at the
Shell Centre for Mathematics Education for the ESRC funded project 'Pupils'
Awareness of Learning'.

REFERENCES

Scott, H. (1991) 'Towards differentiation in mathematics education', *Mathematics Teaching* 134: 2–5.

Skemp, R. (1976) 'Relational understanding and instrumental understanding', *Mathematics Teaching* 77: 20–6.

Chapter 19

Working together

Laurinda Brown

When you were first responsible for teaching a whole class, how in control did you feel? Commonly, PGCE students report feeling that the time passed all too quickly and they felt they were just responding to the problems of individuals within the class. There is a tension between attending to the actual responses of these living pupils to your material and a desire on your part to stay with the security of working with the material you have prepared in the way that you prepared it. How can you work at all within the many complex, inter-related facets of teaching and learning?

I was struck by the following words from a booklet written for people who are practising playing the piano.

> Concentration cuts out and autopilot takes over when you practise without a purpose, be it to develop a particular skill or to realize an interpretation of the music etc. Whatever you are playing at the keyboard, always aim to be *inventive* and *attentive*.
>
> (Asher 1991: 31)

The particular skill you might have decided to focus on, your purpose, could be questioning techniques. Your purpose would provide a filter (see Chapter 9) through which you would view the lesson and interactions. You would attend to particular events and, as well as practising previously prepared questioning routines, you would aim to be inventive and try out other possibilities in response to the pupils' contributions. Left to your own devices you would in this way learn through experience as you become more aware of what works for you in practice. But your mathematics teaching is not done in isolation from all the other mathematics teachers that there are or ever have been! What ways are there of working together to improve teaching and learning?

One way can be to work with a group of teachers who share your interests. I will say more about the various opportunities for finding or creating such a group of people later, but first of all an example. I was a member of a group of teachers who met around the time of the introduction of the GCSE examinations. One of the questions which this group of teachers was working on was 'What are the necessary experiences in the first three years of secondary education to prepare the way for GCSE coursework?' This rather long question became shortened to 'Necessary experiences': we had been interested in the 'handshaking problem' because of an article in *Mathematics Teaching* (Billington and Evans 1987) and had been talking about ways in which we might introduce the problem to a class. We decided to go away and use 'handshaking' with a Year 7 class. In case you would like to try out the problem for yourself, before reading about what happened in two of our classrooms, here it is described with the words Dorothy Buerk used when working with successful women who avoid mathematics.

> If the six of us wanted to meet by shaking each other's hands, how would you envision the number of handshakes?
>
> How would *you* envision the number of handshakes? Try to envision it in more than one way. Think about it for a moment. What questions follow for you as you think about 'hand-shaking'?
>
> (Buerk 1982: 20)

Lesson 1

I was aware that I did not allow enough time for some pupils to think about a problem before directing the activity. Silences always feel so long. What follows is a written account of a lesson with a Year 7 class where, to give myself something to do, I told the pupils that I was going to write everything down – and did. This simple device had the effect of not only keeping me quiet for longer, but also of giving us all the opportunity of checking back over what had been said earlier in the lesson.

> I want everybody to shake hands with everybody else.
>
> (Chaos.)
>
> Put up your hands if you can tell me how many times you shook hands?
>
> 13 times.
>
> 15 times – I shook hands with her 3 times.
>
> Then you didn't do as you were told. I want everybody to shake hands with everybody else.
>
> (More chaos.)
>
> How many handshakes occurred in this room? Not just your own, all of them?
>
> (SILENCE.)
>
> Miss, what's 14 14s?
>
> (I gave out a calculator.)
>
> 162, 159, 169, 196, 169, 196.
>
> Put up your hand if you can tell me how you worked out your answer.

Times.

Pardon?

169.

Times what?

13 times 14.

Put up your hand anyone else who could tell me how they worked it out. Is it 13 × 12, 14 × 14, 13 × 14? We've got lots of ideas. How can we check who is right?

Work it out.

Do it all over again and each person count their handshakes, then add it all together.

OK. Off you go then.

(Chaos again – with counting – pupil wrote on the board 13, 13, 13, 13, until there were 14 of them.)

How many handshakes took place?

162, 196, 182, 169, 182.

What sum did you do?

Add.

Times.

Times what?

Times 14 by 13.

Would someone use the calculator and check?

(182 written on the board.)

Well, I still want to know how many handshakes!

You can't just count for yourself?

26

Why?

Mandy shook Subiya, Subiya shook me, I shook . . . add it all up.

Mandy shook my hand and I shook Mandy's hand.

Stand up and do it.

(Two people shook hands.)

That was two shakes.

I said count how many handshakes.

When two people shake hands, both of them count that shake, but it's really only one shake. So, the answer is half of 182.

If we had a hundred people, how many handshakes if everybody shakes hands with everybody else?

20, 50, 15 !!!

Let's recap. There are fourteen of you, how did we work out how many handshakes?

13 times 14.

(I wrote on the board:

Question: How many handshakes when we each shake hands with everybody in the class?

Method: We added up how many handshakes each person did. 14 lots of 13 = 182. We halved our answer, because we found that we had counted each handshake twice.)

How many in class?

14.

How many hands did you each shake?

13.

Why?

Because we didn't shake hands with you.

Because we didn't shake hands with ourselves.

Now 100 people.

13 times 100.

99 times 100.

(On the board: (100 x 99) then $\frac{1}{2}$.)

247 people?

(247 x 246) $\frac{1}{2}$.

362 people?

(362 x 361) $\frac{1}{2}$.

Now, what if we have any number? Any number times . . .?

One less than the number.

Then. . .

Halve it. I'm too lazy to write . . . any number times one less than any . . . Let's just write n for number, then we can write . . . $(n \times (n-1))\frac{1}{2}$.

Phew! I felt that I was pushing my luck with the formula. I had the recap and results written on the board but rubbed it all out before they wrote up their work.

Morna Kell, Pen Park School, Avon

Lesson 2

I started the lesson with the comment: I want everybody in the class to shake hands with everybody else. After a moment's hesitation there was pandemonium for 5 minutes. I then asked: If we had done it properly, how many handshakes took place? They wrote a number in their books and also how they got their answer. When everybody had an answer I wrote all answers on the board. None were correct. I then asked people to read out an explanation. One child stated:

There are 25 people in the class so I did 25 times 25.

A class discussion followed.

But you don't shake hands with yourself.

25 times 24.

Incorrect.

25 add 24 add 23 add 22 all the way to 1.

Why?

Because the first person shakes hands with everybody else. Then he is out, the next shakes with 24 then is out etc.

But the first only shakes hands with 24, so you start with 24.

At this point I'd noticed that a lot of the class had become lost, so I asked how we can make this problem easier. Eventually we decided to start with less people and work up.

I asked them to work out the answer and write down clearly how they worked it out. I went round helping those who were confused to get started.

At the end of the lesson everyone had the pattern given in Table 19.1. So, 25 people have $24 + 23 + 22 + \ldots + 2 + 1 = 300$ handshakes.

Table 19.1

Number of people	Number of handshakes	Pattern
1	0	
2	1	
3	3	1 + 2
4	6	1 + 2 + 3
5	10	1 + 2 + 3 + 4

Some pupils had written up the discussion and calculated the answer and also worked on the same problem for the whole of Year 7, 304 pupils.

One pupil had written that the number of handshakes was 25×24 divided by 2 because each person shakes hands with 24 others but divided by 2 because each handshake was counted twice.

Since the lesson was 35 minutes long they had to finish writing up their solutions for homework.

I realised afterwards that I was encouraging two different systems of solution.

1 *The thinking solution* – by thinking about the structure of the problem and writing down a formula. In this case:
number of handshakes $= n + (n-1) + (n-2) + \ldots + 3 + 2 + 1$
or

number of handshakes $= \dfrac{n(n-1)}{2}$

2 *The pattern solution* – by building up a pattern of numbers as shown in Figure 19.1.

I feel that both systems have an important part to play in maths and in the approach to the 'investigative' problem, but what concerned me most afterwards was: How do you move from one to the other?

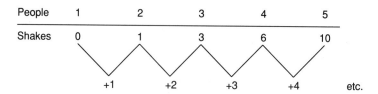

From

x	y
1	0
2	1
3	3
4	6

to $y=x(x-1)/2$ seems a huge step, and what comes in the middle?

John Carr, St George School, Avon

The following observations aim to give some insight into the way this group worked.

1 Even though a group of people talks around a particular problem, e.g. handshaking, and thinks about ways of tackling the idea in the classroom, what actually happens will vary from teacher to teacher. When the group decides to try the idea out, the writing allows sharing of differences and similarities. The writings provoke discussion when the group next meets. With just two people involved from the same department, say, especially when they are both joining in each other's lessons, this might be able to be done by talking through what happened. Here the teachers all worked in different schools.

2 One similarity in the two lessons is the response of 'chaos' or 'pandemonium' to the initial question. In these cases the teachers are recording their reactions to their pupils' initial floundering, especially in consideration of assessment of Attainment Target 1. It is impossible to achieve the higher levels of this attainment target if the problem is structured for the pupils.

3 The writing is also important for the individual teachers in another way. Writing seems to have the function of clarifying and extending thoughts as the writers reflect on their experiences, e.g. from Lesson 2:

> I realised afterwards that I was encouraging two different systems of solution . . . the thinking solution . . . the pattern solution.

These thoughts having arisen in the process of individual reflection also provide discussion items for the wider group which can perhaps then identify new tasks and challenges to work on. The task of 'How to move from one to the other?' – from pattern solution to thinking solution – fed eventually into the work of a group whose focus was specifically 'Algebraic experiences in the first three years'.

4 Each individual is concerned with their own personal agenda of improving their teaching in parallel to group tasks. In Lesson 1 there is an account of a teacher applying one strategy in order to change a particular behaviour pattern. The handshaking problem becomes the vehicle to try out a different style. The writing records the outcomes and the group's discussion focuses on when we direct activities, why, and to what purpose. The detailed write-up allows specific work on questioning techniques and styles of responding to be undertaken.

5 These particular groups were run as part of a curriculum development project and groups were formed for two main reasons:
- in response to government initiatives, e.g. GCSE, National Curriculum, TVEI (top-down);
- from the current concerns of practising teachers (bottom-up).

In effect, most of the groups arose from a mixture of motives, such as a current concern for questioning techniques because of teacher assessment for the National Curriculum.

What was and still is important in initiating such groups is that there is a common focus and, in these cases, a common purpose of producing some support materials for teachers or resources for pupils within a particular time limit. In this way, there could be commitment to the group for a period without the thought that it would drag on forever.

6 In sharing the lesson write-ups and joint tasks, the teachers were often surprised by what they read or heard from other schools and how teaching styles varied. These jolts are useful in that they allow the re-working of previously unchallenged assumptions. Both the lessons described above were single periods although one comment at the time provoked the following comment: 'Someone in my department said they couldn't do handshaking in less than three weeks!' What was it that was being done? Perhaps within that time the teacher was tackling something of the links between the pattern solution and the thinking solution? Is the focus on that problem (handshaking) or the mathematical ideas that are generated from tackling it?

7 Sharing reading from sources other than each other's writing can be equally effective. A book available from Jonathan Press on *Finite Differences* (Seymour and Shedd 1973) and an Open University booklet on *Expressing Generality PM751* (Mason 1988) both have useful ideas to contribute to the work started by John Carr's question to his pupils.

So, if you want to improve your teaching and the learning of your pupils, one way is to work together with other teachers.

What sort of groups are possible?

1 It could be that the department in which you work already gives over parts of meetings to sharing the experiences of the teachers as questions arise. If not, there might be someone else within the department who you naturally find it easy to talk with about your (plural) work. Try some joint activity with them as a focus arises naturally.

2 If your department uses a particular scheme there might be local support groups organised so that the experiences of different departments can be shared and resources pooled. The School Mathematics Project (SMP) would be one energetic example where the materials themselves have been created by working groups of practising teachers. Look out for SMP 16–19, SMP 11–16 and SMP G Users' Groups in which teachers using the materials often meet locally.

3 Use your contacts with people learning to teach in other schools to share ideas, perhaps by writing to each other.

4 The Association of Teachers of Mathematics (ATM) and the Mathematical Association (MA) are national organisations which might have local branches in your area. Look out for meeting dates and use the opportunity of going to a meeting to find out what you can about local groupings and interests. You could suggest your own.

   Nationally there are working groups of teachers meeting through these organisations to address many issues. Find out more about these through the pages of their newsletters or journals, or by writing to their offices. The ATM and MA offices would also be useful contacts if you have other specific interests and want to find out if there is an organisation to support it – history of maths? Yes, a separate group. Research ideas? Yes, again a separate group.

What might the group do?

You might meet together to:

1 produce a product
   producing resource materials, e.g. a mathematical magazine to be sold to pupils in local schools, primary and secondary, to encourage work across phases

2 share practice
   SMP Users' Groups

3 explore approaches to topics
   the teaching of algebra

4 develop theories through practice
   teacher intervention

5 do some mathematics together
   problem solving or updating mathematical ideas such as decision mathematics or statistics

Who with?

The only issue here is whether you work with strangers or friends. Perhaps both? People you work with like this often become friends over time anyway, but you probably learn more where you're being challenged the most and this probably means strangers rather than friends!? Why not both?

So, what are the questions or themes that engage you? Can you find others to work with so that you learn both through your own experiences and by working together? If you find that you are interested in starting your own group you might find the book *Develop Your Teaching* (The Mathematical Association 1991) (which itself was written as the work of such a group!) useful as a focus for finding out about strategies to facilitate its work.

NOTES

ATM, 7 Shaftesbury Street, Derby DE3 8YB; The Mathematical Association, 259 London Road, Leicester LE2 3BE.

REFERENCES

Asher, R. (1991) *Back to the Keyboard*, Bedford: IFS.

Billington, J and Evans, P. (1987) 'Levels of knowing 2 "The handshake" ', *Mathematics Teaching* 120: 12–19.

Buerk, D. (1982) 'An experience with some able women who avoid mathematics', *For the Learning of Mathematics* 3 (2): 20.

Mason, J. (1988) *Expressing Generality PM751*, Milton Keynes: Open University Press.

Seymour, D. and Shedd, M. (1973) *Finite Differences*, Palo Alto: Dale Seymour Publications.

The Mathematical Association (1991) *Develop Your Teaching*, Oxford: Stanley Thornes.

Chapter 20

Changing A level mathematics

Sue Burns

INTRODUCTION: WHY NUFFIELD ADVANCED MATHEMATICS?

When the Nuffield Advanced Mathematics project was set up in 1990, there was a perceived need for change which could be described as having three components: first, there was the need to respond to changes in technology; second, students of A level mathematics were seen to be very passive; third, there were not enough students studying mathematics beyond GCSE. In response to these needs, and the evidence available, I would like to focus on the following four areas of change.

1 *Technology*   Appropriate use of technology could make the content of advanced mathematics accessible to and more enjoyable for a wider range of students.

2 *Content and context*   The emphasis of advanced mathematics could be on building good intuitive understanding of concepts, through experimentation and through using graphical and numerical tools to support analytical approaches. Priorities could adapt; for example, the role of discrete mathematics and approximate methods could grow in comparison with the role of calculus. Mathematical modelling processes and data handling techniques which are widely used in industry, research and commerce could be incorporated into the curriculum. Finally, rigour could be developed through algorithmics and the practicalities of programming.

3 *Ways of working*   Students could be encouraged to work cooperatively, to take more responsibility for their learning and to become increasingly independent in their use of resources, including the teacher. In particular, if it is assumed that students supplement contact time with as much time again in 'private study', better use could be made of the learning time (at least 50 per cent) when the teacher is not available.

4 *Assessment*   The use of assessment devices 'fit for the purpose' could promote investigative and exploratory work, reading and writing about mathematics and the appropriate use of technology.

I shall examine in detail the first two of these, technology and content and context, in relation to the project and within the content of reforms in A level mathematics.

At the time of writing, the SEAC maths committee is involved in producing a new A level core to take effect for the cohort of students coming through the new National Curriculum and starting advanced courses in 1994. The old core, issued in 1983, concentrated on algebra and calculus, and prescribed 40 per cent of an A level syllabus. It has generally been regarded as over full, and has discouraged change in practice at A level to match the changing practices in the 11–16 curriculum. In addition, the emphasis on calculus has been regarded as inappropriate for many in the light of changing needs in industry and business.

In 1985 a committee working under the auspices of the Joint Mathematical Council arranged a conference to explore the implications of new technology for A level. Major A level developers including MEI, SMP and the Northern Ireland Further Maths project were represented.

From 1986, the School Mathematics Project (SMP) embarked on its major reform now available as '16–19 Mathematics'. This has been matched by developments by MEI and Wessex. Since 1988 there has also been a pilot A level in West Sussex which involves 100 per cent portfolio assessment.

In 1986, a subgroup of those involved in the JMC conference made a bid to government to fund a major new development of A level mathematics. The bid was delayed by the expected report of the Higginson committee, and then overtaken by other priorities after the rejection of the Higginson report.

The same group then made an approach to the Nuffield Foundation who committed funds for development. The Nuffield Advanced Mathematics project, based at King's College London, was launched in May 1990 under the directorship of Hugh Neill. The development effort was timed to start with the new core. Hugh invited the Northumberland Supported Self Study Unit and the team at West Sussex to collaborate.

By September 1990, the first of the teachers were seconded to the project. Secondments were made in a variety of ways to suit local needs as well as the needs of the project. Teachers from Oxfordshire and LEAs in London came into London once a week or once a fortnight. Initially, the main aim was to develop their use of technology so that they would be in a good position to trial and comment. They were also asked for advice and comments right from the beginning. Once materials became available, the teachers were able to trial and provide feedback, within the constraints imposed by their existing syllabuses. We know this was a difficult task, as the priorities addressed by the material were very different from those created by the need to prepare students for other examinations.

A different model of secondment was used in Northumberland. Teachers were to be seconded for blocks of time. The Northumberland model had the advantage that timing could better suit the immediate needs of the project. A regular weekly secondment involved teachers in a cycle which was often out of synchronisation with that of the project.

NEW TECHNOLOGY

In 1985, the JMC conference was held against a background claim that new technology would change both the content and the way A level mathematics was taught. However, even by 1990, there was little evidence of large-scale change at A level, despite the availability in some schools of computers powerful enough to run research and industry standard software such as the spreadsheet Excel and the statistics package Minitab. In addition to constraints imposed by the very full mathematics core, I would suggest that the reasons for this were partly lack of access to the technology for students, and also lack of access for teachers in terms of time to develop confidence in using machines and software, and to develop ideas.

Kenneth Ruthven from Cambridge University Department of Education had just finished a major study of the impact of graphic calculators on A level, using Casio 7000g calculators. In addition, some schools in West Sussex had been using graphic calculators in the work for their portfolios. Both projects showed not only that students benefited from using the calculators, but also that the teachers were enthusiastic and inservice training was manageable. It seemed to the Nuffield team in the light of this evidence that by making a minimal requirement that each student have access to a graphic calculator, we would be making realistic demands of money and time on the teachers, while still being able to transform the approach to the A level material.

In addition, we believed that we could ask each school or college to make available by arrangement one computer capable of running a graphing spreadsheet such as Excel, possibly housed in the library rather than in the mathematics department.

It is hoped that such a policy would not inhibit those teachers who were already using more technology from using their existing knowledge as an additional resource in the course. However, it is vital to be aware of the need for teacher confidence in implementing the use of technology, and by concentrating on graphic calculators we are facilitating the provision of appropriate inservice training.

Why spreadsheets?

The rationale for focusing on the spreadsheet as the major piece of software was that it would enable us to offer large datasets such as census data on disc. The spreadsheet had been found to be a very powerful general modelling tool. (See, for example, the work of the Computer Based Modelling Across the Curriculum project, a collaboration between the Advisory Unit in Hatfield and the Institute of Education in London.) The spreadsheet has many other general uses, so once teachers have invested the initial time, the pay-off extends into record keeping and producing worksheets. In addition, it is a tool widely used in industry and consequently well supported in terms of data, texts and new developments.

Once the feasibility of a mathematics curriculum which takes account of the availability of new technology can be established, how would such a curriculum look?

Content and method

One way in which the use of technology can change the curriculum is by enabling students to approach existing topics in a more experimental or exploratory way. For example, students will be able to explore the effect of translations and stretches on functions, explore the gradient function and the area-so-far function experimentally and gain a firmer intuitive foundation on which to build the study of functions and calculus. Polar co-ordinates, parametric equations and the transformations effected by matrices can be explored similarly.

There are additional aspects, which are to some extent specific to the Nuffield course. The content of the Nuffield courses can be described as having two major threads which are not typical at this level of study. The first is the use of algorithms and the second is modelling. In addition, the course incorporates some of the ideas behind exploratory data analysis (EDA) which help to make statistics more accessible and intuitive.

Algorithms

One of the main features of advanced mathematics is an appreciation of the need for more rigour. This has often been approached through the Greek notion of proof. However, with new technology there is an alternative way of looking at rigour, through the construction and modification of algorithms until they work. This is reminiscent of the ancient Chinese way of looking at proof. In the case of the modern student, the calculator or computer offers a chance to design and test algorithms, two essential ingredients being the feedback which comes from trying out an algorithm and the opportunity for refinement.

Let me use the example of the fundamental theorem of the calculus as an illustration. The way we introduce the solution of differential equations is by giving the students the Euler step-by-step algorithm so they can explore approximate solutions graphically on their calculators. For example, the algorithm for the solution of $dy/dx = G(x)$ would include

$$Y_n = Y_{n-1} + h * G(x_{n-1}).$$

The way we introduce integration is by exploring graphically the approximate area so far under the graph of a function, using the algorithm

$$A_n = A_{n-1} + h * F(X_{n-1}).$$

When you compare the two algorithms used there is a correspondence between them which can lead to an intuitive understanding of the fundamental theorem.

Modelling

Mathematical modelling can be thought of as the total process involved in using mathematics to solve real problems. In industry and research it is often experienced as an iterative process within which the results from a model are compared with reality and the model consequently modified. The model has a purpose and is judged by how well it fits the purpose.

There is an existing tradition that many A level students study some aspect of applied mathematics, or mathematical modelling. However, in many syllabuses so-called applied mathematics ends up as pure mathematics in disguise, with mechanics topics offering a chance to explore trigonometry, geometry and calculus, and statistics leading to work in set theory and calculus. There is an increasing demand for students who are more able to use mathematics interactively with the real world.

We have built two kinds of modelling into the Nuffield course, data modelling and the modelling of dynamic systems. In addition, we have tried to build in a final part of the modelling process the writing up or presenting of results.

Why incorporate mathematical modelling and computer modelling into A level mathematics? There are two aspects, the gains for the teacher and the gains for the students.

The teacher gains 'a window into student thinking' as soon as there is any opportunity for students to express their own ideas, whether it be in the writing of a program or in writing or presenting their own work.

The students gain motivation, feedback, reflection and insight.

How can modelling be built into the A level curriculum?

It is often claimed by researchers in the field, such as the team at the Shell Centre in Nottingham, that students are unable to build their own models using mathematics they have just learned. How can this be taken into account in an A level mathematics course while students are also expected to learn new content? We are attempting to do this in two ways. If students are carrying out the whole modelling process investigatively, then they use familiar mathematics, e.g. fitting curves by eye to data collected experiment-ally or from simulations (Figure 20.1).

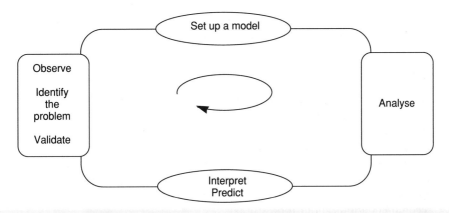

Figure 20.1 Modelling as a whole

Case studies and articles

Throughout the course, case studies are made available to the students as a way of illustrating how a new mathematical concept may be used by someone solving a problem. Frequently, the difficulty with this approach is that modern uses of mathematics assume too high a level of content. We have found two new ways round this.

One is to use historical sources; the other is to use modern disciplines where mathematical modelling is relatively new. In these ways material can be found which is accessible to A level students. I shall describe some examples.

Florence Nightingale

Florence Nightingale had to solve a problem which is readily accessible to students at the beginning of an A level course. She wanted to convince the authorities that midwives be trained, rather than just rely on common sense and doing as they were told, so she set up a midwives' training hospital. However, there was a sudden outbreak of a fatal fever, several women died and she temporarily lost the argument she believed in passionately. The techniques she needed to solve the problem were those of a mathematical modeller, identifying relevant variables, collecting data and analysing and presenting arguments, but using only mathematics very familiar to A level students.

Traffic modelling

In the early days of traffic modelling, there was a need to establish a link between the speed of traffic and the flow, i.e. how many cars per minute passed a fixed point. The problem and the way in which the mathematical model was developed is accessible, and some of the original data is available.

Salmonella

Until recently in microbiology, experiments involving the growth of organisms such as salmonella were done *in situ*, in the type of food under investigation. In the Institute of Food Research, scientists have been arguing the case for using a descriptive mathematical model. They have built a model using pH, water content and temperature as the predictive variables. The data and the mathematics can be made accessible to the students. If the approach is accepted, the model developed may be used as a basis for future recommendations about food storage.

Archaeology

At an excavation of a Roman site in Baldock, archaeologists found many of the skeletons to be incomplete. What they wanted to be able to do was to estimate the height of each skeleton from the available bones. However, reliable data about the relationship between the length of a bone and overall height is hard to come by. In the literature there was a model built by a scientist from data collected after the Vietnam war while bodies were being identified. This model was used to estimate the height of the Roman skeletons, raising all sorts of issues about modelling assumptions.

IMPLICATIONS FOR WAYS OF WORKING

The incorporation of modelling, and of technology, into the A level curriculum brings with it a justification for a change in teaching style. Further justification comes from the need to build on GCSE experience and from research evidence about the effectiveness of group work, discussion and student explanations in making learning meaningful. In addition, it was clear that students needed help in learning to manage their total learning time.

The new developments at A level could provide support for teachers wishing to adapt their methodologies in the light of these opportunities. The teachers we have worked with have been concerned to help the students make better use of their time and become more independent learners. However, there is a caveat here that schemes run a risk of creating a dependency on text to replace their dependency on the teacher.

Implications for assessment

The three major aims of the course are to encourage more students to study advanced mathematics, to encourage students to be more active in their learning and to encourage appropriate use of technology. The guiding principle is that the assessment should be fit for the purpose. However, we have to work within the existing regulations and conditions. Taking those constraints into account, together with an understandable caution on the part of many teachers not to take on too much responsibility for coursework at A level, the project hopes that schools will be offered two alternatives by the board. The first would require students to submit a coursework portfolio for 20 per cent of the A level. The portfolio would be assessed against criteria which encourage students to build their own models, explore areas of mathematics or applications which particularly interest them and carry out extended investigations. Experience of this kind of assessment at A level rests with the West Sussex team who have been working with us. There is similar work in progress in the post-18 sector; for example, at the University of Hertfordshire and at City University.

The alternative we would like to offer to the coursework portfolio is board-marked assignments which cover the same assessment objectives. There is also scope for a comprehension component to ensure that students are encouraged to read about the use of mathematics in context. This device has been used successfully by the Northern Ireland project with further mathematics students and is now being incorporated into some other A level assessments.

A postscript: putting into context

Moves to incorporate technology, modelling, real data and more active learning into the post-16 mathematics curriculum are happening throughout the world, not just in the United Kingdom. For example, the team has been greatly strengthened by the involvement of Mary Barnes, author of an introductory calculus course for Australian schools. Barnes' course is gender inclusive, with a strong emphasis on modelling and solving real problems, working cooperatively and using technology.

Further reading

Higginson Report (1988) *Advanced A-levels*, London: HMSO.
JMC Conference on the Future of A-level Mathematics (1985) London: King's College.
LMS/UMTC (1989) *Mathematics 16–20*, Shell Centre for Mathematical Education.
Ruthven, K. (1992) *Personal Technology in the Classroom*, part of the NCET pack.

Part VII

Research in mathematics education

'To stay alive every teacher must be a researcher' was the title of an address that John Mason gave to the Australian Association of Mathematics Teachers in 1986. Being a researcher in the context of the classroom can mean being aware of the possibilities, reflecting on the outcomes of lessons, noticing particular occurrences and considering the range of ways in which they can be acted on. Being aware of and sensitised to a range of possible courses of actions during a lesson can be construed as research, in addition to the familiar definitions of research.

In this final part, research in mathematics education is viewed from two perspectives, from the position of the teacher in the classroom and from the position of a researcher working with practising teachers. Chapter 21 is a reprint of an article which I wrote shortly after returning to teaching having completed an M.Phil and describes how I 'experimented' with a class and how I evaluated my actions. In the final chapter Barbara Jaworski describes research within a constructivist framework which involved discussion between her and the teachers she observed and working with them. She uses this constructivist perspective to describe what is meant by a mathematical community and how all pupils can become part of such a community.

Chapter 21

Going back

Michelle Selinger

I looked at the envelope.
I tried to remember everything I had written.
Had I attempted all the challenges I had set myself?
Could I expect to be the teacher I wanted to be after only eight weeks back
    in the classroom?
Enough questioning, time to open the envelope and face the truth.

Shortly before completing my secondment, during which I had spent a
year studying for an M.Phil in Mathematics Education, I was encouraged to
write down all the changes I would make in my classroom when I returned
to teaching. I sealed my resolutions in an envelope and re-opened it at half-
term. To my amazement I discovered that I had attempted everything on the
list, albeit some with a greater degree of success than others.

I had trembled at the thought of going back to school. Everyone seemed
to have great expectations.

- You've had a year off, what are you going to offer us?
- Come and tell me about all the developments in mathematics education.
- Will you talk to the special needs department?
- Why have you come back?
- Nobody comes back after secondment!

This last comment made me smart. Why had I come back? Many reasons, I
suppose: the 'right' job did not appear; possibilities of others did not
materialise; and I was unsure of the direction I wished to take. The fact
remains, however, that I did return to my previous post, and although I may
consider the possibility of moving on in the near future, the contents of my
envelope have confirmed that *going back* was the right course of action for
me to take at the time. Returning to the same school has allowed me to view
the changes in myself as a teacher without the complications of establishing
myself in a new environment. It has allowed me to concentrate on my
classroom practice and to interact with colleagues who immediately accepted
me back as an integral part of the department.

How am I different then? I allow the children more freedom. I hope that I am encouraging them to discover the power of mathematics. I am reflecting on my lessons – an act which has sometimes found me surrounded by a class of children who have entered the room unnoticed. I spend less time 'sitting ticking' which leaves me more room to search for new approaches to the syllabus. I've freed myself from the textbook/worksheet syndrome, using these as resources from which I might draw when necessary. I encourage the children to help one another in the hope that the process of putting their thoughts into words will deepen their understanding. I try to answer their questions with a question in the hope that this will allow them to make their own interpretations of ideas put forward during the lesson, and to make sense of the concepts involved in the activity on which they are working. I am no longer afraid of backtracking when I feel that the children have misunderstood a concept, because I believe that if children are uncomfortable with a concept they will not always succeed if and when it is re-introduced. I suppose I feel more confident about what I am trying to achieve in my own classroom and the constraints of the syllabus have become less important than the need to ensure that the children are confident and comfortable with all the concepts they encounter.

I think I also understand now what is meant by comments like: 'children should own their mathematics' and 'mathematics should be real to the children'. These phrases took on meaning when I looked at breakfast cereal packets with a Year 9 group. I asked them to guess what the net of a particular Rice Krispies packet would look like. They all drew their interpretations of the net and then we opened up the box to see who had been correct. I then remembered a conversation I had held at a conference the previous week. We had been discussing the problems of teaching about volume; one teacher told me he had asked children to estimate the amount of water various containers would hold. The children then had to stand with these containers over their heads while he poured in that amount of water! I did not feel able to follow his example but recalled a friend who had recently opened a factory producing breakfast cereals, and who would possibly let me have a box of scrap product. I suggested to the class that they design their own cereal boxes and estimate the weight of Rice Krispies they would hold. I would then pour in that quantity of cereals as long as they promised to clear up the results of any over-estimates. They set to work designing and constructing boxes of various shapes and sizes, arguing over dimensions, discovering the need for flaps, discussing why sides would not meet and much more. Eventually the boxes were complete; some had constructed traditional boxes while others had produced cubes, triangular prisms and even a square-based pyramid with a truncated top. The cereals were brought in, and after the first two or three containers had been filled, the children hastily altered the estimates they had written on their boxes. If their box was not full, they told me how much more it might need and insisted on my filling them to see if they were correct.

These children were owning their mathematics, they were estimating, revising their estimates on the basis of experience and gaining the concept of capacity. They were highly motivated and although the situation was contrived, it had become real to them. We are now examining the different shapes of boxes one can find having the same volume and discussing the marketing aspects of various designs of breakfast cereal packets.

I use this example to illustrate the effect that my year out of the classroom has had on me. I would never have attempted such an activity before, and if I had, I am sure I would have given the children far more direction. That time out of the classroom has provided an opportunity to reflect; to discuss mathematics education without the other pressures that the school environment brings; and to put my years of experience into a theoretical framework. These are all factors which contributed to my metamorphosis.

However, the process was not complete by the end of my secondment; I believe it was important to return to the classroom, to put the theory back into practice and to find out that it really does work. I have developed a self-confidence which has encouraged me to question my previous approach. I have been able to criticise those teaching methods I had once employed and which I now consider inappropriate, and to adapt those practices which complement my new philosophy. I believe it was important to review my previous practice, not just on a theoretical basis, but by comparing and adapting it to my new way of working in the classroom, with real children who would respond in a positive or negative way, and who could confirm the validity of my new approach.

I am not complacent, there is always room for improvement. I still find myself in situations where I regret what I have just said or where I wish I had taken a different approach. But I believe that as long as I am aware of my actions and continue to reflect on my classroom practice, I shall not stagnate.

Chapter 22

Being mathematical within a mathematical community

Barbara Jaworski

What does it mean to *learn* mathematics? Does this bear any relation to *being* a mathematician? In this chapter, I suggest that *all* pupils in mathematics classrooms in schools can be mathematicians, and that this involves *being mathematical within a mathematical community*. My main theme will be the implications which this has for the *teaching* of mathematics.

I believe strongly that a teacher's personal philosophy or view of the nature of mathematics, and its learning and teaching, influences very considerably the way a teacher teaches. I therefore want to introduce briefly a philosophy which I have come to believe underpins much of what I personally regard as good practice in mathematics teaching and learning. It is known as constructivism, sometimes as radical constructivism and sometimes as social constructivism. It is from a constructivist position that I shall talk about being mathematical in a mathematical community.

CONSTRUCTIVISM

Constructivism is a perspective on knowledge and learning which suggests that any person's knowledge is not acquired from outside, but is constructed by that individual. Moreover, individuals adapt what they know in the light of new experiences.

It is not new. It dates back to Kant in the eighteenth century and owes much to the thinking of Dewey and of Piaget in the twentieth century. However, a working definition which I have found particularly useful comes from Ernst von Glasersfeld (1987), who writes:

> Constructivism is a theory of knowledge with roots in philosophy, psychology, and cybernetics. It asserts two main principles whose application has far reaching consequences for the study of cognitive development and learning . . . The two principles are:
>
> 1 knowledge is not passively received but actively built up by the cognising subject;

2 the function of cognition is adaptive and serves the organisation of the experiential world, not the discovery of ontological reality.

(von Glasersfeld 1987)

In terms of the construction of mathematical knowledge in the classroom, pupils are the cognising subjects. It is von Glasersfeld's claim that they do not *discover* some absolute form of knowledge which exists outside of themselves – in the world around perhaps, or in the minds of their teachers – but rather that they learn by *adapting* what they know to *fit* with what they experience in the world around them. What I know is a result of my own experience, of the constructions which I make as a result of all my encounters, and I modify what I know as a result of new experiences. When I see, hear, feel, read something new, I need to fit it into what I know already, and it may be that what I thought was true changes as a result of this. My knowledge might be very different to that of another person.

The social nature of learning alongside others is vital to the development of knowledge. When people talk to each other they share images and perceptions and negotiate meanings. As a result of this they may come to some consensus as to what they believe or understand. From here, aspects of common knowledge can develop. Social constructivism is concerned with development not only of individual knowledge and meaning but of shared meanings within a community. Historically the growth of mathematical knowledge can be regarded as a development of shared meanings in the international mathematical community.

Of course pupils' experiences include those which occur in mathematics classrooms, and in particular what is brought to their attention by their teachers. Of great interest to me is what roles teachers most valuably play in influencing the individual mathematical constructions of their pupils, and shared meanings within the classroom.

As an example of what I mean, I should like to offer a statement from my own research (Jaworski 1991), made by one of the teachers I studied, which led me to conclude that he worked from a constructivist philosophy. He said,

I feel in my head I have a system of mathematics. I don't know what it looks like but it's there, and whenever I learn a new bit of mathematics I have to find somewhere that that fits in. It might not just fit in one place, it might actually connect up a lot of places as well. When I share things it's very difficult because I can't actually share my mathematical model or whatever you want to call it, because that's special to me. It's special to me because of my experiences. So, I suppose I'm not a giver of knowledge because I like to let people fit their knowledge into their model because only then does it make sense to them. Maybe that's why if you actually say, 'Well probability is easy. It's just this over this', it doesn't make sense because it's got nowhere to fit. That's what I feel didactic teaching is a lot about, isn't it? Giving this knowledge, sharing your knowledge with people, which is not possible.

This teacher referred to a lesson in which pupils had been given a formula for the probability of an event as the number of outcomes of the event divided by (over) the total number of possibilities ('this over this'). He seemed to say that if pupils had no means of fitting this formula into their previous experience then the formula might be meaningless to them. He also implied that he could not *give* his knowledge to another person.

One significant implication of constructivist belief is that it is not possible to say something to someone else and expect them to understand exactly the meaning that was intended to be conveyed. You, the reader, are currently making sense of what you are reading here. I cannot assume that the sense you are making is exactly what I mean by the words I have written. In classroom terms, just because a teacher has said something to a pupil clearly and precisely, she[1] cannot infer that the pupil has taken exactly the meaning intended. The pupil's focus might be quite different from the teacher's. The pupil might fit the teacher's words into her own experience to get a meaning different from what the teacher tried to convey. Because people interpret words and gestures differently, any attempt to convey knowledge in an absolute sense must be seen as quite likely to fail. A teacher therefore has to find ways of knowing what sense pupils make of the mathematical tasks they are set, in order to evaluate activities and plan further lessons.

I shall be looking at how this highly complex philosophy might be manifested in practice, and shall consider some of the many implications it has for the teacher of mathematics. I shall begin by offering an anecdote from my experience as a PGCE tutor.[2] My purpose in this is to provide an entry to discussion of what it means to be mathematical, and, in particular, to ways in which opportunities for talking about mathematical ideas can foster being mathematical. I shall suggest that opportunities for talking are afforded by the mathematical community, that being a mathematician is central to learning mathematics and involves being mathematical within a mathematical community.

MAKING MODELS

I recently interviewed a number of applicants for a one-year PGCE course. They wanted to become mathematics teachers. We sat round a table and I offered them a sequence of three 'models' built from small coloured wooden cubes. I indicated 'number 1', 'number 2', 'number 3'. The cubes were arranged as shown below.

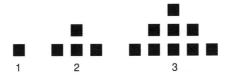

I invited them each to make model 'number 4'. Surprisingly, or unsurprisingly, they *all* built models with the arrangement shown in the figure below.

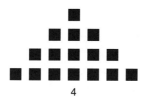

I asked them, in turn, to say something about their thinking in producing this version of 'number 4'. Some of the replies were as follows.

- One said he noticed the bottom rows going up 1, 3, 5, . . . and so he had made a model with seven in the bottom row.
- A second had 'put one brick on each end of each row, and one on top'.
- Another had counted cubes in rows – for model 3 it went 5, 3, 1, so for model 4 it should go 7, 5, 3, 1.
- A fourth had counted the total number of blocks in each model, to find 1, 4, 9. Then she conjectured 'square numbers' and 'just built it up'.

One thing which struck me from these different replies was the very different images which contributed to the similar models. Each time I offer this activity I am made aware of how the perceptions of others can be so different to my own. I have to take care not to assume that students are seeing what I see, even if it looks as if we are all talking about the same situation.

In our discussion, which followed these replies, the students (as they became) commented on each other's perspectives, and recognised the broadening of their own perspective through the sharing of images. For example, one of them said, 'Until Kate mentioned the square numbers, I just hadn't thought of that aspect of it'. Thus, individual perceptions of the models were adapted in the light of interaction and discussion with others in the group.

I then extended the activity by removing my third model, and I said,

I shall now stop here, after number 2, and ask you to construct number 3. However, I want you to construct one different to the one which I had.

The figures below show four of the models which the students built as number 3. I asked them, again, to explain their thinking, and they responded as follows.

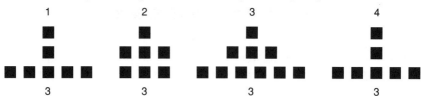

Student 1 said he added one cube in each direction (to model number 2);

Student 2 said she could see the possibility for an arithmetic progression – just adding on three each time.

Student 3 said he saw it increasing like Pascal's triangle. When I asked what he meant by that, he indicated the 1, 3, 6 and said that the next bottom row would have ten cubes.

Student 4 said that number 2 added one in each direction to the original cube, so number 3 should add two in each direction (to the original cube).

Again there was discussion which involved the students sharing images and commenting on each other's versions. Comments like, 'Oh yes, I hadn't thought of that' were frequent. A number of different mathematical notions arose – such as arithmetic progressions, square numbers, Pascal's triangle. It is often amazing how many different aspects of mathematics can be recalled by engaging in even such a simple task. Because of this, discussion of the task can contribute to students' growing perceptions of links between areas of mathematics.

My reaction to one of the above responses was rather salutary for me. In the case of student 3, I was not sure what he meant by comparing his model to Pascal's triangle. After asking for clarification, it seemed to me that the student was perhaps thinking of triangular numbers. I thought he was mistaken in his reference to Pascal's triangle, although I didn't actually say so at the time. However, I felt later that I had jumped much too readily to this conclusion, with very little evidence. How could I be sure just what relationships he was actually seeing? For example, he might have been thinking of a particular *diagonal* of Pascal's triangle. If I had been a teacher in the classroom, how might I have handled this?

My purpose in engaging in the activity with the prospective students had been to provide a situation in which they could become involved and hopefully be able to talk about mathematics, learning and teaching. In listening to and engaging in their talk, I could get a sense of their thinking and gain some awareness of their potential for working on mathematics with children. I now look back at the activity and recognise that it exemplifies for me important aspects of a constructivist view of knowledge and learning. In particular it suggests that knowledge is personal, but, through discussion with others, some common consensus can be reached which enhances individual perceptions. This is one way to view learning.

BEING MATHEMATICAL

The models referred to in the anecdote were not, in or of themselves, mathematical. They were just arrangements of pieces of wood. The context in which they were offered may be seen as mathematical. Since the participants in the activity were applying to be mathematics teachers, it is likely that they had mathematics very much in mind. However, a constructivist perspective of what occurred suggests that any mathematics which resulted from the activity was a product of people's minds rather than inherent in the task of making models. Moreover, mathematical constructions varied from one participant to another, and were modified according to the discussions which ensued. The students were actively being mathematicians, i.e. they were bringing mathematics into being.

David Wheeler (1982) speaks of 'the process by which mathematics is brought into being', calling it mathematisation.

> Although mathematization must be presumed present in all cases of 'doing' mathematics or 'thinking' mathematically, it can be detected most easily in situations where something not obviously mathematical is being converted into something that most obviously is. We may think of a young child playing with blocks, and using them to express awareness of symmetry, of an older child experimenting with a geoboard and becoming interested in the relationship between the areas of the triangles he can make, an adult noticing a building under construction and asking himself questions about the design etc.
> . . . we notice that mathematization has taken place by the signs of organisation, of form, of additional structure, given to a situation.

We might think of the students in the anecdote as mathematising the situation of the models as they looked at individual cases, spotted patterns and sought in some way to express the generalities which they could see. In doing this they referred to aspects of mathematics with which they were familiar. For example, one student's familiarity with square numbers enabled her to express the pattern which she could see, and to conjecture the form of the next model in the sequence. This process of mathematising is a constructive process which includes spotting patterns in special cases and seeking to express some form of generality. It has been a part of mathematical development since ancient times, and might be seen as fundamental to being mathematical.

A MATHEMATICAL COMMUNITY

It seems consistent with a constructivist philosophy that individual mathematisations of a situation, such as the models in the anecdote, are likely to differ. However, in the growth of mathematical ideas over time, there has been wide consensus in mathematisations made. (For example, it is widely agreed that the area of a triangle in the plane may be found as half the product of its base and height.) A great deal of effort has been made to communicate mathematical ideas, and to contrast ways of seeing mathematics in different communities in order to reach common ground. In the situation described in the anecdote, the students each had individual perceptions, but these were developed and perhaps refined in conversation. It is likely that some consensus in the group was reached in terms of mathematisation of the models.

Such a group which fosters the growth and sharing of mathematical ideas has been called a mathematical community (see, for example, Davis *et al.* 1990). This mathematical community seems to mean a group of people committed to the sharing and communication of their mathematical thinking. I like the term because it has positive overtones of a place where someone belongs. It might be seen as a community of mathematicians worldwide, or, more locally, perhaps as the group of people described in the anecdote. In particular it might consist of the pupils and teacher in a mathematics classroom, intent on being mathematical together. The community has many roles which include providing support for individuals in their thinking and acting as a forum for sharing, interchange and critical review of ideas of individuals.

It is on the notion of the mathematical community as it exists in the mathematics classroom that I should now like to focus. I shall consider how such a mathematical community both encourages individual constructing of mathematical ideas and fosters negotiation and social mediation which leads to shared meanings being developed.

IN THE CLASSROOM

The following three examples are of particular classroom situations in which individual constructions of mathematical ideas are seen to develop and shared meanings are encouraged through discussion and negotiation between participants.

Pythagoras' theorem

The first example, from a secondary-school classroom, is from my own research (Jaworski 1991). A teacher, Mike, had set his class (of twenty-eight 13/14 year olds) a two-fold task. One pair, of each group of four in the class, was to undertake one part of the task, and the second pair the other part.

The parts were given to pupils written on paper as follows.

Square sums	Triangle lengths
$1^2 + 2^2 = 5$.	Draw a triangle with a right-angle.
What other numbers can be made	Measure accurately all three sides.
by adding square numbers together?	Can you find any relationship
Investigate	between the three lengths?

Mike told me before the lesson that he hoped cross-fertilisation would take place between the two pairs in a group, so that pupils might start to have a sense of how the two tasks were related. He then hoped to build on their developing awareness to introduce Pythagoras' theorem.

I shall illustrate the nature of the mathematical thinking which occurred by offering two excerpts from my transcript of this lesson. In the first, three boys had been working on the triangle lengths task for some time when the teacher joined them. One boy, Richard, explained what they had done.

MIKE: You three, what's going on?

RICH: Right, well, we're doing the – erm, the triangle problem. And we thought that we (inaudible) looking for a pattern, so we – Robert's doing one to five, I'm doing five to ten, and Wayne's doing ten to fifteen. One by one, two by two, three by three, – then we'll draw a graph, and see if we can spot any pattern in that.

MIKE: You haven't got triangles – does it matter? [They had drawn figures as below.]

RICH: Oh, we're measuring from there to there [i.e. from A to B, my labelling].

The boys had decided how they would tackle the task, and had shared out the labour. Richard's description indicated a high awareness of mathematical process – trying out special cases, drawing a graph, looking for a pattern – which he expressed very confidently.

Another boy, Phil, had been tackling the other task. The teacher noticed that Phil had got twenty-five and twenty-nine ($3^2 + 4^2 = 25$; $2^2 + 5^2 = 29$), and had asked him whether numbers between these two could be found as sums of squares. A little later, the teacher returned to Phil who animatedly referred to his subsequent work:

PHIL: I've got twenty-six, and I'm working on – if I want to get twenty-seven I've, I have to try and get the closest number – to do the sum – I have to use something like 1.5, cause, if I try to get the two, then that'll make four, if I try to use two squared plus five

> squared, er, that'll make twenty-nine, so I have to – cut 'em in half, obviously, cut 'em in half. (Mike 'Right') I'm going to try and keep the five and use 1.5 squared.
>
> MIKE: That's a nice idea. So you're going to try to home in to twenty-seven. Is it twenty-seven you're working on?
>
> PHIL: Yes.
>
> MIKE: Right.
>
> PHIL: I can't do that, I'll take 4.5, I won't take five and a half, I'll take four and a half, and use two here.

The question from the teacher seemed to have caused Phil to move from thinking only in terms of squares of whole numbers to considering fractional numbers. In fact it looked as if his thinking had moved from an operation of squaring and adding to one of reversing this process. Later, conversation moved to consideration of square roots. This was a result of Phil's own mathematical exploration and discussion with the teacher. A mathematical community enables such articulation by pupils and discussion between teacher and pupil. The teacher was able to take advantage of the pupil's evident involvement and enthusiasm to steer towards a technique which he judged appropriate to the pupil's thinking.

The teacher was very satisfied with the outcome of the lessons based on the two tasks. It was not that pupils had dutifully obeyed his every instruction, or that they had responded impeccably to instructions like 'investigate'. In one group, the pupils did not wish to split into two pairs, and so all worked on just one task. In another two girls were puzzled by the square sums task. They said to the teacher, rather incredulously, 'Do we just add up lots and lots of square numbers?' One group became very frustrated because they could not find a pattern. A girl in the group challenged the teacher with having a 'formula in your head, which we cannot find'. The teacher had to deal with these and other situations which he had not necessarily envisaged. However, he felt that he had achieved his main objective which was to get pupils involved in and talking about ideas related to Pythagoras' theorem. His responses mainly encouraged pupils' own exploration, but he was not reluctant to contribute to the thinking himself when he judged it appropriate. As a result of these levels of communication, individual and common knowledge relevant to Pythagoras' theorem developed. I was struck by the ethos in the classroom in which pupils and teacher worked on and talked about mathematics together in an atmosphere of friendly respect. This seemed a good example of a mathematical community, supporting the constructions of mathematics by individuals and groups within it.

Area or perimeter

My second example comes from a secondary-school classroom which was recorded on videotape by the Open University, some of which is published as part of an Open University course (Open University 1992). It concerns a small group of pupils, aged 16 or 17, working with a teacher on a task involved with generating patterns of squares within squares.[3] The small group interaction seems to embody a similar ethos to that in the class which I have described in the previous example.

At the beginning of the sequence the teacher said to the four boys in the group, 'You've described in words for that one; you've described in words for that one; so can you describe in words for this one?'

Pointing to two diagrams, similar to those illustrated below, one boy started to describe, another came in with a different description and then the teacher himself joined in the discussion. All gave slightly different interpretations of the same diagrams. One of the boys seemed not to be taking part as he was busily writing in his own book. However, suddenly he leaned over and contributed to the discussion. Then he went back to his book.

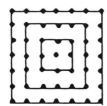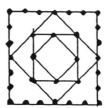

The sequence then showed the boys seeking formulas to describe the patterns. One boy wrote something while the others watched. He then stopped with the words, 'No, that's rubbish!'. However, the teacher intervened, 'No, don't give up. *Why* is it rubbish? Because you've started something . . .'

In the last few moments of the sequence the teacher emphasised some aspects of the discussion, which led one boy to say, 'Oh, it's not area, it's perimeter'. The reactions of the others seems to indicate that this was an important revelation.

The teacher seemed to play two roles in his interaction with the group. The first was to nurture their involvement in the activity in a number of ways, for example:

– encouraging the boys to describe what they saw;
– sitting back and listening as they discussed the patterns and looked for a formula, thus paying respect to their ideas;
– countering the word 'rubbish', perhaps encouraging the boys not to dismiss their own thinking.

The second role was his involvement in the mathematics, expressing his own perceptions, asking questions, emphasising aspects of the boys' mathematics and finally picking up on something they had said to highlight their possible confusing of area and perimeter.

In both roles he fostered individual meaning making and sharing of meanings in the group. The mathematical community was very overt. The boys all interacted, the words of one influencing those of another. Together, they constructed an argument. One boy was able to pursue his own writing between remarks to the group. The teacher joined in or kept silent as he assessed the situation.

The mathematics involved is interesting. At one level it might be seen as pupils grappling with quite simple ideas of area and perimeter, at another it involved tackling the expressing of complex generalities which incidentally involved area and perimeter. The teacher might have been confident on two levels:(1) that pupils' conceptual understanding of area and perimeter was developing through this exploration; (2) that pupils were becoming proficient at expressing mathematical ideas in a fluent way which could then be applicable to other concepts. Thus the mathematical community here overtly supported the construction of mathematical knowledge.

Differentiation

My third example concerns an occurrence which dates back to my own work as a mathematics teacher. I had been working with my Year 12 students on differentiation. I was pleased with how proficient they had become in differentiating quite complex mathematical functions. Then, towards the end of one lesson, a girl, Sara, suddenly said, 'What is differentiation? I can do it all right. But what *is* it?'

I felt my mouth open to launch into an explanation, when suddenly I noticed Tony sitting smirking at the back, as if to say, 'I know all about this. Silly question!' So, instead of offering an explanation myself, I asked Tony if he could explain.

He began with confidence, but then he hesitated and fumbled. Other students started chipping in. Questions were asked, and the students tried to answer them. I cannot remember very much about my own contribution, just that we had one of the best class discussions ever on a mathematical theme. Sara seemed much more happy at the end of it, but it was Tony, finally, who convinced me of the value of the occasion. He hung about until the others had left, and then as he was going he said, 'You know that was really good. I thought I knew what differentiation was, but I couldn't actually say it. Now, I think I can.'

What I learned from this was the value of getting pupils to articulate what they think they know, and the importance of the group as both a listening and a responsive organism. Doing the differentiation had been worthwhile in terms of establishing the technique, but the discussion had been effective in contributing to the establishing of the concept. I had a much better sense of individual perceptions and of the level of common understanding within the group.

BEING A MATHEMATICIAN

From a constructivist perspective, learning mathematics involves the individual construction of mathematical knowledge. Within the social environment of the classroom individual construction takes place alongside negotiation of ideas and construction of common meanings.

In the above examples, the activities in which the learners participated encouraged them to be mathematical, that is to act as mathematicians by mathematising particular situations created by their teacher. The mathematical community, in each case, provided an environment in which individual mathematical ideas could be expressed and tested against others. In each case learners shared perceptions with each other and with the teacher, and their ideas became modified or reinforced as common meanings developed. This enabled learners to become clearer and more confident about what they knew and understood.

Being mathematical within a mathematical community is not an automatic feature of a mathematics classroom. I have been in many classrooms where mathematics was supposedly being done, but where pupils gave no evidence of being mathematical; for example, it was quite possible for my Year 12 students to practice differentiation in a totally mechanical fashion which required little mathematising on their part. They could simply follow a set of rules. There are also many classrooms where the participants could in no way be described as a mathematical community. For example, classrooms where there is little respect for individual perceptions or ideas; where mathematics is routinised, with little scope for creativity; where pupils are required to work mostly in silence or with little mathematical communication. In terms of a constructivist philosophy, in such classrooms little attention is paid to the personal constructions of knowledge by pupils and the importance of sharing perceptions with others in order to build consistent and coherent mathematical concepts. Many assumptions are made about mathematical knowledge and common meanings without providing opportunity to test their validity.

Teaching according to a constructivist philosophy may be seen as creating a mathematical community within which students are encouraged to be mathematicians. This might involve:

– recognising that mathematical constructions vary from one learner to another;
– providing opportunity for individuals to express their own meanings, and

learn from comparing their perceptions with those of others;
- gaining knowledge of learners' constructions in order to prepare appropriate classroom tasks to enable concepts to be developed.

I know from my own teaching experience, and from my classroom research, that it is hard work for a teacher to create an appropriate ethos in which mathematical activity and talk can take place, and where each person's thoughts are respected; to create activities which encourage pupils own mathematization and its articulation; and to listen and respond to pupils' talk in ways which are designed to achieve the mathematical objectives for a lesson.

However, the mathematical community, once established, has many advantages for both teacher and pupils. It supports individual construction of mathematical knowledge through opportunities to develop common meanings with others. In it pupils can find listeners to encourage expression of ideas and test out their ideas, gain new ideas and perspectives and avoid narrow thinking and find support to sustain activity. The teacher can overcome the practical difficulty of making time available for thirty individuals by monitoring groups and listening in to conversations. She can give particular attention where it is most needed, being confident that other pupils will continue to work together and help each other.

It has been said that learning mathematics is very difficult (e.g. DES 1982: 67). I do not believe that this is necessarily true. However, I do believe that teaching mathematics is difficult, particularly if it is based on a constructivist perspective. It is difficult because we cannot see into a child's mind and know what sense she is making of what we offer. We have, therefore, to provide opportunities to gain access to her thinking, and we have to inspect, very carefully, our judgements about pupils. What evidence do we have on which to base any judgement made? How can we evaluate the effectiveness of our own interactions with pupils? How can we become better teachers?

NOTES

1 It is not my intention to imply that all teachers and students are female, rather to redress an imbalance where use of male pronouns perpetuate a male view of society.
2 Many of the examples which I offer in this chapter were first discussed in a talk which I gave at the Edinburgh conference on *Mathematics Teaching* held in 1991, a written version of which appears in the proceedings from that conference.
3 'What do you see?', Bell Baxter High School, Cupar. Teacher – Iain Lochhead.

REFERENCES

Davis, R.B., Maher, C.A. and Noddings, N. (eds) (1990) 'Constructivist views on the learning and teaching of mathematics', *Journal for Research in Mathematics*

Education, Monograph number 4, National Council of Teachers of Mathematics: Reston, Virginia.

DES (1982) *Mathematics Counts* (Cockcroft Report), London: HMSO.

Jaworski, B. (1991) 'Interpretations of a constructivist philosophy in mathematics teaching', unpublished PhD thesis, Milton Keynes: Open University.

Open University (1992) *Learning and Teaching Mathematics*, EM236.

von Glasersfeld, E. (1987) 'Constructivism', in T. Husen and N. Postlethwaite (eds) *International Encyclopedia of Education*, supplement, vol. 1, Oxford: Pergamon Press.

Wheeler, D. (1982) 'Mathematization matters', *For the Learning of Mathematics* 3 (1): 45–7.

Acknowledgements

Chapter 2 Edited version of Chapter 6 in *Better Mathematics* (1987), reproduced by permission of the Controller of Her Majesty's Stationery Office.

Chapter 3 'Small Groups', *SMP User 2*, October 1986, by Steve Turner and Maggie Furness, reproduced by permission of the authors.

Chapter 4 'Teaching for the Test', *Times Educational Supplement*, 27 October 1989: 50–1, by Alan Bell, © Times Newspaper Ltd. 1989.

Chapter 5 'Train Spotters' Paradise', by Dave Hewitt, from *Mathematics Teaching* 140, September 1992, published by the Association of Teachers of Mathematics, reproduced by the author.

Chapter 8 'Assessing what sense pupils make of mathematics', from *Mathematics Teaching – The State of the Art* (1989), pp. 153–66, by John Mason, reproduced by permission of Falmer Press Limited.

Chapter 10 'Critical/Humanistic Mathematics Education: a role for history', by Stephen Lerman, from *Multicultural Teaching* 11(1), reproduced by permission of Trentham Books Limited.

Chapter 11 'Maths Aids: pastoral topics through maths – a case study', by David Urquhart and Graeme Balfour, from *Mathematics Teaching* 138, March 1992, published by the Association of Teachers of Mathematics, reproduced by permission of the authors.

Chapter 15 'Mathematics for the Nineties: a calculator-aware number curriculum', by Janet Duffin, from *Mathematics Teaching* 136, September 1991, published by the Association of Teachers of Mathematics, reproduced by permission of the publishers.

Chapter 21 'Going Back', by Michelle Selinger, from *Mathematics Teaching* 122, March 1988, published by the Association of Teachers of Mathematics, reproduced by permission of the publishers.

Notes on sources

Chapter 1   Commissioned for this volume.
Chapter 2   Edited version of Chapter 6 in *Better Mathematics* (1987), London: HMSO.
Chapter 3   *SMP User* No. 2, October 1986.
Chapter 4   *Times Educational Supplement* 27 October 1989: 50–1.
Chapter 5   *Mathematics Teaching* 140, September 1992.
Chapter 6   Commissioned for this volume.
Chapter 7   Commissioned for this volume.
Chapter 8   Re-worked version of an article in *Mathematics Teaching – The State of the Art* (1989), pp. 153–66.
Chapter 9   Commissioned for this volume.
Chapter 10   *Multicultural Teaching* 10 (4), December 1992.
Chapter 11   *Mathematics Teaching* 138, March 1992: 2–6.
Chapter 12   Commissioned for this volume.
Chapter 13   *The Curriculum Journal* 3 (2): 161–9.
Chapter 14   Commissioned for this volume.
Chapter 15   *Mathematics Teaching* 136, September 1991: 56–62.
Chapter 16   Commissioned for this volume.
Chapter 17   Commissioned for this volume.
Chapter 18   Commissioned for this volume.
Chapter 19   Commissioned for this volume.
Chapter 20   Commissioned for this volume.
Chapter 21   *Mathematics Teaching* 122, March 1988.
Chapter 22   Re-worked version of a paper presented at the Edinburgh conference on Mathematics Teaching, September 1991.

Index